T0267064

PRAISE FOR *THE BUSINESS OF BOTANICALS*

"In *The Business of Botanicals*, Ann Armbrecht brings readers along on a wholly engaging exploration of her questions and hard learnings about whether the healing power of plants can truly make it into the factory-sealed supplement bottles on our grocery shelves."

—KATE WILLIAMS, CEO of 1% for the Planet

"Ann Armbrecht establishes herself as a gifted storyteller, weaving the practical aspects of the global botanical industry with the lesser explored and more nuanced threads that make up the tapestry of sourcing, producing, and selling herbal products. The result is a riveting journey, one that tackles hard questions not explored by most. For those who loved *Braiding Sweetgrass*, this book is a perfect opportunity to go deeper into understanding the complex and co-evolutionary journey of plants and people in creating the herbal products we love."

—ANGELA McELWEE, president and CEO of Gaia Herbs

"*The Business of Botanicals* is a chronicle of the modern-day global herb trade, peppered with historical context, anecdotes, and wisdom from modern pioneers of the herb industry. The quality of the technical information is lovingly translated with practical examples into interesting and relevant guidance for small growers and herb users. And beyond the technical narrative, the author poses philosophical questions about the ethics, authenticity, and sustainability of the modern herb market."

—CINDY ANGERHOFER, executive fellow of
Botanical Research, Aveda Corporation

"I read this brilliant book from cover to cover like a story I couldn't tear myself away from. Like herbs themselves, *The Business of Botanicals* is rich in colors, scents, and flavors and is rooted in the earth—exquisite and messy, beautiful and dirty all at the same time."

—ANNE McINTYRE, MAPA, MCPP, fellow of the National Institute of
Medical Herbalists, author of *Dispensing with Tradition* and *The Ayurveda Bible*

"The high-quality organic herbs in your teacup, tincture, or supplement did not materialize out of thin air. More than fifty years ago, the seeds of an industry were planted by a few unique and talented individuals—farmers, herbalists, and entrepreneurs who have dedicated their lives to improving planetary, human, and animal well-being. This well-researched and fascinating book tells their stories and lays out a clear path for a healthier sustainable future."

—DAVID WINSTON, RH (AHG), dean of David Winston's Center
for Herbal Studies; founder of Herbal Therapeutics Research Library

"Ann Armbrecht acknowledges the racist, imperialist roots of the international trade in botanicals and examines the impressive progress being made to transform this legacy of economic oppression. The evolving supply chain acknowledges the ecology of issues beyond profit. Armbrecht introduces these holistic, ecological perspectives as a sign of great hope for the future and celebrates the rich diversity of people and backgrounds that make the planet's herbal abundance accessible to the West."

—DAVID HOFFMANN, RH (AHG), fellow of the National Institute of
Medical Herbalists, chief formulator for Traditional Medicinals

"Ann Armbrecht has looked under the bonnet and found that the engine of herbal healing is in need of repair. Even well-intentioned conflicts of interest in this industry too often get in the way of quality and sustainability. Ann concludes that the answer here, as ever, is about nurturing relationships and supporting the interests of everyone in the herbal web. Everyone who loves herbs needs to read this book!"

—SIMON MILLS, herbal clinician and elder, author of
Out of the Earth, coauthor of *Principles and Practice of Phytotherapy*

"*The Business of Botanicals* is a thoroughly engaging, must-read book for all herbalists, herbal medicine makers, herb growers, and anyone who turns to herbs for their health. I was immediately drawn into the story of botanical medicines and the complexities within each bottle of herbal tincture on store shelves."

—ROSALEE DE LA FORÊT, herbalist and
author of *Alchemy of Herbs*, coauthor of *Wild Remedies*

"Ann Armbrecht writes with deep respect for the essence of plants and their capacity to heal, seeking to reconcile the spirit of botanicals with the realm of brands and tradeshows."

—JUDITH D. SCHWARTZ, author of *The Reindeer Chronicles* and *Water in Plain Sight*

"Ann Armbrecht's engaging book provides perceptive and important insights into what is too often an invisible trade despite its immense importance to the livelihoods, traditions, and interests of a great many people around the world."

—STEVEN BROAD, executive director of TRAFFIC
and member of the Board of the FairWild Foundation

"A vastly important and enlightening dive into the complexities of the botanical industry that is a must read for conscious consumers and industry professionals alike."

—ERIN SMITH, director of Herbal Science & Research, Banyan Botanicals; co-chair
of the Sustainability Committee at the American Herbal Products Association

"This well-written and well-researched book provides fascinating and important insights into how herbal remedies make it into our homes. Ann Armbrecht's passion for the subject shines through."

—SUSAN CURTIS, director of Natural Health, Neal's Yard Remedies

The Business *of*
Botanicals

EXPLORING THE HEALING
PROMISE OF PLANT MEDICINES
IN A GLOBAL INDUSTRY

Ann Armbrecht

Chelsea Green Publishing
White River Junction, Vermont
London, UK

Copyright © 2020 by Ann Armbrecht.
All rights reserved.

Unless otherwise noted, all photographs copyright © 2020 by Ann Armbrecht.

William Stafford, "Deciding" from *An Oregon Message*. Copyright © 1987 by William Stafford. Reprinted with the permission of The Permissions Company, LLC on behalf of the William Stafford Family Trust.

No part of this book may be transmitted or reproduced in any form by any means without permission in writing from the publisher.

Project Manager: Alexander Bullett
Editor: Fern Marshall Bradley
Copy Editor: Laura Jorstad
Proofreader: Diane Durrett
Indexer: Shana Milkie
Designer: Melissa Jacobson
Page Layout: Abrah Griggs

Printed in the United States of America.
First printing January 2021.
10 9 8 7 6 5 4 3 2 1   21 22 23 24 25

Our Commitment to Green Publishing
Chelsea Green sees publishing as a tool for cultural change and ecological stewardship. We strive to align our book manufacturing practices with our editorial mission and to reduce the impact of our business enterprise in the environment. We print our books and catalogs on chlorine-free recycled paper, using vegetable-based inks whenever possible. This book may cost slightly more because it was printed on paper that contains recycled fiber, and we hope you'll agree that it's worth it. *The Business of Botanicals* was printed on paper supplied by Sheridan that is made of recycled materials and other controlled sources.

Library of Congress Cataloging-in-Publication Data
Names: Armbrecht, Ann, 1962- author.
Title: The business of botanicals : exploring the healing promise of plant medicines in a
    global industry / Ann Armbrecht.
Description: First. | White River Junction : Chelsea Green Publishing, 2021. | Includes bibliographical
    references and index.
Identifiers: LCCN 2020045617 (print) | LCCN 2020045618 (ebook) | ISBN 9781603587488
    (hardcover) | ISBN 9781603587495 (ebook)
Subjects: LCSH: Materia medica, Vegetable. | Medicinal plants. | Medicinal plants—Economic aspects.
Classification: LCC RS164 .A753 2021 (print) | LCC RS164 (ebook) | DDC 615.3/21—dc23
LC record available at https://lccn.loc.gov/2020045617
LC ebook record available at https://lccn.loc.gov/2020045618

Chelsea Green Publishing
85 North Main Street, Suite 120
White River Junction, Vermont USA

Somerset House
London, UK

www.chelseagreen.com

Deciding

One mine the Indians worked had
gold so good they left it there
for God to keep.

At night sometimes you think
your way that far, that deep,
or almost.

You hold all things or not depending
not on greed but whether they suit what
life begins to mean.

Like those workers you study what moves,
what stays. You bow, and then, like them,
you know—

What's God, what's world, what's gold.

—WILLIAM STAFFORD

CONTENTS

Introduction

I have never liked shopping of any kind, but especially not shopping for food. As I walk down an aisle and put a can of beans into my cart, I imagine farmworkers and factory workers tumbling in as well, pulled by invisible threads attached to my hand. It is worse in the supplement aisle, even the supplement aisle of my local food cooperative. I stare at shelves lined with brown glass bottles and white plastic containers. Most, though not all, bear an image of the plant, a flower or leaf. While some list only the plant name, many also claim to be the best quality, the most sustainable, the most fair. I wonder which product will live up to its promises. I worry about the people and places behind those products. By putting this box of tea instead of that one into my cart, am I actually keeping pesticides out of the water? Am I really helping a wild harvester earn a fair wage? Or is it all simply trick mirrors of feel-good marketing, letting me pat myself on the back for being an enlightened consumer? Do my choices, in fact, change nothing?

Perhaps the best thing is to choose nothing, to simply walk away. But I recall what nature writer Barry Lopez said when describing Pacific Northwest landscapes destroyed by clear-cut logging in the mid-1990s. Unless our hands were doing something to stop that logging, Lopez said, we were part of that destruction. Inaction, in other words, is also action.

The global dietary supplement industry has grown significantly over the last few decades, reaching a little over $143 billion in annual sales in 2019, increasing 5.7 percent from 2018.[1] Due to COVID-19, *Nutrition Business Journal* projects that supplement sales will reach the highest level in 20 years, surpassing $50 billion at a growth of 12 percent.[2] The United States is a major player in this industry, representing $46 billion: 34 percent of total sales. Asia's market is nearly equal in size, making up 33.9 percent of the global market in 2018.[3] The global market for herbs and botanicals, a subset of the broader dietary supplement category, in 2019 was estimated to be $37.2 billion with a 5.7 percent growth. Herbal supplement sales in the US were a total $9.6 billion, an 8.6 percent increase from 2018, slightly down from a 9.4 percent increase in 2017. This represents the strongest growth in US sales of herbal supplements since 1998.[4]

In a 2019 study, Natural Marketing Institute (NMI), a strategic consulting firm specializing in natural health and sustainability, found that approximately seven out of ten US consumers reported using supplements in the past thirty days, a percentage that has remained relatively stable for the past five years.[5] Market researchers study these users extensively, dividing them into segments—Well Beings (26 percent), Magic Bullets (20 percent), Eat, Drink & Be Merrys (17 percent), Food Actives (14 percent), and Fence Sitters (23 percent)—based on their shopping choices. Studies indicate that purchase decisions are moving toward what the NMI calls a "whole health" perspective in which individual health concerns merge with concerns about the health of the planet. NMI found that 69 percent of herbal supplement users "embrace a healthy and sustainable lifestyle"; 86 percent of these users prefer supplements made by an environmentally friendly brand. Not only do consumers care about socially responsible business practices, they want evidence that a company is truly walking the talk and not just greenwashing.[6] In their 2019 sustainability report, the Hartman Group, a consumer marketing firm focused on the American food and beverage culture, found that in 2019, 51 percent of consumers reported purchasing sustainable products because they were better for the earth and the environment, up from 32 percent in 2017. The report also found that 26 percent of consumers say they will pay more to support companies that support a worthy cause. And 28 percent say they will pay more to support companies that share their values.[7]

Despite this data, conversations in the herbal products industry about the crucial connections among quality, traceability, and sustainable and ethical sourcing are still in the early stages compared with changes that have already been initiated in the food industry. Because of the way the herbal supplements industry has developed, it is very difficult to find accurate information about the numerous supply chains or about the human and environmental costs of producing a specific product. Companies increasingly claim to be ethical and sustainable. Yet for the most part, consumers are asked to trust those claims even though companies reveal little information about how their sourcing decisions and manufacturing processes affect the people and environments involved in and impacted by that production.

―――――

I began studying herbal medicine in the late 1990s, shortly after returning to the United States from an eighteen-month sojourn conducting ethnographic research on the connections between people and the land in Hedangna, a village in northeastern Nepal. Even though I was back at home, I felt "homesick" for Nepal. I missed the simplicity of living in a remote village, life pared down to the essentials. Like many returning from living overseas, I felt a profound sense of culture shock on returning to a culture and society so driven by consumption. In herbal medicine I found something that filled my yearning for the way of being I had discovered in Hedangna—a sense of reciprocity with the natural world, an understanding of the earth as something more than a resource to exploit, a recognition of the spiritual and cultural dimensions of healing. I signed up for an apprenticeship with Rosemary Gladstar, the "godmother" of the American herbal medicine renaissance, and immersed myself in the study of what felt like the indigenous knowledge of my home.

Yet as I learned more, I realized that the primary places in which medicinal plants entered mainstream American culture were the supplement aisle and the herbal tea section (and today, thousands of internet sites). To most people, herbal medicine was a product to consume, not a set of practices to follow. This commercialization seemed to threaten the heart of herbal medicine, and I wanted to bring the values and practices behind the products into the public eye. And so my husband, Terry Youk, a filmmaker, and I co-produced a documentary celebrating the philosophy of traditional Western herbalism. We called the film *Numen*, a Latin term that means "the animating force in all things living." To us, this concept expresses what is most important about herbal medicine in any tradition—that it is a way to encounter the mystery of nature, an encounter that is healing not just for ourselves, but for the world.

We began screening the film across the country in 2010, and the audience response was striking. Viewers either immediately understood the film's message about the healing power of plants, or they didn't. They either were open to the idea that they could make herbal medicines themselves, or were not. It was a time when many people were beginning to question everything about how food was grown and processed, but far fewer were asking those questions about the medicines they ingested. Parents who would not feed their children anything other than organic food had never questioned the wisdom of giving them Tylenol or Advil, or considered how those medicines were made and with what ingredients. And although they shopped at local farmers markets, those conscientious parents never asked whether "medicine" could be found there as well. Medicine was what you bought at a drug store, not something you could learn to prepare in your own kitchen with plants you had grown yourself, the way I had been taught to do by Rosemary Gladstar. During the screening tour of *Numen*, I came to realize that one small documentary film was not going to change that consciousness on the broader scale. In order to reach people who couldn't conceive of medicine as something other than a pill or powder, I needed to meet them on their ground—in the supplement aisle.

The Importance of Intention

Most herbalists believe that the efficacy of herbal medicine depends on more than the chemical constituents in the plants. Whether and how plant medicine works also depends on what herbalists refer to as the *spirit* of the plant and the relationship of a healer to that spirit. *Intention* matters, too—the intention felt by those who grow, harvest, and process herbs; the intention of the people who make the medicine from those herbs; even the intention of the person who ingests or applies the medicine. Many of these herbalists expressed ambivalence about the commercialization of herbal products, yet they still recommended those products to their clients. They often got around this seeming contradiction by recommending specific companies to buy from, implying that these companies brought intention to their products. Still, as I learned more, I saw it was almost impossible for a company to bring that quality of intention and attention to each step of the process when producing products on a larger scale.

Moreover, much of that production was invisible to the end user. During herb classes, my teachers talked about the uses of chamomile or nettles or echinacea, but they didn't mention any potential differences in the effectiveness of herbs as medicine based on where plants had been sourced and how they had been cared for along the supply chain. Yet, I wondered, in what ways were certified organic nettles grown on a thirty-acre farm in Vermont different from those wild-harvested in places such as Bulgaria or Romania, where the collectors are paid pennies for their labor? Would it change the quality of the medicine if those harvesters were paid a more equitable rate for their work or I could be assured that the plants had been sustainably harvested? And how would you even measure these differences?

At the Watershed Gathering in 1996, writer and farmer Wendell Berry said, "As a nation we are struggling with a profound lack of imagination. We don't see the forests being cut down to build our homes, the lakes being drained as we fill our tub. We live on the far side of a broken connection." Not seeing the people and places on the other side, not seeing the moral and ecological consequences of producing these products, he continued, makes it easier to consume them. "Healing this broken connection," Berry concluded, "begins with seeing beyond what the market wants us to see."[8] This begins with an act of imagination.

Inspired by Wendell Berry and haunted by my shopping experiences, I decided to follow medicinal plants through the supply chain, from the woods and fields where they grew to the facilities and warehouses where they were processed and stored to the factories where they were heated, treated, and packaged. I wanted to tell the stories of the people and places that feed the supply chain, especially those on the far end from the supplement aisle. I wanted to see whether I could find intention in a global supply chain (which I later learned is really more of a network than a linear chain) and, if so, what I might discover in the process. And I wanted to understand how knowing the stories of the people involved in growing, harvesting, and producing these products and those working to source herbs responsibly might make a difference.

Like most commodities, plants are complex entities that have different meanings and values, especially to different stakeholders. They can be a source of healing or of profit, an item of trade, or a foundation for biodiversity. Yet unlike most commodities bought and sold in an international market, plants are alive. They are not simply inert objects to use as we please but rather have adapted to grow in particular habitats and are used in specific ways in systems of medicine around the world. They are embedded in cultural and ecological frameworks of meaning that include guidelines about how to harvest plant parts and prepare medicines from them in ways that respect the plants and their ecosystems. Can connecting these plants with these cultural and ecological worlds, with the people and places that came tumbling into my grocery store cart, lay the foundation for building structures of reciprocity rather than of exploitation?

"We can't be well until the planet is well," Bioneers co-founder Kenny Ausubel told us when we interviewed him for *Numen*. In other words, herbal supplements can promote wellness and health only if the systems that produce those supplements promote health and wellness for all of the stakeholders involved. That depends, as Wendell Berry says, on reconnecting the end product with the people and places behind the production. Yet, is that even possible in an economic system based on that disconnection?

The Sustainable Herbs Project and Program

I began with a simple question: Can the life force of a plant find its way into products manufactured according to the requirements of capital? I knew that to answer this question, I would need to visit collecting sites and manufacturing centers around the world. I made a preliminary trip to eastern Europe. In February 2015 I launched a Kickstarter campaign to fund production of a series of videos that would tell the stories of the people and places on the far end of the supply chain. I decided to call it the Sustainable Herbs Project (SHP). My objective, I explained, was to educate consumers about issues of sustainability, quality, and fair trade in the botanical industry. The outpouring of grassroots support, primarily from the herb community, was overwhelming. I raised $65,000, with an average donation of $35.

Over the next two years, Terry and I and our children, Willow and Bryce, visited farms and factories where we met and interviewed collectors, farmers, business owners, and many others from the key herb exporting regions of the world. We primarily visited producer companies, which were typically located in the country of origin of the herbs and had direct relationships with farmers and collectors from whom they purchased dried or fresh plants. Producer companies carried out minimal processing (drying, sorting, storing) of the plant material before shipping it to other companies, sometimes called secondary processing companies, that further processed the herbs for incorporation into the form in which consumers would purchase them.

Starting in the Pacific Northwest, we visited some of the first certified organic herb growers in the United States. We then headed to the United Kingdom, Germany, Bulgaria, and Poland. In what proved to be one of the most productive trips of the project, in the winter of 2016 Terry and I joined the co-founder and the sustainability manager of Pukka Herbs (a finished-product company) while they met with producer companies in Karnataka state in southern India. In particular, this trip brought into starker relief the cultural dimensions of navigating different standards of quality control as well as the importance of and challenges to developing and maintaining relationships along the supply network. We visited the manufacturing facilities of Banyan Botanicals, a company that produces Ayurvedic herbs and products, and Vitality Works, the leading certified organic contract manufacturer of liquid herbal extracts, both in Albuquerque, New Mexico. From January to June of the following year, Terry, Bryce and I spent six months following the chains of Ayurvedic herbs in India. Willow, who was eighteen at the time and traveling during a gap year before college, joined us for the last month we spent in India. I had hoped to include a trip to China, which is one of the leading suppliers of botanicals around the world. Logistically it just was too difficult and costly, however, and so I had to rely on what I could learn from published reports and by talking with those who have been to China.

Though we visited a number of different companies, I had the most access to Traditional Medicinals and Pukka Herbs. These two companies produce high-quality certified organic teas and other supplements and were both earlier adopters and advocates of the FairWild Standard. Individuals at these companies invited me to visit their supply networks, allowing me a more in-depth, behind-the-scenes view than was possible with any other firm. Other companies are also leading in this work, but because of this access, Pukka and Traditional Medicinals are more heavily featured in this book.

On returning home, I launched a multimedia website to showcase videos and photo-essays based on our travels. The following year I formed a partnership with the American Botanical Council (ABC), an international NGO dedicated to providing education using science-based and traditional information to promote the responsible use of herbal medicine. SHP became a program of ABC, and for clarity I changed the name to the Sustainable Herbs Program. SHP began as a grassroots project rooted in the herb community and the plants. This partnership with ABC brought it into an entirely different world, one where few people would consider that commercialization of herbs might not be a good thing or would ever wonder whether intention can be preserved in a global supply chain. This was not the world I knew, but it was one I needed to take part in if I truly desired changes in the industry to take hold. ABC has given me a platform to initiate and join conversations about sustainability in the herb industry happening on this much larger scale.

I conceived of SHP to inspire change in the herbal products industry. The first step of any change, however, involves understanding the system and the stakeholders involved. And so while this book is not a product of the Sustainable Herbs Program, the two are related in that in it I recount my journey to understand the challenges and issues in the industry from the perspective of those working in that industry, not simply as an outsider. I also explore the questions that drew me to herbalism in the first place. If, as I believed, herbal medicine offers insights into how to live in right relationship with the earth, can those values stand up to capitalism? Can plants be both living entities with which humans can have a sacred relationship *and* commodities governed by the laws of capital? If that is possible, what are the conditions that allow for right relationship within a commercial enterprise?

As I stood in the grocery store many years ago, the idea of following herbs through the supply chain seemed fairly simple to me. But I soon found out that it was not. Unlike other plant commodities such as coffee, cacao, or cotton, which follow a fairly straightforward trajectory from harvest to market, sourcing medicinal plants is more like a spiderweb than a chain. A single herbal products company may source anywhere from thirty to several hundred species of plants. They may need to find roots or resins of some species, leafy parts or flowers of others, and even the bark of certain species. Roots must be handled differently from flowers or barks. Each species and plant part must be harvested at certain times of year, dried at specific temperatures, and processed in unique ways. Plants contain a particular combination of constituents based on where they grow—the soil, the weather, the altitude. Change the growing location and the constituents may change, too. All of these factors impact whether the plants being sourced have the necessary qualities to be effective. Because of this, sourcing herbs is challenging, even on the open market where there is no need to trace the plants to the source. Sourcing high-quality, sustainably harvested or certified organically grown herbs—and verifying that the workers are paid a fair wage as well—requires so much attention to detail that it boggles the mind.

Given this complexity, I rarely received simple answers when I asked questions about the issues of ensuring fairness to workers, minimizing the impact of wild-harvesting, developing sustainable methods to cultivate herbs on a commercial scale, and assessing and ensuring product quality. More often than not, I was told, the answer depended. It depended on what country I was asking about. It depended on the species of herb being harvested. It depended on what part of the plant would be used and what type of finished product it would be used for.

I originally envisioned structuring this book around each step of the journey that medicinal plants make from seed to shelf, but the reality of so much variation in that journey made it difficult to create a narrative that held together. Instead, I discovered that the thread weaving through the stories that interested me most was relationship: a commitment by an herbal product company to establish and maintain relationships with the producer companies that in turn had direct relationships with farmers and collectors. Maintaining the relationships was essential to ensuring the plants were high quality and that people and places were well cared for. These relationships were established and preserved through one-on-one conversations in a farmer's fields, visits to processing facilities, or while negotiating price and the terms of trade at a company's display booth during a trade show. They brought in a human dimension, making it possible for a transaction to be about more than profit—a way to also care for humanity and the earth. These one-on-one connections didn't make that transformation inevitable. They simply made it possible.

CHAPTER ONE

Making Medicine

Our gaze has become so narrow—
we no longer feel 10,000 trembling things
at the periphery of our gaze.

—MARTIN SHAW, "Trailing the Gods Back Home"

I first recognized medicine as a process rather than a product at a tincture-making workshop in the mid-1990s. The young teacher showed us a twisted echinacea root she had dug from her garden the previous day. "It's easy to wash the roots," she said. "Just use a strong hose." She demonstrated how to break the root into smaller pieces to remove dirt from the crevices. "Cut up the root as small as possible," she added as she chopped it into tiny pieces. She explained that the greater the surface area that comes into contact with the *menstruum*—the solvent used to extract compounds or constituents from the plant material—the more constituents would be extracted. She dumped the root bits into a mason jar, covered the roots with vodka, put a lid on the jar, and shook. Let it sit in a dark place for six weeks, she said, then strain off the liquid, which is the medicine. The leftover bits of root, called the marc, can be composted.

The demonstration lasted only ten minutes. For the remainder of the hour-long class, the instructor talked about the uses of various medicinal plants. I only half listened. I was still marveling at the simplicity of the medicine making. It would be one thing if making a tincture was difficult or time consuming, but it isn't. The process is a bit messy, but it is easier than making a cake, even a cake from a packaged mix. And yet I had never before considered the possibility that I could make my own medicine. To me, medicine was what I bought at a pharmacy, what a doctor would prescribe for me, not something concocted with roots and leaves and some vodka in my kitchen. Why hadn't anyone ever told me how easy this was? Or that I could do it myself? In my own home? With the root of a plant I could grow in my own garden? And that it was so inexpensive? I was preoccupied by the cost and by another more confounding question, which I had never considered before. When— and how—had medicine become a product to buy instead of a skill we could share?

Restoring Balance

The following year I met Deb Soule at a retreat to envision an organization that would honor of the work of simple-living advocates Helen and Scott Nearing. Deb ran a small apothecary selling remedies prepared from herbs grown in her biodynamic gardens in Downeast Maine. She brewed pots of tea from loose dried flowers and leaves. I was used to my coffee strong and my tea in bags, and so I was curious. It tasted a bit like grass. Deb talked about her gardens and the medicines she made in her kitchen and the community clinic where she met with clients. It all sounded small-scale and right-sized. She mentioned that she was buying some land up the road from her house to expand her gardens and that I should come visit.

Later that summer I did visit. Deb and I gathered nasturtiums and greens from her garden for dinner. In her house, jars filled every open surface: counters, wooden shelves, tables by a futon couch. Some jars were filled with dried orange flowers or green leaves, others with what looked like chopped roots soaking in a brown slurry. Still others held a deep golden or crimson oil. A sticky note on the oven door proved to be a reminder to check inside before turning the oven on, because there might be medicinal oils within, being slowly warmed by the pilot light. Deb's house smelled earthy and slightly sweet, a greenish smell that is hard to describe but which I recognized immediately in every herb warehouse I subsequently visited on my travels for the Sustainable Herbs Program.

When I was growing up, I never would have found medicinal oil in the oven in our family's kitchen. More likely it would have been Hamburger Helper or minute steaks on the stovetop. The salads of my childhood were a chunk of iceberg lettuce with a dollop of bright orange French dressing from a bottle. Nestlé's chocolate chip cookies were as homemade as we got. This wasn't because my mother was negligent or didn't care. This was the 1960s in West Virginia. The promise of the modern era was for women to spend less, not more, time in the kitchen, and I was born into a social class where that shift was possible. What mattered about food was that it was convenient and quick, not where the ingredients came from or how they had been processed. I grew up thinking of my body as something to exercise and to fuel as needed, like a car. I depended on my body, but didn't think much about how it worked. When I was a college student at Dartmouth, a tree or a plant was what I passed as I hiked—or better yet, ran—up the trail to reach the top of the mountain.

Deb went on walks, not runs. She drank teas that nourished her body, not ones that kept her awake. She ate the foods she could grow in her garden, and whole grains she could grind herself.

Being with Deb, I was reminded of what I'd experienced in Nepal—in the way she talked, in the little things she noticed, in the pace at which she worked. She didn't let the hurry around her change her rhythm. Her hands, like the hands of the women in Hedangna, were rough from a lifetime of working the soil. And she talked about plants as if they were alive—as if they were people with whom she could have a relationship, with whom she did have a relationship.

At Deb's suggestion I attended the New England Women's Herbal Conference, which took place in August at a summer camp in New Hampshire. Hundreds of women joined hands and sang, attended workshops to learn about using echinacea and goldenseal, and discussed the differences between dry and wet coughs and the best medicines for each. It was an astounding change of scene from Cambridge, where I was completing my dissertation at Harvard, a place where people decidedly did not stand in circles or sing songs or hold hands. At Harvard knowledge was what you learned with your head, not what you discovered in your heart. At that herb conference, though, the openness of so many people unafraid to speak of what they loved reminded me of what I missed most about Nepal. And so without much thought I signed up for Rosemary Gladstar's apprentice program on the art and science of herbal medicine at Sage Mountain Retreat Center in north-central Vermont.

The apprenticeship took the form of eight weekend classes over as many months. Each weekend focused on a different system of the body and included a mix of lectures about the specific plants to use for ailments of that body system, hands-on medicine-making classes, and plant identification. We camped in a field and shared potluck meals in a communal kitchen. We began class each morning by gathering in a circle to drum, and we sang songs and chants throughout the day. Several weekends included taking sweats in the sweat lodge built in a clearing in the woods.

That first weekend Rosemary stood in the yurt before an altar with candles, stones, feathers, and a bouquet of fresh flowers. Her wavy auburn hair hung down the back of her long, maroon velvet dress. She spoke about health as wholeness, and healing as a way of restoring balance. She explained that medicinal plants strengthen the immune system by nourishing and supporting the body's capacity to heal itself. She gave examples of plants used to support the immune system, for anxiety, for broken bones, and for broken hearts. But she didn't stop there.

Echoing the tradition of healers and mystics from around the world, Rosemary then described how plants are complex beings with their own role and purpose in the ecosystem. When we use plants as medicine, we tap into that larger sense of connection, she explained, into the weave of every thing with every other thing. When you ingest plant medicine as a tea or tincture or even as a capsule, you take in the life force of the plant. And that life force is healing. All of the natural medicine traditions of the world embrace this healing force of nature, she continued. It is only modern Western, or allopathic, medicine that does not.

The heart of my research in Nepal was speaking with Yamphu priests and shamans about their journeys through the world of the ancestors and the ways their relationship with this unseen world sustained the world of the living. Their stories and practices opened me to a world beyond what I could know with my rational mind, a world that acknowledged mystery and spirit, one that recognized traditions that placed limits on human use of the land.

In the herbal medicine taught by Rosemary, I discovered a way to practice these values at home, in my own culture, in my own kitchen. I stepped in with both feet. My daughter, Willow, was an infant at the time, and I placed moist tea sachets of chamomile on her eyes to treat a case of pink eye. We drank nettle tea from a mason jar each day. I gathered red clover from fields and tried, without much success, to dry the flowers and retain their vibrant purple. I made echinacea tincture with roots harvested from a friend's garden. I collected St. Johnswort from a nearby meadow to make a salve for my sister to use during childbirth. Each month, on the evening of the full moon, Willow and I gathered calendula, peppermint, lemon balm, and petals from whatever edible flowers were blooming at the time. We placed them in a bowl filled with water and added a special object—a ring, my moon necklace from my apprenticeship at Sage Mountain. We set the bowl outside to steep in the rays of the full moon. First thing the following morning, we drank the whole bowlful of brew and felt we were drinking in the mystery of the night sky. Retrieving the object from the bowl, we could wear that mystery around our necks or on our fingers. Working with these plants was something lovely to do with and for my daughter. Even more important than the physical constituents of the tea, I felt, was the way I could fill her with memories of moments that were like a prayer, even if those moments seemed, to her, more like a dream than a memory.

I loved the sweat lodges, the drum, the prayers we spoke while gathered in a circle. Herbal medicine promised a way for me to find the sacred in my own culture and in the land that was my home. I didn't question the sources of the teaching, the cultural sources or the mystical dimensions that I experienced during my apprenticeship. Growing and using medicinal plants was purposeful—an occupation, like growing food, that was simpler, more connected to values that mattered to me. And it was also a way to connect with the spiritual dimensions I witnessed in Nepal. As Rosemary told us in that yurt, "Plants offer so much more than that." That more-ness got me hooked.

The Mystery in Herbal Medicine

Rosemary's classes at Sage Mountain often ran over the time allotted, and she would postpone a topic to the next class or next weekend. The year I took her course (and perhaps every year?), the class that kept getting rescheduled was about chemical constituents. It was one of the classes I had most been looking forward to, because I hoped it would unlock the mystery of how herbs worked as medicine.

In Western herbal medicine, phytochemistry and pharmacodynamics are the primary systems of reference for explaining how herbs affect the workings of the human body. *Phytochemistry* is the study of the chemical constituents in plants; *pharmacodynamics* is the study of the pharmacological effects of phytochemicals and their mechanisms of action. One well-known example is echinacea. When taken in the proper doses at the onset of symptoms, echinacea has been shown to boost the levels of macrophages (cells that function in destroying foreign invaders such as bacteria and viruses) and some types of white blood cells. This in turn stimulates phagocytosis (one of the body's innate defense mechanisms), which enhances the body's ability to attack pathogens that trigger illness.[1] Even though scientists have been able to document this effect, however, there is no consensus on which constituents in echinacea cause these particular actions.

The number of chemical constituents in a plant is immense. This is one challenge scientists face in trying to identify which chemical constituents in a medicinal plant are the ones that produce a healing effect. But the complexity is not simply that there are billions of chemicals in plants, and that it is impossible to predict the ways those chemicals may interact in the body. An additional dimension is that a plant is more than simply a passive container for its chemical constituents. I asked herbalist David Winston, the president of Herbalist & Alchemist and director of a well-established herb school in New Jersey, about this when I interviewed him at their production facility in New Jersey. Large and complicated systems demonstrate "what is called emergent behaviors, behaviors that arise from the way the system—the pieces—come together," David explained. Or synergy. It seems obvious that life is more than a sum of the parts—yet it is hard to talk about this less tangible dimension. I asked David how he would describe this other quality of the plants. "If you could identify every single chemical in nettles—you couldn't," he said. "No one has. But say you could, and you put those chemicals into a bowl in the same proportion they are found in nettle plants and then mix them up, the results wouldn't be nettles. There is a deeper organization beyond biology; there is a spiritual nature to these things. And a bowl of chemicals doesn't have a spiritual nature."

Rosemary explained it this way: "Echinacea increases the body's white blood cell count, so we can use it in that simplistic way. But unbeknownst to us it's working on a very deep level. It's grounding us. It's building our relationship with the world around us . . . The constituents don't really explain the whole personality of that plant.

"It's like knowing a person," she continued. "The longer and deeper you know someone, the more you begin to see the different levels of who they are. At first, you may see that they're a good mother or an artist or play music. As you get to know them and your relationship deepens, your ability to understand all they can do in the world deepens. It's much the same with plants. I mean, why would it be different?" she concluded, laughing.

The work of making medicine from plants is to transfer this complexity into forms—teas, tinctures, capsules, salves—that our bodies can utilize. A medicinal plant can be eaten whole as food, but more traditionally herbalists extract the plants' constituents in a menstruum— alcohol, water, glycerin, vinegar, oil—to preserve the medicine. The extraction methods used depend on factors such as whether the desired constituents are water-soluble or are better extracted from fresh versus dried plant material—as well as the medicine maker's preference.[2]

Extraction occurs until homeostasis is reached between the concentration of constituents inside the cells and outside the cells. Shaking or agitating the mixture helps change this balance to extract more constituents. The presence of constituents in the menstruum can often be detected by a change in the menstruum's color, taste, or odor. These indicators are also increasingly the basis of lab testing of medicinal extracts—to show that the active constituents that will make the remedy effective have passed from the plant into the menstruum. That menstruum can then be delivered as tea or a tincture, or it can be spray dried to make a powder that can be encapsulated.

The mechanics of extracting medicinal constituents is fairly straight-forward. The art of making *good* medicine is something else altogether.

As traditional practitioners around the world know well, the process of making medicine begins long before the chopping of roots or leaves. For wild-collected plants it begins at the moment of harvest. With cultivated plants the process starts much earlier, with the decisions about where and when to plant. Tibetan and Ayurvedic texts include guidelines that specify the appropriate time of day, stage of the moon, and month of the year for harvesting plants to be used as medicine, and even which side òf a slope to harvest from. Anthropologist Calum Blaikie writes that practitioners of Tibetan medicine (*Sowa Rigpa*) in Ladakh harvest "when most flowers are in bloom, and again on the fifteenth day of the sixth moon when later blooming flowers are at their peak."[3] Dhansing Rana, a village elder in the Indian Himalayas and one of the most active wild collectors I've met, described how villagers relied on a particular late-blooming plant that grew near the village as a signal of sorts for when to collect the roots of kutki (*Picrorhiza kurroa*), an herb that must be harvested above the tree line. When the signal species began to bloom, the villagers knew that the kutki would have finished its life cycle and started to die back, and thus it would be the right time to hike up through the forest to harvest. The timing was important because the energy of a plant goes to the roots as the aerial parts die back. It also ensured that harvesting happened only after the kutki plants had set their seeds, increasing the likelihood of regeneration.

Behind all these guidelines lies the fact that the chemical constituents of a plant, and so the activity of the plant as medicine, vary depending on environmental stresses—the amount of rainfall or sun or wind, whether the plant is fighting insect attacks and other threats. Plants demonstrate what is known as *phenotypic plasticity*, a term that refers to the changes organisms make in response to the environment in which they grow. These changes include things like variations in the thickness of their leaves, density of pores, and the amount of chlorophyll in the leaves.[4] "There are no characteristics without a context," wrote Craig Holdredge, director of The Nature Institute.[5] Each plant develops what Holdredge called the "signature" of place.[6] This signature is the way the larger context—seen and unseen—is expressed in the structure of the plant.

These qualities are particularly important with plants used as medicine. The primary constituents of a plant are those considered essential to the survival and well-being of the organism, such as proteins and starches necessary for respiration, photosynthesis, growth, and development. Plants also produce secondary constituents, also referred to as *secondary metabolites*: substances that are not essential to the plant's direct survival, but that play a larger role in the ecosystem, such as attracting pollinators, helping the plant adapt to environmental stressors, or serving as chemical defenses to protect the plant from attack. Secondary constituents are typically responsible for the medicinal activity of plants.[7] They are often found in greater quantities when plants grow under stress because the soil is poor or there's a drought or other environmental problem. When we interviewed him for *Numen*, well-known medical herbalist David Hoffmann explained what humans receive from these constituents: "Secondary plant metabolites are the way in which the plant interacts with its ecology, with other plants, with other animals, with the soil. So when we're using herbs, we're not just getting their nutrition. We're partaking in this ecological interface. We're embracing nature and nature is embracing us, whether we're aware of it or not." Ultimately this embrace is part of what drew me to herbal medicine, an embrace that is built into the chemistry of the plant.

Traditional systems of medicine have developed based on the ways particular plants growing in particular places have been found to be effective, on their signature of place. Not all individual species of *Echinacea* are equal as medicine, in other words. Both formal modern medical systems and most traditional medical systems of the world capture this type of knowledge in a book called a pharmacopeia. A *pharmacopeia* is a book of standards that may outline the uses of plants and how to harvest and process them to ensure that raw plant materials meet the quality necessary to make effective medicine. The information in a pharmacopeia is quite detailed and includes descriptions of what a plant should look like whole as well as under a microscope. It includes various methods for testing identity and purity (testing the microbial load, ash content, and so on), which are often unique to particular species. For dandelion root, for example, an important test is its bitter value. For slippery elm bark a key indicator is the swelling qualities, which indicate the presence of the desired mucilage. A pharmacopeia is based on the recognition that the way plants are handled is integral to the efficacy of the finished product. When a species is grown in a new ecosystem, it must be tested to determine whether there are measurable differences in phytochemical composition, quality, and strength—and if so, whether the plants can be expected to produce the same effects as described in traditional use.[8]

On the last weekend of the apprenticeship at Sage Mountain, Rosemary assured us that we would get to the class on chemical constituents. It was a brilliant Indian summer day, the kind of weather you know won't last long before late fall and winter arrive in Vermont. The leaves on the mountain were turning deep red and yellow and orange. The sky was blue and the air was cool, but not too cool. The thirty students, twenty-eight women and two men, slowly straggled back through the woods toward the yurt after lunch. Rosemary was sitting on the porch beating a drum to call us back. The first of us to arrive picked up drums and rattles and joined her. Soon everyone was there, and it was time to start class, but Rosemary kept drumming. No one said anything; we all just continued to drum in that early-autumn sun.

After some time she stopped and put down her drum. Laughing, she said, "I know we were supposed to have class now. But it is so beautiful out."

Sitting outside in the sunlight that afternoon, filling ourselves with the beauty—the blue sky and warm sun—was a memory we could return to during the winter months, when the days were gray and cold and the ground covered in snow. "This, too, is a kind of medicine," she told us. And then she rose and went into the yurt. We followed, sat in a semicircle in low chairs around the altar, and continued with the day of teaching. I can't remember anything else from that weekend. I just remember that in lieu of studying the chemical constituents of plants, we had drummed in the beautiful autumn sun.

Learning to See Double

In his essay "The Invitation," Barry Lopez described an encounter with a bear while hunting with a group of Athabascans in Alaska. He was struck by the differences in how he and his companions described this encounter. To Lopez it was all about watching the bear. He didn't pay much attention to the landscape or the events that led up to or followed the encounter. The Athabascans, however, were aware of the bear in the larger context. For example, they noticed signs indicating where the bear had come from and where it was going. They experienced the encounter not as an isolated moment but as an event unfolding in time. The two modes of perceiving the bear—his seeing it as a single object of focus versus his companions' seeing it in relationship with its environment—reminds me of Holdredge's observations about how plants are expressions of the environment where they grow. Lopez concluded that unlike his experience, which was simply an isolated event, for the Athabascans the appearance of the bear was an invitation into the stream of life, "offered, without prejudice, to anyone passing by."[9]

I encountered a similar way of seeing in Nepal, where the priests and shamans in Hedangna were distinguished from everyone else in the village by their ability to "see double." They could see the concrete, material world, of course. They could also see the nonliving, or more than living, such as the ancestors. The priests and shamans knew when these ancestors arrived at ceremonies held in their honor. These village healers could also visit and interact with the ancestors while searching for the lost souls of villagers who had fallen ill. This ability to see beyond the physical world requires a different quality of attention and of listening, one that allows for something unknown to emerge rather than adhering to the belief that the physical environment is all that is there. By seeing how our lives depend on a web of non-visible relationships, we enter a relationship with that broader frame, or web. We see ourselves as part of the unfolding of events and act accordingly. Although I didn't realize it at the time, my apprenticeship at Sage Mountain was the beginning of a journey of steeping myself in this other way of seeing.

———————

Deb Soule once told me that, often, as she listens to a client talking, a plant will appear in the periphery of her vision. Deb said she took these occurrences seriously and trusted in them as signs that the plant she saw had something to offer that client, whether to heal their physical ailment or to provide succor for something more elusive, something emotional or spiritual.

I wondered aloud why she was able to have these visions. Deb said she spent so much time working with the plants in the garden through the seasons, she knew them intimately; how they moved and reseeded, whether they liked dry or moist or shady soil, and how they grew—tall and weedy, tight and clustered, or solitary. She knew plants better than she knew most people, she said. The depth of that relationship, she believed, is why they showed up for her in this way.

I believe it is also because Deb makes room and takes the time. Perceiving the essence, or spirit, of a plant takes a particular type of work. It is like exercising a muscle we don't use much, one that, without practice, can easily be misused.

One morning at Sage Mountain, Rosemary sent the apprentices into the forest with the instruction to speak with a plant. It's a familiar practice to me now, but it was new to me at the time. Afterward the group shared their experiences. A young man said he sat with a plant that encouraged him to take a bite. "Eat me," he said he was told. And so he did. Rosemary responded more firmly than usual. "There is water hemlock, a poisonous plant, down there," she said. "Listen to the plants. But also always have a field guide. Know without a doubt the identity of the plant you choose to eat."

Next, a woman shared her experience, but I was listening with only half an ear. Then another woman, the one who struck me as most knowledgeable in the class, spoke up and said her experience had been very similar. Each of them had brought back a leaf to identify, because they didn't know what their plant was. On comparing the leaves, they discovered they had each connected with what turned out to be blue cohosh. Even to a trained eye, the leaves of blue cohosh can be hard to identify. Now they had my attention.

My curiosity aroused, I wanted to learn more. About a year later I attended a workshop at Sage Mountain on sacred plant medicine offered by herbalist and scholar Stephen Buhner. Stephen led us on a guided spiritual journey to what he called "an inside house." On some plant journeys like this one, I have taken a drop of a tincture of a particular plant (not hallucinogenic) beforehand, but most of my experiences with plant spirit medicine are reached through visualization. On this particular journey, my first of what has been many, I found myself in a clearing in a forest of evergreens. As Stephen guided the group with his voice, I followed a packed-dirt path leading out of the clearing, through the forest, onto a rocky slope, and across a stream. I then headed uphill and began to see a stone cottage high in the mountains, on the edge of a meadow filled with wildflowers. A little girl, probably three or four years old, stood shyly by the stone wall of the cottage, watching as I climbed toward the ridge.

Stephen recommended that we visit our inside house daily for a full year to strengthen that "muscle." I took him at his word and made it a daily practice. I would close my eyes and concentrate on my breath. I would suddenly find myself alone in the clearing surrounded by tall evergreens. I would rise, walk along a path leading from the clearing down through a forest, also evergreen, and into the meadow. I would follow the path, jumping across the stream, and then climb the rocky trail to the stone cottage in its high mountain pasture. Time and distance had little relationship on this journey. Whether I arrived quickly at the cottage depended on the quality of my attention. Below the house was a waterfall with a shaded pool; sometimes I would swim there. Other times I would climb through the fields behind the house, high up the ridge. Most often I would enter through the wooden door, ducking my head. Allowing my eyes to adjust to the dim light, I would sit down by the dying coals of the cooking fire on the ground, like in the homes where I had lived in Nepal. There was a wooden table with wooden benches on one side. Vases filled with flowers from the meadow sat in the windows, which were simply openings in the stone.

The little girl would greet me. When I first encountered her, she was aloof and suspicious. She asked where I had been all these years. I didn't know how to respond. But I kept coming back, and soon she would come running to greet me. Sometimes she brought flowers from the meadow—deep blue larkspur, yellow buttercups, whatever was in bloom. She would reach for my hand, eagerly leading me to something that delighted her or scared her or something that made her sad. Later, when we went inside, she would lean against my side as we sat cross-legged by the fire.

Dhanmaya was in the stone cottage as well. Dhanmaya was the mother of the family with whom I had lived in Hedangna. She and I hadn't talked much then; nor did we talk much in the cottage. She would bring me tea and warm soup. She would tell me to rest.

During that year of visiting the inside house, I was in the middle of a drawn-out, contentious divorce. My husband of thirteen years, partner for eighteen, and father of our two-year-old daughter had just left to try something new with a younger woman who had no child. He and I were fighting over custody of our daughter. My closest friend was dying of breast cancer. And I had moved three times in the last ten months. I had never felt more alone in my life. In that stone house by that cook fire, Dhanmaya let me rest. She prepared food for me. And that rest and that warmth—nourishment I couldn't find anywhere else in my life at the time—provided what I needed so I could rise, walk back down the hill, cross the stream, and reenter my outer life.

These experiences paved the way for me to see more deeply into the world around me. Equally important, they helped me begin to trust what I saw. What started as learning about preparing herbal teas and tinctures became something much more, an invitation into a world that was more magical and mysterious than I had ever known and more deeply healing than I imagined possible. That is the invitation and the medicine that plants offer.

Twenty years on from my first herbal medicine-making class, I have a floor-to-ceiling cupboard lined with mason jars filled with tinctures. I've taken countless courses on medicinal herbs and making herbal medicine, but I still do what I learned how to do in that first lesson. I chop and fill a jar with roots, leaves, and flowers freshly harvested from my garden or that I've dried or purchased from someone else. Though I always intend to follow the very specific instructions on how much alcohol to add when extracting a particular herb, I rarely get around to looking up the details. I just make sure the herbs are covered by the liquid and then store them in a dark cupboard. I shake the jar when I remember and decant the tincture when I have time—always at least six weeks later, though sometimes as much as a year.

I trust that if I follow this process, using high-quality herbs that have been handled correctly, the medicine will carry the components needed to stimulate the intended result. I see the clear alcohol change to a dark muddy brown or greenish color, depending on whether I'm tincturing roots or fresh leaves. I feel the tingle of echinacea on my tongue or taste the bitterness of motherwort and trust that something of the plant has infused into the menstruum and that the medicine will be effective in ways I can and cannot know.

Making herbal medicine as a product to sell is an entirely different story, however. The focus shifts from a living plant growing in a meadow or field to a finished product on a grocery store shelf. What matters is that the material in the bottle is what the label claims it to be. The integral connections among process, *how* that material has been sourced and handled, and quality, are invisible—and so not considered relevant—to most buyers of these products.

What is lost when the product matters more than the process, when all we see is the bear isolated from the context? My journey to follow herbs through the supply chain was perhaps simply a quest to see double, to see the products within their context. Not necessarily to see the invisible world of spirit, but to make visible the invisible processes that must take place in order to fill all those store shelves with perfectly packaged products. I wanted to see what might be regained by observing the entire journey.

I was drawn to herbal medicine because it allowed me to connect with the source of healing. The process—the experience of growing and harvesting the plants and making the remedies—mattered as much as the remedy itself. When I took a tincture of motherwort I had made myself, I took it as much for the memory of the motherwort plant growing in my garden as I did to experience the herb's bitter flavor and receive its benefits. I wondered how this dimension of healing might translate to a global scale of herbal medicine. I also wanted to understand how herbal medicine had become transformed from the traditional practices of kitchen medicine that we learned at Sage Mountain to an incredibly complex, mechanized, sanitized global supply chain. How did the herbal supplements aisle come to exist in the first place? To answer that question, we need to explore the rebirth of interest in herbalism in the United States and how that resurgence shaped the botanical industry of the twenty-first century.

CHAPTER TWO

The Modern Renaissance
of Herbal Medicine

*The seed is the whole potential of the plant
contracted to a single point.*

—RUDOLF STEINER

A history of what philosopher Paul Lee coined the "herbal renaissance" in the United States has yet to be written, but a book titled *Herbal Pathfinders* captures the diversity and creativity of that period of time.[1] The book is a collection of interviews with men and women active in the herbal revival of the 1970s as well as brief introductory essays by the book's authors, Robert Conrow and Arlene Hecksel. Each essay traces the lineage of learning—from Shakers to Rudolf Steiner to Native Americans to Ayurvedic texts to elders to *curanderos* to books. The diversity of the contributors captures the creativity of the herbal movement at that time. The voices were eclectic. There were essays on vision quests, responsible harvesting practices, medicinal uses of herbs, the spiritual dimensions of herbalism, and more.[2] No one claimed to have the only valid perspective. Each was one thread in reintroducing practices that had been lost—or simply weren't visible—in mainstream culture.

The common theme across all the interviews in the book is the power of learning directly from the plants: from the spirit of the plants or by experimenting with using plants as medicine. The relationship is at the heart of the healing.

There are many ways to tell the story of the herbal renaissance. Unlike countries where the traditional systems of medicine that relied on plants never died out, in the United States herbal medicine had fallen from mainstream use by the early mid-1900s. Even so, in rural communities without access to formal health care, in African American communities in urban areas, in Native American communities, in pockets of Appalachia and more, these methods were kept alive and passed through the generations. Just because no one was talking about plant medicine in mainstream circles didn't mean no one was using plants as medicine. These communities became the sources of inspiration for the women and men who "rediscovered" these practices in the 1970s.

Because there was no strong cultural framework for learning about the practice of plant medicine, the individuals rediscovering it played a large role in shaping how traditional Western herbalism reemerged. Those eager to learn gathered knowledge wherever they could and in turn shared that knowledge with whoever would listen. In this chapter I describe what I learned of this revitalization by tracing the stories of the teachers with whom I studied, particularly those who went on to create the companies that many other herbalists in turn now advise their students to support.

This account is based on my experience, and as such, it is not a complete history of herbalism or of the herbal renaissance in the United States. I present it in this way because the herbal medicine that was widespread in the late 1990s and early 2000s primarily catered to white audiences who, because of their economic class and ethnicity, had the resources to access this information, either by attending conferences or enrolling in in-person apprentice programs. Similarly, those with resources, financial and cultural, were more likely to start businesses than those without. Other voices and stories are now entering the conversation, revealing the ways that people of color have been excluded and their practices ignored or taken without acknowledgment. An entirely different book can, and I hope will, be written about these practices, historically and in the present, and the movement to bring this diversity to herbalism in the United States.

Rosemary Gladstar

For me the story begins with Rosemary Gladstar. "As a child, I was infused with the plants," Rosemary once told me. As she said this, I imagined an infusion of nettles, steeping overnight in a mason jar. By morning the clear water has turned a dark green. I think of Rosemary infused in the same way, filled with the colors and vibrations of plants.

We were sitting in the cozy, comfortable living room of her home at Sage Mountain on a rainy autumn day. Herb books were stacked on the coffee table and on bookshelves. Potted plants sat on a bench by the row of windows. Candles, small statues, rocks, an incense burner, a vase of dried flowers, photos of her grandson filled the mantel.

Rosemary spent uncounted hours as a child with her grandmother, Mary Egithanoff, in the garden, weeding and gathering herbs for cooking. Rosemary's grandmother had escaped from Armenia in the early 1900s, fleeing starvation and persecution. Her grandmother showed her amaranth, chickweed, purslane, the native plants they had eaten in Armenia when they were starving. "She loved purslane," Rosemary said. She paused. "I grew up being nurtured on this cellular level by this ancient information. That was important. It kind of encoded me."

Rosemary told me about the earliest childhood dream she could remember, when she was four or five years old. "I'm in this kind of foggy place, and I'm running through the mist and then into a beautiful meadow of violets. The feeling I had—I can still feel it as if it were yesterday—was like, *I've come home.*"

Another time, in an experience that wasn't a dream, she and her brothers and sisters were in the field with the cows from their dairy farm in California. Suddenly the cows started running toward the children. "We thought they would trample us to death, so we ran across the field and climbed an enormous willow tree. It was dark and the cattle were coming, and what I remember, again, it's just like yesterday, was sitting completely protected and held by this giant willow and feeling this incredible oneness with that tree."

Rosemary graduated from high school in the late 1960s, just as the back-to-the-land movement was beginning. "It was incredible, you just got pulled into it," she said. But she didn't need to go back to the land, because she already lived in rural America. Instead she went to the wilderness. Rosemary spent three years in the Sierra Nevada, living out of a backpack in the woods and learning from the plants, her books, and the people she met. Herbal medicine was still alive and well as a system of folk healing in this area. "These teachers were just people living," Rosemary said. "They weren't teaching from a book. They were just like, here you go, let me show you what is around here and here is how you make this."

Each summer she came down from the high country to town to earn some money. She cared for the children of the Roma people who worked in the circus. She cleaned toilets at the Guerneville natural food store. Once she'd made some money, she headed back to the mountains. She recalls it as a time of grace, a time when she was able to drink deeply of the world, to fill herself with adventure. It wasn't a way of life she could continue, though. And so when she came back to town to stay, she was ready to "give back."

———

Baiseti *thuma* (which translates as "grandmother") was a tiny woman whose hands were gnarled from years of working the soil in the remote Himalayan village of Hedangna. Rosemary has the same direct, clear presence that Baiseti thuma had, like a forest-spirit. She would have been a shamani, Baiseti thuma once told me, had she been a man. Being a woman didn't stop Rosemary.

Rosemary's joy and apparent lightheartedness belie an incredible depth of knowledge and an equally incredible capacity for hard work, for doing what it takes to get things done. She can make it seem like everything is easy. At one of the countless conferences she has organized, in a moment when I could see Rosemary's weariness showing through, she told me that she *chooses* joy. She sees the good in people, not necessarily because that good is always easily available, but because she intentionally chooses to focus on it.

In 1972 Rosemary began working in the herb section at the Guerneville natural food store, mixing herbal medicines. People began buying her custom formulas. Seeing how well the formulas worked, their friends came to buy them as well. Soon she made arrangements to rent a small wing in the store. "It was like a closet, really," Rosemary said. That was her first business, Rosemary's Garden. Like many of Rosemary's creations, it still operates today (under different ownership).

Rosemary continued mixing formulas in her small shop. Customers who came in would describe the symptoms of their ailment, and as they spoke Rosemary's hands would begin gathering a pinch of this herb and a pinch of that, her body intuiting what each individual needed. "It wasn't like I wasn't thinking," she said. "It was that I was moving into a part of myself that knew more than my brain alone knew. My brain could help understand what I was doing, but the process was happening on some deeper level.

"Some people have a knack for aspects of herbalism, maybe a knack for making things or listening to people. I found I had an incredible knack for formulation." More and more people began to request her formulas. Rosemary was also giving public lectures and being invited to teach. Filling bags of the same formula for customers was becoming repetitive, so her partner, Drake Sadler, suggested that she pre-package the blends in brown paper bags, the type used to hold bulk coffee, and label the bags "throat formula" or "nursing formula," as appropriate. A mutual friend told Drake and Rosemary they should create a brand with names for the formulas that people would remember. One evening Rosemary, Drake, and two of their friends (one also named Rosemary and her partner, Warren), sat around a woodstove drinking tea, brainstorming names for the formulas: Smooth Move, Mother's Milk, Throat Coat, Gypsy Cold Care. Warren drew images—for Smooth Move, a sketch of a person in an outhouse.

I didn't meet Drake until well after I first got to know Rosemary. Terry and I interviewed him for *Numen*, and then I also talked with him again by phone while researching this book. I asked Drake how the business evolved after that first meeting around the woodstove. He told me that he was an astrologer at that time, and he traveled along the California coast each fall to sell his silk-screened astrology calendars. He suggested taking along some bags of the bulk tea on his next trip to see whether they would sell.

According to Drake, Rosemary was not interested in creating products to sell beyond her store, fearing that selling their teas would be the "further dissolution of herbalism and commercialization." He convinced her by suggesting that he would try to sell ten thousand bags at $1 a bag, and then they could use that $10,000 to travel to Mexico. "It was a hippie dream," Drake said, "to make $10,000. But Rosemary loved to travel almost as much as she loved the plants, and so she agreed."

It was an era when the established institutions of political and economic power were showing their vulnerability. Close to half a million people had attended the three-day music festival at Woodstock, New York, in the concert that has come to epitomize the counterculture of the time. In 1970 four unarmed students were shot by members of the Ohio National Guard during a mass protest against the Vietnam War at Kent State University. The Pentagon Papers were published. In 1972 five White House operatives were arrested for burglarizing the Democratic National Committee offices, marking what became the Watergate scandal. Antiwar demonstrations drew an estimated hundred thousand people in US cities. Three hundred thalidomide victims were offered nearly $12 million in compensation after a twenty-year fight in court. Richard Nixon made an unprecedented visit to China and met with Mao Zedong, after years of impasse. The last US ground troops withdrew from Vietnam. In 1973 the American Indian Movement (AIM) occupied Wounded Knee, South Dakota, in a seventy-one-day standoff with federal authorities. In August 1974 President Nixon resigned from office.

Amid so much unrest, change on many fronts suddenly seemed possible. For California hippies like Rosemary and Drake, the right response was to seek a way to live simply, off the land, using one's hands and reconnecting with all that had been cast aside in the pursuit of profit and power.

There was a lot of mixing and mingling of traditions—Tibetan Buddhism or Zen, tantric yoga or hatha yoga or Transcendental Meditation—and a lot of drugs. Young men and women pursued what worked for their own spiritual transformation and discarded the rest.[3] Herbal medicine was no different. For better and for worse, the men and women who were rediscovering plant medicine didn't worry much about documenting the genealogy of their inspirations. It was a time of loosening and breaking rigid traditions; there was an openness and sense of freedom that made possible a tremendous amount of creativity.

Dressed in a long cape, with what he called his Charles Manson beard, and driving a Volkswagen van filled with herbal tea, Drake headed up the California coast in 1974 and into that awakening. He sold all ten thousand bags in eleven days. He called Rosemary from a pay phone by the side of Highway 1 and told her to order more herbs and brown bags.

Rosemary recalled Drake's "orders for so many tea bags, and then another stop and more tea bags! And I remember thinking, *Oh, that's going to be a lot of mixing and bagging!*" She told him to come back home. They talked things over. Rosemary agreed to try selling the tea for nine months, since that had been their original plan, but only if they used the bags to educate consumers about herbalism. And so they started including leaflets along with the herbs with instructions for making infusions and salves, information on the history of wild collecting in America, promotion of good causes like clean water and their local birth clinic and community center, and poems and quotations. "There was more information than tea in those bags!" Drake exclaimed.

The images on boxes of Traditional Medicinals tea are no longer hand-drawn sketches, and the wording on the label speaks about details of sourcing and certifications that weren't part of the picture in the 1970s. And the details of the Traditional Medicinals origin story have blurred a bit, depending on who is telling it. Yet regardless of the specifics, what emerges is that Rosemary and Drake had vision, and they had stamina. There was plenty of room in the 1970s for that combination—room to start a business, room to set up a school, room to teach. Listening to the stories of that era, it's easy to feel envious. There was so much possibility. Drake saw the potential and jumped in. Nine months later they were managing a warehouse and twelve employees and had invested $100,000 into the business. "It just exploded," Drake said. The company filled a unique niche in the United States at the time. Celestial Seasonings, another herbal tea company that came out of the back-to-the-land movement, had begun to focus exclusively on beverage teas, not medicinal ones. Alvita Tea, a family brand that dates back to the 1920s, sold single herbs as medicine, so it was up to the customer to know how to use them as teas. Rosemary and Drake's teas were the only pre-blended formulas available as a consumer product. They created a niche for themselves that they hadn't even known existed.

After a few years it became clear to Rosemary that Drake had an amazing sense of how to develop a business and that he really loved the work. It was equally clear that she did not. "I remember thinking, *This is not fun*," she told me. "*It's not what I want to be doing*." She loved sharing information and helping people. "Part of my fascination is with the healing aspect of the plants, their wildness, their spirit. And also with the people I met—they were just incredible characters. People who had missions in life. They were brilliant and wild and passionate and willing to be different. The plants were clearly directing them and they were willing to follow. That's who I wanted to spend time with."

Rosemary and Drake separated. In 1978 she set up the California School of Herbal Studies, the first herbal school in the state. She also founded Mountain Rose Herbs as a mail-order company to provide bulk herbs to students who wanted to prepare their own remedies. By 1987 she decided it was time for a change and moved to five hundred acres of wilderness in Vermont. Once there, she became aware of and concerned about the impact of the herbal renaissance on wild plant populations of North America. She turned her new home, Sage Mountain, into an herbal retreat center and botanical sanctuary where she continued to teach. In 1994, with a group of concerned herbalists, she founded a nonprofit organization called United Plant Savers, a nonprofit dedicated to the conservation and cultivation of native medicinal plants. Though many men and women were part of and leaders in the herbal renaissance, Rosemary stands out. Herbalist David Winston said it this way: "The amazing thing about Rosemary Gladstar is that she has vision *and* she manifests that vision."

Ed Smith

Around the time that Rosemary was starting Rosemary's Garden, Ed Smith started reading a borrowed copy of Jethro Kloss's book *Back to Eden* while riding on a bus in Colombia. First published in 1935, *Back to Eden* was the bible for the natural living movement in the late 1960s. It introduced Kloss's method of natural self-healing based on herbs and a diet that eschewed meat, fat, and eggs. (By the 1980s almost three million copies had been sold.)

Ed read the book cover-to-cover. It was his first exposure to the use of plants as medicine, and he was hooked. He began visiting the village markets to speak to the curanderos who sold fresh herbs, and he tried preparing the remedies they described for himself. For several years Ed traveled between his home in Cambridge, Massachusetts, and South America to continue studying herbal medicine. Although he wouldn't have predicted it at the time, this initial exposure to plant medicine in Colombia would eventually lead him to start an herb business, Herb Pharm, that has thrived for decades.

Ed and his then-partner, Sara Katz, founded Herb Pharm in 1979. I met Ed and Sara when Terry and I visited Herb Pharm to film the farm and production facility in Williams, Oregon, for *Numen*. Ed was a regular teacher at herb conferences at the time, and like Traditional Medicinals their company was among those most often recommended by herbalists. I also spoke with Ed and Sara separately about their memories of the company.

Ed told me that on his first time back in Cambridge after being in Colombia, he visited a local health food store to buy some herbs. He was disappointed with what he found. Colombian healers used vibrant, vital, fresh herbs. In the stores in Cambridge, though, the herbs were overdried and stale. The arnica had gone to seed. Mints didn't smell like mint. "The herbs were just good enough to keep people interested," Ed said. "But that was all."

Ed got a Peterson field guide and began gathering wild plants from the woods around Boston, continuing to learn about their medicinal uses from whatever sources he could find. A few years later he and Sara moved to Oregon, where they helped Dr. John Christopher, who was starting a naturopathic school of medicine. Often called the father of the modern herbal tradition, Dr. Christopher was a naturopathic physician from Utah known for his teachings on herbs and natural healing especially among the Mormons in Utah, during a time when few people were teaching about the use of plants.

In Oregon, Ed continued harvesting wild plants, and he also explored secondhand bookstores. On one visit he stumbled across the entire collection of a retired pharmacist, which included books about liquid extracts written by the Eclectic physicians. Ed couldn't believe his good fortune and told me he spent his last $300 on the books.

The Eclectic physicians were a group of nineteenth-century sectarian medical practitioners marginal to the history of allopathic medicine but central to that of herbalism. Their practice emerged in response to the growing dissatisfaction in communities in America with the harsh, heroic healing therapies—especially use of leeches and heavy metals like mercury and arsenic—common among medical providers in the mid- to late 1800s.

In the late 1880s and early 1900s, Ed said, you could walk into any pharmacy, apothecary, or doctor's office and find liquid extracts, bitter-tasting liquids in brown bottles. These extracts were made by the leading drug companies of the time, such as Eli Lilly and Parke, Davis and Company.[4] John King and John Milton Scudder, the two leading Eclectic physicians in the late 1800s, developed a theory of medicine making based on analyzing the specific medicinal qualities of individual plants.[5] They then hired a gifted young pharmacist, John Uri Lloyd, to manufacture liquid extracts based on these formulas. Lloyd, along with his two brothers, developed Lloyd Brothers, which was best known for making extracts for use by Eclectic physicians. King and Scudder's formulas were produced from raw materials supplied by a robust trade of what were called raw drugs or crude drugs.[6] These plants were cultivated by the Shakers (the largest growers of herbs in the United States in the nineteenth century) or wild-harvested from Appalachia.[7] Most of these plants harvested from Appalachia passed through supply houses in North Carolina. In the late 1800s the largest wholesale botanical drug dealer in the region, Wallace Brothers, in Statesville, North Carolina, stored more than two thousand varieties of leaves, roots, barks, and berries in its forty-four-thousand-square-foot botanic depot. Historian Gary Freeze describes "rows upon rows of ginseng, sassafras, and cherry bark, stacked in baskets or wrapped in bales awaiting shipment."[8] An 1883 North Carolina Agricultural Department report noted that "the bales [of medicinal herbs] seen in the country stores of the mountains were similar to the bales of cotton seen elsewhere." According to Freeze, Statesville became known "as the place where more medicinal plants are collected and prepared for the trade than in any other [place] in the world."[9] By 1875 the root trade, which had been "looked upon almost contemptuously" generated more than $50,000 (equivalent to over $1 million today), and provided a living to many people.[10]

These plants were shipped to the Lloyd Brothers in Cincinnati, a center for the botanical trade in the late 1800s and early 1900s, to be manufactured into the liquid extracts that King and Scudder used in their practice.[11] The two doctors treated tens of thousands of patients over the course of almost fifty years. Their success was in large part due to the quality of these formulations.

This information faded from public view, only to reemerge when aspiring herbal practitioners discovered books written by King and Scudder, which documented their clinical practice and formulas in great detail, while rummaging through secondhand bookstores. Herbalists often return to the Eclectics as the source of information about high-quality material and herbal medicine. This is both because of the quality of their clinical work and the botanical medicines they produced *and* because, unlike many others from whom they acquired their knowledge—early American settlers who drew on European traditions, Native Americans, African American slaves, midwives, homeopaths, physiomedicalists, and others—the Eclectics were some of the only ones at the time who wrote books about their practice.[12]

Though not part of mainstream medicine, as educated white men, the Eclectics had the access to resources that allowed them to codify their knowledge, the freedom to practice, and the available time to document their learning. They were educated in institutions that valued written culture over oral traditions and had access to circles and audiences who could further and perpetuate their beliefs. When I spoke with Richard Mandelbaum, the director of the ArborVitae School of Traditional Herbalism, about the legacy of the Eclectics, he told me that they rarely attributed the foundational sources of their knowledge, or at least not more than in passing, instead presenting it as if they had discovered this knowledge themselves. Even if they didn't intend to exclude the sources of their knowledge, by translating that knowledge into their own words and books, often without citations, in fact they did.[13]

Ed gathered herbs by day. At night he pored through the books of King, Scudder, and others, taking notes longhand on yellow legal pads, noting which plants and formulas were used and how. He gathered herbs and ground them in a coffee grinder, mixed them with alcohol and water in mason jars, and left them to stand until he had time to strain and bottle the finished tincture. As every budding herbalist discovers, extracting herbs produces a lot of tincture. Ed ended up with ten ounces of arnica tincture, nine ounces of yarrow. He shared the extra with friends, who saw the tinctures were effective. As with Rosemary's tea blends, they told their friends, who came to purchase some for themselves. And without intending to, Ed realized he had started a company.

The key to the success of his remedies, Ed believes, was the attention paid to the quality of the raw material; he wanted to match the kind of vitality he had seen in the herbs displayed at the Colombian markets. He made a pegboard to use during classes he taught at Dr. Christopher's school. He divided the board in two, and on one side he attached yarrow from a local health food store. On the other, he displayed yarrow he had picked himself. He pointed out the silvery green leaves and vibrant white flowers of the yarrow he had harvested and dried, and the faded, brown and gray leaves and flowers of the yarrow from the store. "You didn't have to be a master herbalist to tell the difference," he told me.

Ed is quite well known for making this point at every opportunity when he has an audience. Sienna Craig, an anthropologist, described meeting Ed at a conference on traditional systems of medicine in Bhutan in 2009. Ed pounded a fist on the table as he told the audience of academics, "You don't have to have a PhD to tell good-quality plants!"

Rosemary recalled sitting in on one of Ed's classes back in the 1970s, a time when no one was really thinking or teaching about the importance of herb quality. She invited him to teach at Orr Hot Springs Resort in the California redwoods. After his class Ed displayed bottles of his tinctures on a Guatemalan blanket. Students bought every bottle. He left with $300 in cash. Rosemary invited him to teach again, at another hot springs site in Northern California. He brought along a bigger blanket—and left with $600 in hand. As he was packing up, a student who ran an herb store asked whether Ed had a wholesale catalog. "No," he said. "But we will next week!" He and Sara immediately registered the name Herb Pharm and made a logo. Sara typed up two pages describing twelve to fifteen herbs. That was their first catalog.

More orders came in. Herb Pharm, which made its mark by knowing the "pedigree" of its herbs and selling only "organic, custom, wild-crafted plants," began to take off. Ed and Sara made enough money to pay the rent and put food on the table. They took a weeklong vacation to Mexico. Sara said they were never goal-driven. They had the good fortune to be doing something that wasn't widespread but had widespread popularity, which meant they never had to be clever about marketing or sales. "The whole industry was so fledgling and naive. We were always just ahead of the curve. We showed up all day, every day, and did the work. People loved the medicine we made. It was thrilling—we would say to each other, 'Let's go home and make some more!'

"You couldn't do that today," she continued after a pause. "We were able to get where we did because of hard work and passion and because of the times."

"When we first started Herb Pharm, we never dreamed it would turn into a multimillion-dollar business," Ed explained. "We were basically two hippies trying to avoid getting a job. Not that we didn't want to work—we just didn't want to work for The Man. We were trying to earn a right livelihood, to do work we believed in, work that was good for our fellow citizens and good for the planet."

Phyllis Light

Realizing that we needed to diversify the voices we were recording for *Numen*, we headed to Arab, Alabama, to interview Phyllis Light, a fourth-generation practitioner of what she calls Southern Folk Medicine. Our conversations with Phyllis brought in the perspective of the practice of herbalism passed through family in a tradition that was never broken.

Phyllis is more rooted in the physical and cultural place of her home than anyone else I have met in the North American herb community. She still lives in Arab, the town where her ancestors lived and where what she calls the mishmash of cultures that make up her heritage came together. Phyllis's entire family—on both sides—was involved in folk healing, a mix of Native American knowledge about plants and the spiritual knowledge of African slaves who had been brought to North America by the Spanish. Europeans added their system based on the ancient Greek humoral methods made popular by Galen. The Scots-Irish, who came to the area in the 1700s and 1800s, brought in a superstitious or magical framework that they combined with what they found in the Bible and Christianity.[14] "So we have about a four-hundred-year history of folk medicine in the South. Other parts of the country can't say that," Phyllis told me with pride.

The Civil War helped solidify herbal use in the South, she continued. "I'm not going to get into the politics of it. We all know slavery was not a good thing." But the South was blockaded by land and by sea and so certain foods and medicine weren't available. Southerners had to go back to using herbs as medicine, she explained, adding that some of the best herbal books were written during the Civil War.

After the Civil War, the land was ruined: "The barns and houses had been burned. The fields and crops and soil had been burned. The land was in waste and devastation. The slaves were free, but they had nowhere to go. Reconstruction was a really horrible time. Then, too, herbs were the only thing people had as medicine. Every woman had to know to care for her children and her family using herbs, because that was all there was. No one could afford to go to the doctor, and there weren't many doctors even if they could."

Just as the South's economy was beginning to stabilize, the Depression hit. Phyllis recalled that her grandfather used to say, "I read in the paper that there is a Depression, but we couldn't tell any difference in our family."

When Phyllis was ten years old, she began gathering herbs with her grandmother, who was part Creek and part Cherokee and had been taught by her own mother and grandmother. Phyllis's father took over after her grandmother died. "On my dad's side, I'm part Native American, German, and Jewish German. I'm a little Oriental and definitely Scots-Irish," Phyllis explained.

Phyllis has thin, straight blond hair, cut just below her ears, that ripples as she shakes her head to emphasize her points. In a photo taken when she was seventeen, Phyllis's set jaw shows her determination—like the shake of her head, her expression seems to say, *Don't even think of crossing me.* Sitting at the linoleum table in her kitchen that she uses for teaching, Phyllis described growing up in Arab at a time when everyone lived off the land because that's all they had. "We all had gardens. We all raised our own animals for food. We all farmed and hunted and went to the woods to gather wild food and herbs. That's just the way life was in that part of the South. Drop me in the woods with a knife and I'll make it. I know how to eat, how to make a shelter, I know what foods to eat. I know what herbs I'm gonna need for medicine.

"When I heard people talking about the herbal renaissance, I was like, *What in the world are they talking about?* We didn't need any renaissance because we already had it. We didn't know we were holistic," she added. "We were just poor."

I asked Phyllis about her relationship with plants. She answered by telling me a story.

One morning when she was seventeen, her father told her they were going to the forest to find ginseng. It wasn't the season for digging ginseng, she said, they were simply venturing out to locate some plants. By that time Phyllis had spent plenty of seasons with her family "sanging," as hunting ginseng is called, but she had never tried to find a ginseng plant without the red berries that are its signature. She and her father walked and walked. Finally, after what seemed a long time, he stopped and told her that "between that creek, them rocks, and that tree, there's some ginseng plants, and I want you to find them." And then he pulled out his paperback western from his back pocket, sat down, and began to read.

"There I was standing in the middle of all these plants that all hit around my knees, and they all looked exactly the same. They were all green, and they all had leaves," Phyllis said.

She looked and looked. She couldn't see any ginseng. She asked her father for some help, but he ignored her and continued reading his western.

She kept looking. Eventually her father told her, "You better hurry up, we have to get home for supper."

"And I am so frustrated that I'm starting to cry," Phyllis told me, her voice inflected with the accent of her home. "I'm getting mad at myself, and I just stopped and took a breath. Right in the middle of all this green stuff, I just paused. And suddenly I didn't care anymore if I found those ginseng plants or not. I was done. I closed my eyes. I could hear the birds, and I could hear my daddy turning the page in the book, and I could hear the creek bubbling over the rocks, and I could hear the wind flowing through the trees, and in that instant I really couldn't tell the difference between myself and the wind, and myself and the creek, and myself and the pages of that book. And when I opened my eyes I saw seven ginseng plants, outlined in light. It was the most amazing experience of my plant life.

"And I looked at my daddy and I said, 'Here's one, here's one, here's one!' I was so excited! And he stood up, and he said, 'Yep. Let's go eat.' He put his book in his back pocket and started walking toward home.

"And that was my teaching. That's how my dad always taught me. That's how my grandmother taught me. They taught me by making me learn. They didn't teach me with a lot of words. Those were the teachings I had all through my early years of herbalism: *How do you connect? How do you see what isn't there?*"

The herbal medicine Phyllis learned came from her relationship to a particular place, to the plants that grew there, and to the people who knew those plants and how to use them, steeped in knowledge that had been passed down to them from their mother or father or grandmother.

It wasn't a product separate from the source. It was knowledge rooted in connection.

David Winston

To the north, in New Jersey, David Winston was also becoming interested in herbs. David described the 1930s to the 1960s as the "herbal dark ages." In the late 1960s and early 1970s, he recalled, he would tell people he was an herbalist and they would ask, "You mean like spices? Potpourri?" They thought he was wasting his time. "It was like saying I delivered ice for the icebox or used gas in my lamps," David said.

"My friends were all interested in *one* herb, and I was interested in all the rest," he told me, laughing. He thought he was the only person on the East Coast interested in herbs, but gradually he began to meet other people who used plants as medicine—Tommie Bass of Georgia, Catfish Gray in West Virginia, Adele Dawson in Vermont. They were members of the generation who kept herbal medicine alive. He fell in love with the way these wise herbalists talked about using plants for healing.

While visiting Goddard College in central Vermont in 1975, David stopped in a general store and noticed an announcement for a book sale tacked to the bulletin board. Intrigued, he stopped by the sale, where he discovered a collection of vintage leather-bound books about herbal medicine—books written by Eclectic physicians including *King's American Dispensatory* by John King and *American Materia Medica, Therapeutics and Pharmacognosy* by Finley Ellingwood. David told me that he was blown away to discover that medical doctors in the United States had used herbs in their practice as recently as the early 1900s. He thought their use had died out hundreds of years ago. Yet on page after page, he found accounts of a rich clinical record using herbs not only to treat conditions like headaches and cramps, but for the most serious diseases of the day. He thought all of this knowledge had been lost—or that it had never existed. It was incredible, he said, to discover a whole history of plants as medicine. All the books were half price. He spent almost every penny he had buying two shopping bags full of the treasures, reserving only enough cash to pay for his bus ticket home, with a dime to spare.

A Community Forms

Many of the social and cultural movements of the 1960s faded or transformed beyond recognition as the front-line individuals grew up and realized they needed to find conventional jobs. What made the herbal movement a true renaissance turned out to be one of the many pivotal projects Rosemary decided to embark upon—organizing a conference. She was inspired by a retreat she attended in the mid-1970s organized by Baba Hari Dass, an Indian guru who, among other accomplishments, was an early proponent of yoga and Ayurveda in the United States. Rosemary decided to do something similar for the herb community.

As Rosemary described that first herb conference to me, it struck me how similar it sounded to conferences I have attended for the past twenty years. Everyone gathered for an opening circle, holding hands. We sang together. There were classes on the uses of plants as medicine and on making remedies with those plants. At these early conferences, in between sessions, the participants took off their clothes and soaked in hot tubs.

Rosemary had grown up with Adventists with a strong sense of family and community. "When I look back on it, I think I brought in some of that sense of community from church, singing together, holding hands, praying over meals, washing each other's feet. I brought the sense of holiness that I loved in church into what became my spiritual family. Otherwise why would I start off with singing? We didn't sing or hold hands at the Baba Hari Dass conference. I didn't make a plan, now we're going to make a circle and hold hands, even if you are uncomfortable, you're going to stand here and hold hands. I just thought that's what we should do—and people did it!" She burst into her huge laugh. "They joined hands and sang—and then we saw that it was good so we kept doing it."

She paused and then added, "Even if people hadn't been interested in standing in a circle and singing, I would have continued doing it because I knew gathering in a circle was important. I always felt that these conferences were about more than just educating. Plants bring something deeper than that. They bring the sense that we are connected. We are part of that mycelium. To me, that's the biggest teachings they offer."

Rosemary went on to organize a second conference, this time at Breitenbush Hot Springs, southeast of Portland, Oregon. Photos of these early conferences periodically show up on the internet. Some of the key teachers in herbal medicine today are in those photos, too, men with full, bushy beards and thick heads of hair, women with long, flowing hair and long, flowing dresses. Thirty years on, when herb conferences take place regularly all over the world, it is hard to imagine the impact of these early gatherings. David Winston was the only herbalist east of the Rockies to attend that second Breitenbush conference. "It was amazing to be in a room of people, seventy people in a circle, all in love with the idea of using plants as medicine," he told me when we spoke.

Herbalist Paul Bergner attended his first Breitenbush conference in 1986. I spoke with him on the phone years later. He was living in New Mexico at the time, he said, where there was no social or cultural support for herbalism. Anyone interested in plant medicine was accused of being a fraud. Paul felt like a sailboat "sailing into the wind, an oddball wherever I went." Attending Breitenbush was like being struck by lightning: "It was electrifying to be in a room where everyone talked to the trees *and*—where the trees talked back."

David Hoffmann moved to the United States in 1986 from the United Kingdom, where he had studied clinical herbalism in the mid-1980s. He met Rosemary while traveling in California in 1985, and she offered him a job teaching at the California School of Herbal Studies. I first met David when he taught a weekend course in the advanced program at Sage Mountain. Terry and I later interviewed him at the campus of the California school, where he still teaches. He is also chief herbal formulator for the Traditional Medicinals company.

As herbalism became more popular, a core group of herb teachers such as David Hoffmann were able to make a living from their work through teaching, practicing, or selling herbal products. These herbalists didn't have to grow out of their love of plants; that love could be the foundation of their work. The US herb community had something he hadn't encountered in the U.K., David told me during a phone conversation.

Rosemary "infused the movement with hippie love and peace without talking about it in those terms." There were a lot of different flavors of herbalism then, David mused, including Wise Women, Mormons with Dr. Christopher, hippies from the West Coast, and people like him who leaned more toward clinical herbalism and science. As David said, at conferences "we were all in a room with nothing in common except our love of herbs." That joy of being with the plants is the heart of herbal medicine. Rosemary's gift and one of her main legacies was to create bridges between the differences, a container that helped give birth to a viable movement that has grown and developed for decades. "We overcame our differences by not looking at them," David said, "and that helped give birth to a viable movement that has grown and developed."

Of course ignoring differences doesn't make them go away, and herbalism was no exception. David Hoffmann soon found that things weren't perhaps as "glowy" as he initially thought. Herbalist David Winston shared similar reflections on the herbal renaissance. He described it as the most creative, vital, imaginative blossoming of herbal medicine that has ever occurred, but, echoing what others told me about this period, David went on, "It was sloppy. There was a lack of discernment." There was no science, he added. In many ways, my own journey with herbalism has followed this trajectory, through my deepening exploration of the industry.

As herbs became more popular with consumers, a disconnect grew between the celebratory joy of plants and the reality of sourcing herbs on a scale needed to meet the growing demand. As demand kept on increasing, the companies started in hippie kitchens in the early 1970s grew. Production spilled into barns and then warehouses. Their demand for plants with which to formulate their products also grew. This entailed finding more sources, processing more plant material, and storing and shipping more dried herbs. The gardens and forests near their homes could not supply enough to meet their requirements, which meant herbalists and those starting companies had to turn to other sources of materials—wholesale companies that imported herbs from around the world.

The pioneers of the herbal renaissance had a vision of changing the world through using plants as medicine. They brought their imagination and intuition and activism to the formulas, the packaging, and more. But as the scale of production ramped up, more and more of the herbs in those packages—the raw material for the revolution—came to them from networks that had been supplying herbs and spices for hundreds of years. A trade that was founded on slavery, theft, and war.

When I began studying herbal medicine, herbalists downplayed their connections with the industry. Herbalists tend to have a high ecological consciousness, David Winston told me, but the industry is an entirely different beast. For a long time, he was embarrassed to be part of it, he admitted, even though his company produces some of the highest-quality products available.

Herbalists criticize people in the industry for compromising on their values. Those in the industry criticize herbalists for being naive. The promise, implicit or explicit, was that herbs offered a "natural" and thus safer and more environmentally responsible alternative to conventional medicine. And that, it followed, buying from companies making these products was better for humanity and the earth. When she taught in the advanced course at Sage Mountain, medical doctor and herbalist Dr. Tieraona Low Dog admonished us to think more critically about herbal medicine. Don't just repeat what nettles were good for, she told us. Find out where that knowledge originated and whether it was a valid source of information. I asked her about this when we interviewed her for *Numen* at the Andrew Weil Center for Integrative Medicine in Tucson, Arizona (at that time, she was head of the fellowship program). She elaborated, "We must bring the same critical edge that we bring to the drug industry to our own industry of herbal medicine. One is big and one is small. But even so, we can't have a separate set of ethics. We can't suggest in any way that just because you're in the field of herbal medicine, just because you dance with the plants, you have high integrity by default."

I realized I had set aside my own critical lens in my embrace of herbal medicine and the criticisms of the industry. I needed to understand politics and economics, not just culture. And to do so required going further back in time.

CHAPTER THREE

Digging Deeper

How does one speak about connection in a
culture of separation and isolation?

—FRANK GOLLEY, *A Primer for Environmental Literacy*

*T*he first thing I noticed in Drake Sadler's office were the artifacts: intricately painted *thangkas*, a large statue of the Buddha and another of Shiva, bronze bowls, and woven wall hangings. Photographs of Drake kneeling next to an herb farmer or collector in remote regions of the world sat atop bookshelves. The office was a mini museum of objects collected from his travels around the world sourcing plants for his medicinal tea company. Terry and I were there to interview Drake for the *Numen* documentary. Traditional Medicinals is known for its integrity and good intentions. The company has high standards and impressive systems of quality control, and the individuals sourcing plants for the company are actively involved in improving the international standards for the trade of medicinal plants.

Yet the artifacts reminded me of the global trade of herbs and spices, and that in turn led me to think about colonialism: ships and cannons; barrels of cinnamon, nutmeg, cloves, and pepper; silks and rubber and opium. Those artifacts whispered to me that the legacy of herbal medicine is rooted not only in the soils and welcoming community of Sage Mountain, but also in the spice trade and the unsavory commerce of colonization.

As our cameraman set up for the interview, I tried to review the list of questions I'd prepared. But my mind wandered to images of wooden ships loaded with barrels, sailing out from low wooden buildings flanked by palm trees. I imagined bodies scattered on white sand beaches in what is now Indonesia, slain by the bullets of Dutch traders seeking a monopoly on the nutmeg trade.

As life turned out, Drake never took Rosemary on that trip to Mexico he'd promised. He was busy with the growing business and Rosemary was busy teaching. One day Rosemary exclaimed, "Hey, you never took me to Mexico!" Drake suggested they visit the farms in Guatemala instead to see where the lemongrass they were using came from. Always ready for a trip, Rosemary readily agreed.

They were horrified by what they found. "It was like indigenous slave labor, women and children working in the fields!" Drake told me. Drake has a background in community development, and one of his first jobs had been opening a Head Start family planning center in the 1960s. His work had always been about alleviating poverty, but on that trip to Guatemala, he realized he now was running a business built on the labor of people in poverty.

When they returned to California, Drake shared his impressions with the buyer who had suggested they visit those fields. The buyer told him the conditions he'd seen weren't unique to lemongrass production: "That's how the botanical supply chain works. And if you don't like what you saw in Guatemala, don't go to India."

Drake sought advice from his mentor, Eddie Mae Sloan, who was a leader in community development in Northern California and dedicated to improving the state of those living in poverty. She spoke sternly, Drake remembered. "You didn't learn anything from me," she admonished him. "You bring about change by changing one village at a time."

That visit clarified his vision for Traditional Medicinals. From then on, he told me, he would produce boxes of medicinal tea as a way to *address*, not to perpetuate, the social and environmental injustices caused by capitalism. This is the vision that brought Terry and me to Traditional Medicinals in the first place, to include a section in *Numen* on social and environmental responsibility in the botanical industry.

Yet as I sat in Drake's office, I thought about the ways market forces erase history as well as geography. In what ways, I wondered, do so-called responsible businesses depend in part on these erasures as well? How does legacy of that trade, the way it shaped people's lives and the terms of trade established during those times, matter in understanding conditions in the present?

Green chemist John Warner once said that if we want to attain a world with no toxic chemicals, we first have to understand how we ended up in a world so filled with toxicity. We need to investigate not only the systems that create and perpetuate the need for those chemicals, but also why the toxicity wasn't seen—why it wasn't considered an impact worth developing the tools to assess and quantify. And so, it follows, if I wanted to tell a story of whole supply chains, of plants embedded in communities and landscapes, I had to understand how they became disconnected from those communities and landscapes in the first place.

Where do we begin? Perhaps in the way that poet Rebecca Seiferle responded to a question from a conference-goer about what she, as a white person, could do with the legacy of colonialism. "Acknowledge it," Seiferle responded, without hesitating. She paused, and then added, "Which most whites haven't done."[1]

The Legacy of Herbal Medicine

So much has been written about the devastation caused by the European plundering of the Earth in search of spices, and yet this book would not be complete without some mention of that history. And so I embarked on my own research into that history, and along the way, I stumbled over an unexpected echo of Drake and Rosemary's experience in Guatemala in my own family history. In 2017 I received a Fulbright scholarship to study sourcing and processing of medicinal plants in India. Terry and Bryce accompanied me. Halfway through our stay we visited Fort Kochi, what had been one of the biggest spice trading centers for the British East India Company. Early in the morning, I would leave them behind in the coolness of our air-conditioned room to wander the backstreets, looking for signs of the history of that trade.

Before I visited India, the name Malabar Coast evoked images from stories I listened to when my children were young, tales of a hundred camels crossing deserts, bearing gifts of jewels, silk, spices, and woolen carpets to court a bride. The names of the spices—cinnamon, cloves, nutmeg—conjured an exotic and mysterious world in my imagination. I didn't know then where such plants grew or what they looked like. I didn't know that the Malabar Coast was the southwest coast of India or that this was where the Portuguese explorer Vasco da Gama landed in 1498, the first European to reach India in search of a direct trading route to the source of the spices.

Little about Fort Kochi today retains any sense of the exotic. I walked carefully along the side streets, avoiding the trash piled on the edges of the potholed, narrow roads and the dogs and occasional cow rummaging for food. Hawkers tried to catch my eye. My skin was covered in a thin layer of grime from the heat and the exhaust from the cars and tuktuks. I skirted beneath jumbles of electric wires wrapped around electric poles leaning precariously over the road. I realized that I was walking through the legacy of colonialism. Everything around me—the garbage, the beggars, the narrow winding streets—was part of this history. The abandoned trading houses along the shore, now fallen into disrepair, as well as the ornate homes, with their cool and inviting verandas set beneath towering trees, were all remnants of the spice trade and the British Empire in India. The signs of wealth and the signs of poverty are especially impressive in India, given the extremes of each, and all are products of the terms laid down by the Portuguese and the British colonizers, plundering what was not theirs to plunder.

The colonial legacy is brutal. Even though I already knew the outcome, it was shocking to read page after page of the deception and the ruthlessness. Mostly it was shocking to read of the greed. Entire cultures wiped out by guns and cannons, victories secured by treaties that were little more than an excuse to grab control of resources: huge tracts of land, forests, minerals, and people.

I pored through books and images online, trying to get behind the scenes of a history that focuses on ships and ports. I finally came across photos of warehouses in the Indian port cities of Kochi and Calicut, turquoise doors on yellow buildings, terra-cotta tile roofs above open stalls filled with sacks of spices for sale. I realized they were the same as the buildings I had seen on my morning walks in Fort Kochi, the turquoise and yellow faded, the cement and terra-cotta chipped. And I imagined that the peppercorns I passed drying on woven mats in mud courtyards by thatched-roof homes in the hills to the east could just as likely have been drying there one or two hundred years prior. I imagined the dried pepper being carried in sacks or baskets on someone's back, or perhaps on a donkey, to a warehouse in a nearby town. Men dressed in lungis hitched up above their knees, haggling over prices. I imagined the sacks of cardamom or pepper or cinnamon then stacked in the warehouse until there were enough to transport to the nearest port, likely on the backs of porters, down steep, narrow footpaths. (But these days, the sacks would be piled in the back of a brightly colored truck.) At the port they would be stored in even larger warehouses until a sale was negotiated to ship overseas on a Chinese junk or an Arab dhow or, later on a Portuguese, then Dutch, and then British ship. It's not more exotic than that. It's just trade, and it has never been very fair.

———

The first transnational traders are said to be the Nabataeans, nomadic clans who raided caravans in the Arabian deserts two to three thousand years ago. They gradually began to carry frankincense by dromedary camels.[2] When their camels reached the sea and were unable to go farther, the Nabataeans built small dhows to sail across the Indian Ocean. They eventually supplied markets throughout the Middle East with black and white pepper, cassia and cinnamon, nutmeg, cloves, star anise, and mace from the Molucca Islands and the Malabar Coast, a monopoly they held for several centuries.[3]

In a move that has shaped global commerce ever since, wrote ethnobiologist Gary Paul Nabhan in *Cumin, Camels, and Caravans*, the Nabataeans secured their control of this supply chain by insisting that the buyers of frankincense had no direct contact with the men and women who tapped the frankincense trees. By hiding the source, Nabhan argued, the Nabataeans were able to control the trade and set the price, often a hundredfold more than what they paid for the product to begin with. The end buyer could neither go around the trader nor bargain for a better price.[4]

Hiding the source wasn't the only way the Nabataeans secured their control of the value chain. The true genius of the Nabataeans was "imbibing the incense, spices, salves, and silks destined for Europe, Africa, and Asia Minor" with a sense of wonder. "They were marketing mystique as much as they were materials," Nabhan wrote.[5] By spinning a good tale, the Nabataeans made sure that these spices were sought after and a sign of status as well as a useful product.

Portuguese explorer Vasco da Gama's arrival on the Malabar Coast in 1498 is often cited as the moment when the nature of trade shifted. He launched the Age of Discovery and of modern colonialism. At the time of this encounter, trade along the Malabar Coast was largely in the hands of Muslim merchants. The Calicut bazaar, the "greatest spice emporium on the subcontinent," was loaded with spices, precious stones, silk carpets from China, gold, and more. It had been a center of the maritime spice trade in southern Asia as well as the overland trade for more than two hundred years. Most important, Nabhan wrote, it was "the mother lode of pepper on the Malabar Coast that the Christians of western Europe had been waiting to mine for a very long time."[6]

The most widely available painting of da Gama's first arrival in the busy port of Calicut shows the *samuthiri*, the hereditary ruler of the Malabar Coast, sitting cross-legged on a throne.[7] Brass animals are carved onto the armrests. The samuthiri and his attendants wear lungis and turbans, his made of elaborate cloth. Everything—the throne, his clothing, the carvings—is bejeweled.

Da Gama, dressed in a royal blue tunic edged in gold under a crimson robe with a border of white fur, holds out a scroll to the samuthiri. It is a letter from the king of Portugal, demanding permission to build a trading post with exclusive rights to the trade of pepper and cardamom.[8] In exchange, da Gama offered barrels of olive oil, cane sugar, casks of honey, and some cloth—gifts considered so common they were an insult, sufficient perhaps, it was said, for trading on the coast of Africa but not for the kingdoms of the Malabar Coast.[9]

Da Gama was dismissed, empty-handed. Some accounts say he had to fight his way out of the harbor. Not easily turned away—the stakes for his success were high—he returned, this time with cannons. Thus began a series of battles that the Portuguese eventually won, securing a monopoly on the trade.

Da Gama's voyage gave the Portuguese direct access to the source of the spice trade, and it also marked a shift in Europe's place in the world. Europe had been the terminus of the silk and spice roads, far from the heart of trading markets, but it now became the center of this world instead. Spices that had been an elite luxury business became part of the cultural and commercial mainstream, making their way from the drawing rooms of the wealthy in Venice to the kitchen tables of the European middle class.[10]

Within a few decades of da Gama's expedition to India, the Portuguese had set up a series of trading posts. They secured trade along the coast of Africa to India and eventually as far as what were known to outsiders as the Spice Islands, but to those in the region as the Banda Islands. This archipelago located in the Banda Sea off Indonesia comprises more than one thousand small mountainous islands. Because these islands were the only place in the world where nutmeg grew, they were considered "the lodestone" of the spice trade, wrote historian George Masselman.[11]

Nutmeg was valued for its flavor and as a remedy for fever. It was also valued because of its rarity. Thus the Banda Islands became the site of a series of battles not just between traders and the indigenous population but between colonial powers fighting for a monopoly of the lucrative nutmeg trade. In the end it was the Dutch who secured control, with disastrous results. Not only did the Dutch decimate the population of the islands, they also pulled out by the roots any nutmeg trees on islands whose trade they didn't control, especially Run, the one island that the English still dominated.[12] To secure their monopoly into the future, the Dutch traders dipped the nutmeg seeds in lime to prevent them from sprouting, thus preventing their competitors from planting nutmeg elsewhere in the world.[13]

In a sign of just how important the Banda Islands and the nutmeg wars were, the Dutch considered it a good bargain to accept Run and part of the Guyana coast from the British in exchange for the Dutch settlement in New Amsterdam (which the English called New York). For many decades, writer Amitav Ghosh said these islands provided the

Dutch East India Company with "huge and easy profits."[14] But then European tastes changed and the price of spices began to fall. In 1760, in a last-ditch effort to maintain the value of nutmeg and cinnamon, the Dutch burned large amounts of the spices stored in warehouses in Amsterdam.[15] Despite the Dutch's effort to control the market, their monopoly finally ended in 1817 when live nutmeg trees were success-fully transferred to Ceylon, Singapore, and other colonies not controlled by the Dutch.[16]

I have read and re-read this history so many times, trying to make sense of its significance for the contemporary trade of herbs and spices. On one hand, reflecting on how the current terms of trade derive from colo-nialism can be useful in correcting that ongoing legacy and addressing those historical inequities. Yet the enduring impact of colonialism on the modern herb supply chain is more nuanced and harder to disentangle.

The legacy of colonialism, which side we and our ancestors were on, shapes the opportunities we do or do not have, where we can or cannot live. We are literally the lands in which we are born and raised. Those environments determine the quality of air we breathe, the vitality of the soil that grows our food, the presence or absence of the toxins in our soil. In much the way plants are, as ecologist Craig Holdredge has written, a conversation between the genetics of the species and the environment, the political and economic circumstances of our lives are written into the tissue in our bodies. What is in the soil now depends on what was in that soil in the past, which depends on how that land was used, which has to do with economics and politics as much as, if not more than, biology or chemistry. Whether and when forests were chopped down, whether crops were grown—and if so, which ones and how intensively and with what inputs—determine the makeup of that soil. It matters where industries were located, what wastes those industries produced, and how and where those wastes were disposed. Droughts matter, floods matter, what happens upstream and upwind matters, the severity of storms, the direction of the wind—what the wind carries in and what the wind carries away.

Discerning the ways in which the history of the spice trade matters or doesn't matter when analyzing the contemporary herb industry requires a kind of double vision that allows us to see the present as linked to the past. Harvesting pepper and cloves is not the "traditional" way of living for collectors in the Western Ghat mountain range of India.[17] Rather, once the market existed, the people who lived there reorganized their strategies of survival to include the possibility of selling spices to traders. The economies of countries at the origins of the herbal supply chain today developed as they have because the forces of trade relegated them to the periphery and not the center of that trade, which shaped and limited the opportunities available to them moving forward.

In countries that European colonial traders viewed as a source of wealth, the native men and women had few options other than to enter the international economy on their knees or, in some cases, on their backs. They were always working in a system of trade established in rooms where they had no voice. And the systems of decision making, trade relationships, and ways of negotiating prices and contracts that shape the herb industry today are also an outgrowth of those established by the European colonial traders.

It feels impossible to untangle the wrongs that have been committed. Is it possible to acknowledge those past wrongs in a way that doesn't simply re-create them? Can we create relationships in which trade actually can be beneficial to all involved, not just because a company claims it to be?

Learning from Legacy

Ethnobotanist Claudia Ford doesn't consider herself an herbalist, but she is a part of a growing movement in the herb community that is examining the ways herbalists have appropriated knowledge not their own, knowledge that includes West African drumming, sweat lodges, and Native American chants, songs, and rituals. This work builds on her research into the ways that knowledge and stories of using plants as medicine have been not only hidden but also erased from the record.[18]

Claudia began her research by following the plants, she told me when we spoke on the phone, letting stories about how African Americans used these plants in Africa and as slaves in America guide her. She focused on herbs used in childbirth because of her own experience as a midwife. She found that childbirth was a liminal space, an in-between moment in which knowledge was shared across cultures. If a slave was the best midwife available, Claudia said, she would be the midwife called to deliver the baby, whether of a slave or the mistress of the plantation. What mattered was the outcome—that the baby was born and the mother survived—not the identity of the individuals involved. If, during that encounter, someone suggested a plant to use, then everyone present at that birth gained that knowledge, regardless of its source or the cultural framework or place from which that knowledge originated.

As Claudia read historical accounts of such sharing, she wrote down the names of plants mentioned. Certain names kept appearing. "I realized they were telling me a story," she told me.

I asked if any surprised her.

"The cotton story," she answered. "It blew my mind. I didn't know anything about cotton. I found references to criminal abortions and so I did some poking around. I found out about the use of cotton root and seed for abortions, and how black haw was used to reverse those abortions."[19]

Claudia has written about her research, as well. "The conditions under which African female slaves would desire to abort a pregnancy," she wrote, "were many, including rape, maltreatment, brutal labor, and the tragedy of enforced separation from young children sold away to other masters."[20] When Congress passed a bill in 1807 abolishing the importation of slaves into the US, plantation owners realized that their only source of new future slaves would be babies born to current female slaves. The owners established breeding plantations for that purpose.[21] And so slave women decocted cotton roots and seeds to induce abortions. "Cotton root induced abortions could be seen as an act of African American women's resistance. Even as slave women bloodied their hands picking the masters' bolls, they could chew the roots of the cotton plant to impede unwanted conception."[22]

Claudia dug deeper and found medical journals in which surgeons in the United Kingdom, Scotland, Canada, and the United States wrote to one another over a period of about two years in the 1800s about ways to prevent cotton-induced abortions. The planters had complained to the doctors that these abortions were an economic issue. The plantation owners were breeding these women, Claudia told me, like breeding an animal, and they were upset because they suspected the enslaved women were trying to thwart their plans. Herbalist Karen Culpepper, who has also researched the use of cotton and black haw, wrote, "White physicians, who took their commands from plantation owners, had a single goal in mind: save the slave mother if her life was at risk because she could always produce more 'property.' They administered black haw to stop contractions of miscarriages and abortions that were underway."[23]

"Here was a case where one plant expressed the agency of the women, and another was used to undermine that agency. It was an important reminder that plants are also used for nefarious purposes," Claudia said. She paused and then added that these plants don't just show up in our gardens with the intention of urging us to learn and deepen our understanding as we learn to prepare remedies. She believes these plants are a key part of this history, and that they showed up for her as a way of inviting her, and through her, us, to bear witness to that history.

"Why is that important?" I asked.

"Because it becomes a little less transactional," she said. "It becomes a little less appropriative if we respect there is a history."

I thought about what it means to be less appropriative by respecting that there is a history. And how plants offer an invitation, a path forward. I began to listen to how they showed up in my own past where, surprisingly, they led me to a twisted story involving salicylic acid from willow bark and derivatives of coal, which also originally comes from plants.

After the presents had all been opened on Christmas Day, the living room of my childhood home would be filled with scraps of wrapping paper and ribbon, and there would always be envelopes waiting on the mantelpiece, next to the hand-carved crèche. To my siblings and me, those envelopes were an afterthought. We opened them, quickly skimmed the message saying we had received a gift of American Home or Sterling Drug or Bristol Myers stock, and then handed them to our mother and went back to playing with our gifts. I never thought much about the contents of those envelopes, or the source of the stock in the first place. I certainly didn't consider what had and hadn't been done in the past to earn that stock, or whether those actions would ever impact my life.

I'd been told stories about William Weiss, who married my great-grandmother's sister in approximately 1901. He came from an established family of German immigrants in Wheeling, West Virginia. I'd seen the big stone town houses on the outskirts of Wheeling on family trips during the 1960s to visit my grandparents, signs of a past prosperous era in that city, which was no longer the center of the steel industry and was in decline. But the present was always more engag- ing to me than the dark, musty-smelling stories of my ancestors from Wheeling, a place that seemed forgotten.

Many years later, while researching the early days of the pharmaceuti- cal industry for this book, I picked up *The Aspirin Wars* by Charles Mann and Mark Plummer, a book I'd borrowed from my father's bedside table long ago, planning to skim through it when I had time. On page one of that book, I came upon the name William Weiss. I vaguely remembered that my great-great-uncle William had had something to do with Bayer Aspirin and the pharmaceutical industry, but I didn't know much more than that. As I read, I discovered that in fact Weiss had begun his career as a pharmacist peddling a patent medicine called Neuralgine.[24] "An old-time remedy, and a good one," announced the placards attached to the horse-drawn painted wagon that pulled boxes of the remedy through the countryside around Wheeling.

So much for my wistful longing for a grandmother who could have taught me to harvest plants and brew herbal medicines on the kitchen stove. Not only had my grandmothers done nothing of the sort, here I was confronted with a great-great-uncle who made his living—indeed, his fortune—first in the shady world of patent medicine, and later by running not just any pharmaceutical company but Sterling Drug, a company, chemist Kevin Dunn wrote in *Caveman Chemistry,* that "changed the way that drugs are marketed." Part of Sterling's legacy, Dunn said, was to distinguish over-the-counter and prescription drugs sold by big drug companies from the untested patent medicines of the past—a realm now claimed, Dunn writes in an interesting twist on the story, by herbal remedies and food supplements.[25]

The middle and late nineteenth century were the age of patent medicines and medicine shows, a time when snake oil was sold from the back of wagons by so-called Indian doctors, men who were neither Indians nor doctors, but who promised miracle cures with remedies that had names like Wizard Oil and Kickapoo Indian Oil. I picture the traveling salesman and his covered wagon in *The Wizard of Oz,* the con man extraordinaire.[26] According to historian Susan Strasser, many "root doctors" or "herb doctors" roamed the frontier on their horses, saddlebags filled with herbal remedies claimed to be "compounded by red men from the bounty of forest and field with the wisdom learned from their forefathers."[27] True to their name, some of these doctors may have sold genuine roots and medicine plants. But few of the Indian doctors selling patent medicine actually had any ties with Native American healing traditions. And though they were called doctors, they had little of the training and rigor of the Eclectic physicians. Most of their nostrums were simply factory-made drugs purchased wholesale from pharmaceutical firms in the backstreets of New York City.[28]

William Weiss was a twenty-one-year-old graduate of the Philadelphia College of Pharmacy working at Hill Pharmacy in Canton, Ohio, when he and a friend acquired the rights to Neuralgine in 1901. Weiss and his friend, Arthur H. Diebold also of Canton, moved their business across the river to the steel town of Wheeling, where, it was said, people were "more open to patent medicine," which typically meant they were "poor and the climate was conducive to disease and so people were more inclined to trust the so-called empty promises of these purveyors of snake oil remedies," wrote social historian James Harvey Young.[29]

The two friends set up their business in two rooms on the second floor of an old building in town. I can picture worn rough-hewn pine floors, unsanded pine walls, cold air blowing through cracks in winter.

Long wooden worktables. A brass scale. Handwritten account books. And sacks of acetanilide, caffeine, and sodium salicylate, believed to be the three ingredients of Neuralgine, likely shipped from a New York wholesaler that had imported the chemicals from Germany, the center of chemical and drug manufacturing before World War I.[30] Three days a week Weiss and Diebold produced dime-sized round white tablets from these ingredients and packaged them in simple cardboard boxes with NEURALGINE printed in bold letters on the side. They traveled the West Virginia countryside the other two days a week, selling Neuralgine for 25 cents a box.[31]

Unlike most patent medicine makers who stayed on the move from county to county, leaving town before word got out about the true quality of their medicines, Weiss and Diebold stayed put, perhaps because their remedy actually was effective in relieving pain. Whether that was the case or not is impossible to say, since no records exist on the efficacy of Neuralgine. Their advertisements, however, made them famous. Weiss and Diebold reinvested their first $10,000 profit into advertising in two Pittsburgh papers, an unheard-of investment for a patent medicine maker at the time. Ads for Neuralgine announced that it "Sells on sight when kept in sight. And it is a fine repeater. Keep it in sight, out in front where all can see it and put your *PERSONAL PUSH* behind it and it will pay you."[32] With the profits from sales, Weiss and Diebold began buying other companies and adding more medicines to their wagon: a dandruff nostrum, a nicotine cure called No-To-Bac, and a laxative formula developed by the California Fig Syrup Company.[33]

Weiss and Diebold likely would have faded—as did many peddlers of patent medicine—were it not for their stunningly bold purchase in 1918 of the US rights to manufacture and market Bayer Aspirin. In October 1917, six months after the US entered World War I (on April 6, 1917), the country passed the Trading with the Enemy Act, giving the newly created Office of Alien Property Custodian power to take over enemy property to hold in trust during the war. A subsequent amendment allowed the office to seize patents, copyrights, and trademarks owned by the enemy. A later amendment to the Trading with the Enemy Act allowed the Office of Alien Property Custodian to sell the enemy property they had seized directly to Americans. Bayer Company was one of the companies to be seized. The company was put up for auction in December 1918.[34] Bids began at $1 million, Mann and Plummer wrote. Well established companies like DuPont, the biggest chemical firm in the country at the time, and PaineWebber, representing a consortium of banks, joined the bidding. Sterling Products, under the direction of Diebold and Weiss, outbid PaineWebber, the last company in the running, at $5,310,000 to become the new owner of Bayer Aspirin, shocking the pharmaceutical world. The purchase also horrified the German owners of Bayer, who prided themselves on the rigor of the company's scientific research.[35]

The rights fee of $5 million was paid in part by selling stock certificates to Weiss's relatives in Wheeling, in companies that came to be known as Sterling Drug, American Home Products, Bristol-Myers Squibb. Stock in these companies was passed down through the generations and eventually ended up on our mantel on Christmas morning.

Weiss and Diebold expected the sale to be clear and clean. Yet they soon discovered that Bayer Aspirin was far more complex to manufacture than any of the patent remedies they had purchased to date. The two men were in over their heads, and they realized they needed to develop an ongoing relationship with the German manufacturers to master the technical details of the process.

In order to understand the manufacture of aspirin, it's first necessary to understand something about coal. To a West Virginian, *coal* is a loaded term. The legacy of this black, slightly greasy mineral is outside the scope of this book. I always thought it was outside the scope of my family history as well. It never occurred to me that it was the source of the material that fueled much of my family's wealth. That was because I knew little, if anything, about the manufacturing of pharmaceutical drugs.

In the mid-1700s the British began manufacturing gas from coal and developed the steam engine, which famously launched the Industrial Revolution. Less well known is what happened to the coal tar, a thick, black, nasty-smelling liquid that was considered a useless by-product. Coal tar is now known to be a human carcinogen. That wasn't known in the 1700s, but even then disposing of this by-product was considered a problem. While searching for solutions to the problem of its disposal, chemists in Germany and the United Kingdom discovered that coal tar was an incredibly complex mix of organic chemicals. "Like the nuts, bolts, and metal flanges in an untidy toolbox, the substances in coal tar could be combined into all manner of interesting things by a scientist who didn't mind a bit of trial and error," wrote Mann and Plummer.[36]

Synthetic dyes—brilliant reds, yellows, greens, and blues—were the first products developed from this coal-tar waste. Acetanilide, a waste product of the dyeing process and a coal-tar derivative, was first given to humans by accident, because a bottle was mislabeled. The substance was found to reduce fevers. At the time, the compounds in use to treat fever included salicylic acid, derived from the bark of *Salix alba*, the white willow tree. Unlike willow bark itself, though, salicylic acid produced undesirable side effects, which led doctors to search for alternatives. Other compounds that effectively relieved fevers were also unsatisfactory because of side effects or cost.[37]

No coal-tar derivative had ever been given to humans before and, according to Mann and Plummer, this accidental discovery opened up an entirely new use for the barrels of coal-tar waste from synthetic dyes. "Faced with the disposal of thirty thousand kilos of waste para-nitrophenol," Dunn wrote, Carl Duisberg, the head of research and patenting for Farbenfabriken vormals Friedrich Bayer (Bayer), "challenged his chemists to turn that waste into a drug."[38] From acetanilide, other derivatives were discovered, each with fewer side effects, until eventually in 1899 a new drug was developed with the chemical name acetylsalicylic acid. Because chemicals could not be protected by patent, Bayer decided to market it under the brand name Aspirin, which could be legally patented and in turn became the world's first blockbuster drug.[39] And two peddlers of patent medicine in the small town of Wheeling, West Virginia, had just acquired the US rights to it.

It must have been exciting for Weiss and Deibold to have gone from a run-down building mixing drugs by hand to flying to Germany to negotiate trade deals with the leaders of the world's most advanced chemical manufacturing companies. It must have been gratifying to be so financially successful, to be able to live in such comfort, and to move in circles Weiss otherwise never could have imagined. Mann and Plummer describe how

Weiss, "the brazen American dynamo, a rich man who still spoke with a poor-boy country accent," met with Carl Duisberg, now the chairman of Bayer in Germany, a man "who was proud not to 'just' be a businessman." Weiss, in contrast, "was just a businessman and proud of it."[40] "He was always a guy from Wheeling, West Virginia," one of his co-workers later told Mann and Plummer. "You have to understand that about him—he was a small-town guy, suddenly playing in the big leagues."[41]

For a time, Weiss was a grand figure in the booming city on the banks of the Ohio River. Every Fourth of July he threw a huge party that extended behind his house to a park on the hill, with cotton candy and pony rides, a party my father still remembers with nostalgia. A picture in my parents' home shows a collection of young children all dressed in white party clothes, sitting in a formal garden before an elderly woman (my great-grandmother) also wearing a formal white dress.

Weiss's business dealings didn't end well, though. Bayer became part of the German conglomerate IG Farben that, among other things, produced nerve gas for Auschwitz. In May 1941 the muckraking tabloid *PM* accused Sterling Drug of "fulfilling Goebbels's 'boast' that 'Americans would help Hitler win the Americas.'" Elsewhere Weiss was accused of being "an active soldier for the Nazi cause," and he became the object of an FBI investigation to search for any ties with Nazi Germany. My father remembers that Weiss was horrified. "Never intending to be more than just a businessman," Mann and Plummer wrote, "he had worked himself into a situation where his name was becoming a synonym for 'Nazi collaborator.'" They continued, "From a powerful man who singlehandedly ran an ever-growing corporation, he had become, almost overnight, an irrelevant, ghostly figure." No evidence of collaboration was found. Regardless, Weiss was forced out of the company ownership. A few years later, at age sixty-three, he died in a car accident near his summer home in Michigan.[42]

The Elusive Dividing Line

What relevance does this story have to the herbal supply chain? Was it just a coincidence that I had an ancestor whose story wasn't so different from Rosemary and Drake's, and Ed Smith's, and the many others who began by formulating concoctions in their kitchens and later became successful business owners? Or was it something more, like the plants showing up in Claudia's research, trying to capture my attention, helping me to see perspectives I hadn't yet considered?

As with the lingering effects of the spice trade and colonialism on the contemporary botanical industry, once we start digging into the past, we find connections we may not have expected and may not welcome. And although we often wish to present history in black and white, when we look deeply we find that the lines dividing right from wrong aren't what they appear from afar. Environmental sociologist Rebecca Altman began an essay on benzene with an image of what is called the coal tree, which was commonly used in the nineteenth and twentieth centuries to represent organic chemistry. Altman is drawn to these diagrams because she is interested in the moment when the natural is divided from the unnatural, a line we police so closely and with such judgment. But the difference between what is synthetic and natural, she explained when I spoke with her about her research, is often something as trivial as the placement of a single hydrogen molecule: "When [the benzene ring] is incorporated into certain molecules, it is essential to life. But in other configurations, slight tweaks in the composition and arrangement of atoms render benzene part of a toxic, possibly carcinogenic, molecule. And on its own, there is ample evidence that benzene causes cancer."[43]

One of the main selling points of herbal medicine is that these remedies are natural and thus superior to medicines synthesized in a lab. A tremendous amount of energy is spent claiming, if not carefully defining, this boundary between what is natural and what is unnatural (synthetic). Yet as Altman pointed out, the crucial difference is not whether a substance is natural or not, but rather how the arrangement of chemicals in the substance affects the body. In other words, you can't just assume that natural is good and unnatural is bad. What matters is how the substances are produced and used, with the intentions and attention of those producing the medicines. Which, as Claudia Ford wrote, can be for good purposes as often as for nefarious ones.

Given this entanglement, what is the path forward? I was dismayed to discover one of the key figures in launching the pharmaceutical industry (an industry I loved to hate) in my past. Yet, digging further, I came across veterans of the Indian wars and slaveholders in Virginia among my ancestors as well. At first I was quick to distance myself from these connections with the source of the violence and racism that continues to rack our country, a legacy that is no better than that, it seems, of da Gama plundering the Indian Ocean and beyond. But then I wondered what I might learn from being on what is now the wrong side of history.

No matter how much research I could have done, I could never discover the motivation and actions of these ancestors, what they did and didn't do about the injustices they were part of. I can ask, though: What did they see and not see about how to live in right relationship with others and the earth? What if these blind spots linger in my own ways of perceiving and judging right and wrong? Good and bad? I have benefited from what these ancestors did see and create. What I make of that legacy depends on what I choose to listen to and the ways I engage with the world around me; like Claudia Ford, following where the plants lead.

CHAPTER FOUR

The Herb Industry

*M*y vision of herbalism started out local, grassroots. I imagined people growing pots of thyme, sage, and rosemary in
pots on their back porches, echinacea and garlic in their gardens. Adults
and children alike would know where and when to gather St. Johnswort
and stinging nettles. They would know how to dry them for tea, prepare
an oil or salve, and when to use each one. Herbalists and farmers would
offer classes in their community; share medicinal plants and resources.
Everyone would learn this basic knowledge to keep themselves and
their family well, as important to the sustainability and viability of their
communities as growing their own food and producing their own energy,
as important to the education of their children as learning to read and
do math. They would collect medicinal plants growing in empty lots in
town, in community gardens, in meadows and fields and forests outside of
town. Much of the herbal medicine dispensed in the community would
come from these plants. And there would be community herbalists in
the town, too, to whom people could turn for treatment of more serious
conditions and who would know when the best course of action would
be to send them to the hospital to consult with specialists.

I imagined that I wanted to be such a community herbal practitioner,
and so after the apprentice program, I enrolled in an advanced program
at Sage Mountain. As part of my training, I sometimes observed as
Rosemary's more experienced students consulted with clients at a free
clinic once a month in the town of Barre, Vermont. One evening two
of the students met with a slightly overweight middle-aged man. They
listened for about half an hour as the man described his symptoms
and talked about his sleep and his health overall. One of the herbalists
asked what supplements he was taking. Reaching for his backpack, the
man emptied out fifteen to twenty white plastic containers of dietary

supplements, herbal products, and vitamins, all purchased, he said, from Rite Aid, GNC, and Walmart.

We were stunned. As Rosemary's students, we had learned that one path to healing could be through teas and tinctures, but lifestyle and diet were important, too, and so much more. Finding time to do things you love. Connecting with others. Getting rest and exercise. As I listened to this man and witnessed his health-in-a-bottle approach, I began to understand that my vision of herbal medicine was very far from the mainstream.

The enormity of the dominance of big companies in the herbal industry hit home as I walked the floor at the SupplySide West (officially SupplySide West & Food ingredients North America) trade show in Las Vegas, where these companies gather to negotiate contracts, forge new relationships, and wine and dine customers at extravagant gatherings. I asked Steven Dentali, a former scientific officer for the American Herbal Products Association (AHPA), about the impact that herbalists and their vision have on the part of the industry that attends these trade shows. We were speaking on the phone in one of several conversations. He said dismissively, "They pretend Walmart doesn't exist." He acknowledged that herbalists do bring about changes in their home communities, but they will never bring about change on a national and international scale. Achieving large-scale change was my goal, though, and that meant I needed to understand what the herb industry was doing to, and with, plants in the name of herbal medicine.

When I began this research, I was entering a whole new world, and I realized I would need help in understanding its complexity. So I sought information from many people within the industry, and my interviews with them proved fascinating and challenging. I particularly relied on the expertise of people such as Steven Dentali, along with Josef Brinckmann, formerly the sustainability director at Traditional Medicinals and now research fellow for the company; Steven Foster, author of numerous books and field guides on medicinal plants and a widely recognized plant photographer; and Mark Blumenthal, founder of American Botanical Council (ABC) and a leader in educating about the responsible use of herbal medicine. I also spoke with Lynda LeMole, co-owner and president of Traditional Medicinals from 1982 to 2003 and an early president of the American Herbal Products Association (AHPA), and Roy Upton, an herbalist and head of quality control at Planetary Herbals and founder of the American Herbal Pharmacopoeia (a nonprofit educational organization dedicated to promoting the responsible use of herbal products and herbal medicines).

For a long time I referred to and thought of the industry as singular and monolithic. Mark explained to me that, in fact, "the herb industry" is quite diverse, layered, fractionated, heterogeneous. There are companies in various positions along the supply chain (including all the stakeholders) that are owned and/or operated by people committed to quality, integrity, good business ethics, and the health and welfare of their customers, employees, and partners in the supply network. These are the companies that tend to start and/or belong to trade associations and that help to generate and promulgate best practices within their sectors of the "industry." And, Mark continued, there are companies that are committed to and focused solely on maximizing profits, with little or no regard to responsible and ethical practices, or to product quality. The "industry," he concluded, includes both kinds of companies as well as some that can be seen perhaps in the middle, with moderate commitment to best practices, to the extent that they can find a compelling business reason or justification to do so.

Herbal Medicines at the Industrial Scale

My first visit to the kind of company that processes herbs on an industrial scale was a trip to Naturex in Hoboken, New Jersey. A French company, Naturex was founded in 1992 and over the years has steadily bought up businesses in the industry. In 2018 it was acquired in turn by the world's largest flavor and fragrance ingredient supplier, Givaudan, a Swiss company founded in 1768.

To enter the Naturex factory, I had to call the front desk on a phone by the gate in the tall green chain-link fence that surrounded the strip of windowless buildings. Once through the gate, I spoke through another intercom at the door of a white vinyl-sided building. The door opened and I walked into a white-walled waiting room decorated with two ficus trees. There was no natural light in the room, and I checked to see whether the trees were real, but I couldn't be sure. Several ferns, obviously plastic, were placed around the base of the ficus trees. Individually wrapped breath mints sat in a dish next to a plastic bottle of pink hand sanitizer on what looked like a reception desk, though no one was there. A steel door with a security keypad marked the other exit from the room.

Two workers dressed in blue pants, blue tunics, and hair nets came through the steel door. One carried his lunch. Another carried an oxygen tank. Neither took notice of me.

After some time a thin, pale man with slicked-back dark hair and wearing a white button-down shirt with black square buttons came through the door. This was David Yvergniaux, the sales director, with whom I'd communicated by email to set up my visit. I guessed that David was in his thirties, and he spoke with a strong French accent. I couldn't imagine anyone choosing to move from France to live in this part of New Jersey, but he said he didn't mind. He led me to a conference room where he had set up a PowerPoint presentation about Naturex's work. Though I feared I would simply get a sales pitch, David was remarkably candid about the industry. At one point, looking at my tape recorder, he said he probably shouldn't say what he was about to say, but he went ahead anyway. He talked about the intentional adulteration of raw materials, how US buyers tended to care more about price than quality, and contaminants in the Chinese supply. Doing business with China was very difficult, he said, but it was almost impossible not to.

We talked for almost two hours, and then he introduced me to Florian Bernodat, the operations manager, for a tour of production. I put on a disposable hairnet and a white paper coat, per industry regulations, and followed him through heavy steel doors that bore warning signs prohibiting access. We entered a soccer-field-sized area with a cement floor and huge, stainless steel vats along the far side. Pipes branched off from the top and sides of the vats. I had to yell to be heard over the racket of the machinery. My guide explained the process, beginning with the correct identification of the plant material. Once that had been done, the cut material was brought in for extraction. He then described what happened: The plants sat in a mixture of water and ethanol in the huge vats—eighteen hundred kilograms of raw material per vat—for two hours. Then the slurry would be extracted, passing through the pipes to another container, while more solvent would be added to the original raw material, and it would be allowed to sit for another two hours. This slurry would pass out of the vat into a storage container, and one more round of extraction would be done. Three rounds were completed to recover as much of the constituents from the raw material as possible. The process was spread out over nine days, he explained.

A heater evaporates the solvent, using the same technology used for drying milk. They remove the solvent, which is then stored in another container to be reused. During this process, the extract is standardized to a particular marker compound. (Marker compounds are standardized as a quality control measure, indicating the presence of particular constituents in the extract.) This dried extract is then mixed with a compound like maltodextrin, a water-soluble carrier used in spray drying that can also be added and mixed in to normalize or standardize the content of the final extract. The powder then drops to the bottom of the storage container and passes through a tube into a box lined with plastic. This is the dried powdered extract that Naturex sells to its customers.

I found most of the terminology my guide used to describe the process pretty confusing. Though I took careful notes, I still had a hard time understanding the process. On top of that, whenever he mentioned "customers," I kept imagining men and women like me standing, perplexed, in the supplement aisle. But Naturex is just as invisible to the end consumer as the slurries of herbs he described were to me as I stared at the huge steel vats. Naturex's customers are other large, medium, and small companies that manufacture herbal products.

The US dietary supplement industry generated $42.6 billion in retail sales in 2018, with herbal dietary supplements contributing $8.84 billion to the total.[1] These numbers don't include herbs sold as teas. It is difficult to get accurate numbers on the scope of the international trade, because different countries use different tariff codes for classifying commodities.

Thus they aren't necessarily documenting the same information. Figures on one country's trade could leave out a whole category that another includes; these numbers thus wouldn't necessarily be comparable.

To illustrate this complexity, Josef Brinckmann responded to a question about numbers in trade by saying, "In the years that I put together annual global export trade data for the medicinal and aromatic plants sector (for International Trade Centre and the United Nations Conference on Trade and Development), the reports normally took me about five work days (after I got the hang of it), accessing databases of not only the United Nations Statistics Division but national import/ export trade databases of the major players, some freely available (like India's) while some available for a considerable fee (P.R. China). It is not as simple as one might think, because some countries, like India, report in agricultural seasons (say, March to April), while other countries, like China, report in calendar years (January to December), and some use strange weight measurements (like quintals in India) vs. pounds in the US vs. kg in China, etc., then all of the currencies need to be converted to a uniform currency for comparing. For determining the value of trade, I generally converted all of the currencies to either US dollars or to Euros, depending on the target audience of the trade report."

This is the kind of reply that made my head spin. His comments drive home the complexity of this industry and the attention to detail that is required to do the work well. They also drive home how difficult it is to make generalizations about the industry as a whole.

Globally, some thirty thousand plant species are said to be used for medicinal purposes, and four to six thousand are traded internationally. While estimates vary, on the basis of number of species, 60 to 90 percent of the herbs in commerce are thought to be sourced from the wild.[2]

The International Union for Conservation of Nature's (IUCN) Red List of Threatened Species brings together the world's most comprehensive information on the global conservation status of animal, fungal, and plant species. The IUCN Red List measures the pressures on species based on a set of quantitative criteria that estimate the risk of extinction. This list is an important indicator of the health of the world's biodiversity and a powerful tool to educate and catalyze action for biodiversity conservation.

Unfortunately, many medicinal and aromatic plants have not yet been assessed. At the time of this writing, of the approximately twenty-eight thousand species that have well-documented uses as medicinal and aromatic plants, only about 17 percent have been assessed against the extinction threat criteria of the IUCN Red List (and nearly 20 percent of those that have been assessed are believed to be in urgent need of reassessment). Based on these assessments, one in ten (11 percent) of the world's medicinal and aromatic plant species is threatened.[3] The proportion of threatened plants varies considerably from region to region, and more comprehensive assessments are needed and are currently under way.

Most medicinal plants are used by people who live in the region where the plants are grown. The greatest amount is used in Asia, where there is a long history of traditional herbal medicine, especially in China and India. China is the largest producer of the three thousand or so species in commerce, both for use domestically and for export, followed by India. Historically botanicals were exported from Asia or eastern Europe into Germany, which is one of the biggest importers of medicinal plants in the world. Ninety percent of plants destined for the U.K., Canada, or the US are channeled through Germany, which has a well-established system for processing, sorting, and grading medicinal plants. India, China, Germany, and other countries in which traditional medicine is popular and respected keep the highest-quality material for their own use and often export the rest to countries that have lower quality control standards. Typically the United States has been one of the major destinations for poorer-quality material, but this is changing as US standards become more rigorous. The most important medicinal plants grown in the US include various species of echinacea (roots and aerial parts), peppermint, and hops. Wild-collected plants include black cohosh, American ginseng, goldenseal, and slippery elm bark (all from Appalachia), saw palmetto from Florida, and cascara from the Pacific Northwest. More US farmers are beginning to cultivate medicinal plants, so a wider range of domestically grown species are becoming available.

Fewer than a thousand of the medicinal plant species in trade are cultivated, and some of these species are both cultivated and wild-collected. The significance of this is that overall, only a very small amount of the plant material used by the industry is being grown on farms. This is a concern because it means that a large and undefined amount is being harvested from the wild, and thus a significant portion of herbs being used by the industry are coming from sources that are perhaps overharvested. It is also a quality concern because it is more difficult to ensure the quality of wild-harvested plants bought and sold on the open market.

———

Herbs change hands as many as ten to fifteen times on their journey from source to shelf. Each of those hands take some of the money, usually in exchange for adding some value, though sometimes that value is simply putting the herbs into a different container with a new label. More often it involves some kind of handling, such as drying, cutting, sifting, and storing. Those at the bottom of such a long supply chain typically make pennies for their work. "The supply chain starts with very little money and ends with a lot of money. The people doing the most work—the collectors and then the farmers—those folks are getting the short end of the stick," Peg Schafer, a California grower of Chinese medicinal plants and author of *The Chinese Medicinal Herb Farm*, once told me. Studies in Mexico found that wild harvesters receive only 6 percent of the retail price of what they collect.[4] Wild asparagus in China brings collectors less than 1 percent of the retail price in Germany.[5] The ratio is similar for collectors of devil's claw (*Harpagophytum procumbens*) in Namibia.[6] In a research report, Kerry Ploetz, a Peace Corps volunteer who studied household use of medicinal plants in Bulgaria, described how herb companies would drive collectors to a particular region of the country to harvest particular herbs. The companies paid by weight, which "encouraged the herb gatherers to pick the entire plant, including the roots, and to pick all of the herbs in a given area."[7] (In chapter 10 I explain why this style of harvesting can lead to the demise of wild plant populations.) In interviews with collectors in Bosnia and Herzegovina, researchers found that 85 percent said they were underpaid for the raw material, and that is why they harvested larger amounts of herbs. Sixty-five percent of the collectors said they would quit collecting if they could find another source of income.[8]

The Promise of "Goodness"

When I shared the Kickstarter page for the Sustainable Herbs Program (SHP) with the head of a US herbal products trade association, he cautioned me against using the photos I had selected of a processing facility where wild-collected herbs are gathered and dried. "They look dusty," he said. *They are dusty*, I thought, and I left the photos there.

This conversation highlighted to me a key tension in this book project: I did not set out to write an investigative exposé on the botanical industry, yet I also did not want to naively accept claims about socially and ecologically responsible practices that were for marketing purposes only. There were risks on either side. First, I was concerned by how the media sensationalizes negative stories about the industry, perpetuating the trend of describing it in monolithic terms as all-bad, instead of the reality, as Mark described it, of a diverse and heterogeneous mix of companies. Yet I also believe that herb companies do get away with a fair amount of fuzzy messaging because many consumers naively accept the word *natural* on a product label as a promise of goodness, even though the term has no official meaning when used in describing herbs or cosmetic products. I discovered that claims of being natural were often far from true. As I navigated this line, I mostly spoke with industry leaders who were well aware of the issues and challenges the industry faces and who are working in various capacities to bring more rigor to industry practices for quality control, adulteration, and social and ecological sustainability. Even they weren't clear about how much to reveal.

Roy Upton said he sees so much more garbage than good in his role overseeing quality control. He asked me if I was going to talk about the negative side of the industry. I said I wasn't sure. "It's hard to know what is in the best interest of the community overall," he commented.

The companies that focus on quality may differ in how they extract the constituents from the plant material or in how they set specifications for the finished products they produce, or whether they source plants through intermediaries or form direct relationships themselves. Despite these differences, these companies know that the key to quality is controlling the source of the raw material. Some go beyond that, understanding that quality also means addressing environmental and social issues. This attention requires additional investments of money and time. Roy told me he guessed that most companies aren't guided by these values. Yet regardless of the investments a company makes in quality and social issues, its products have to be able to compete on the store shelf. And there is only so much a customer—even a socially responsible customer—will pay for a box of tea or a bottle of capsules or tincture, especially when cheaper ones are available.

"Maybe it is important to tell the positive story," Roy told me. But, he added, I should probably also touch on what was wrong in the industry—to make it clear what ethical companies are up against. Also, he said, consumers need to understand the bad quality in order to understand why investing in good quality material is so important.

On our first trip to India, Terry and I visited a wholesale herb company in the heart of Bangalore, one of the most crowded cities I have ever visited, with a researcher from the University of Trans-Disciplinary Health Sciences and Technology (previously FRLHT). We got out of the car on the side of a busy street and followed the researcher down a narrow passage, winding around motorcycles, pedestrians, and porters carrying huge sacks on their backs, and entered a narrow shop. Several men gathered around a desk at the entrance to the store. The researcher explained why we were there, and one of the men nodded and led us into the back section of the store. Open sacks of dried plants were piled from floor to ceiling on both sides of the long, narrow room. He reached into an open sack and pulled out a handful of dried leaves to show us. He reached into another open sack to show us a dried root, which he put in a tin container so we could take a closer look. He then left the plants in the tin on top of the sacks and looked for something else to show us. Other clerks came back to fill orders, reaching with their bare hands into the sacks (none of which were labeled as far as I could see), and filling tin containers with material to show to customers at the front of the store.

There are thousands of wholesale companies in India like this one, where buyers on the open market might purchase herbs. I thought about how many hands had touched the contents in each bag and wondered when those hands had last been washed. I thought of how easily the contents of one sack could spill into another or how one type of plant material might be mistaken for another because the bags weren't labeled. I pictured the bags left sitting open all night and what might crawl inside. The utter lack of care and concern about quality was astonishing. I was equally astonished that our guide, who worked for one of the leading research organizations on medicinal plants in India, was not the least bit surprised by the conditions we were witnessing.

The following year when I returned to India as a Fulbright scholar, I visited an herb broker south of Madurai, a hot dusty cow town whose main claim to fame is the Meenakshi Amman Temple dedicated to Shiva and Parvati. I had first met this broker, who was introduced to me as Mohan, when he gave a keynote presentation at a conference on the medicinal plant supply chain at Tamil Nadu Agricultural University. Wanting to learn more about his work, I scheduled this visit and also invited Dr. Aruna Ramachandran, a botany professor I had met at the conference. Mohan met us on the side of a busy road. He climbed aboard his motorcycle, a lungi pulled up over his knees, to lead us out of town to his factory.

The landscape was flat, dry, and hot. The sky was white from the ever-present heat of southern India. Mesquite trees, planted by the government, were scattered in an otherwise empty expanse that spread out from either side of the road. Following Mohan's motorcycle, we drove past depressions that had once been lakes, now empty, and riverbeds now dry. Garbage and trash filled ditches along the road. After some time we pulled up alongside a field of bright pink and crimson periwinkle flowers. We got out of the car to talk with the farmers who grew the flowers on contract for the European phytopharmaceutical market. The farms looked fine, the splash of purple and pink flowers brightening the drab, dusty south Indian landscape. We spoke with the farmers about the inputs they used, how much labor they needed to hire, and the challenges they had faced this season. Then we got back in the car to follow Mohan to his warehouse on the edge of a small village of mud huts. We drove past a group of women sitting on a porch filling small matchbook boxes with individual matches that they lined up neatly by hand. I realized I had never considered how matches ended up inside the boxes, nor considered whether they might have been placed there by hand by women in rural India.

Mohan led Aruna and me into a dimly lit room filled with piles of dried roots, twigs, and leaves. These conditions were nothing like what I'd been taught about how to store medicinal plant materials: the importance of making sure they are covered and not exposed to fluctuating temperatures, moisture, and dust. I remembered the strict rodent control system I had observed at a processing facility in Poland, and I was dismayed by the gaping holes in the walls of this warehouse, imagining the rodents that bedded in there at night.

Standing by a pile of brownish, old-looking stalks and leaves, Mohan explained that if a customer asked, he would provide them with bigger, greener, better-quality leaves than these—leaves that were stored elsewhere. But if they didn't ask—and most don't, he added—he gave them these older stalks and leaves. (Others have also told me about this practice.) Mohan walked across the room to a pile of dried roots. He broke off a bit of the root to taste, gesturing that we should as well. I almost put it in my mouth, but then copied Aruna, who pretended to nibble on a piece before dropping it discreetly to the ground.

Next we visited a collection center, also part of the uncertified supply chain that provided wild-collected plants to some of the leading Ayurvedic companies. A woman dressed in a red sari sat cross-legged on the edge of the dirt road, sifting twigs or pebbles from a mound of dried leaves piled higher than she sat. Just beyond her was a large cement water tank, the water surface covered with green algae. Plastic bags and trash rolled across the road whenever the wind blew. Nearby a thin, tired-looking woman in a faded pink sari sat by the scales while the head of the collection center weighed the dried roots the collector had brought to sell. I asked where these herbs were from. Mohan gestured to the stretches of scrubland we had driven through. As I was told again and again, all bets are off when you buy on the open market.

From the collection center, Mohan then led us on another drive about fifteen minutes farther to the south to show us a new business, his sparkler factory. We stopped on yet another dusty, flat Indian road, seemingly in the middle of nowhere. We walked through a gate and then passed some small cement buildings scattered randomly on the packed stretch of land. The buildings were small and separate, Mohan explained, to prevent any accidental explosions from causing a bigger explosion.

In a clearing behind the buildings, three men dipped a tray filled with individual straight wires into a vat of silver slurry. Their arms were covered in the dried silver paste as they dipped in tray after tray of sparklers. I was horrified. I had been worrying about heavy metal contamination of the air and soil, but these men were dipping their entire arms into vats that must have contained powdered metals (aluminum, magnesium, titanium, and iron are commonly used in sparklers). All day long, every day. Madurai is known as a fireworks manufacturing center, and though he mostly traded herbs, Mohan told us, he had recently started this business as well to make more money. Aruna, who looked as shocked as I felt, asked him why he was so focused on making money. Most people do it for their children, she said, but he had said he didn't have any. Mohan replied that he just wants to make money for himself.

We left the sparkler factory and headed back to Madurai. I had taken notes all day, but I never bothered to transcribe them. This was the most shocking of the many journeys I made to the source of an herb supply chain—as far from the yurt in the forest of Sage Mountain as I could go. The lack of concern for quality I saw in Madurai isn't inevitably the end point. But unless you find out for yourself, there is no way to know for sure what is happening at the far end of a supply chain. You may find a fairly paid farmer or wild harvester carefully tending the aliveness of the plants. Or you may discover a trader for whom it makes no difference whether he is trading a plant to be used as medicine or producing sparklers soaked in aluminum.

Complex Standards for a Complex Industry

The food industry understands that quality is cultural and is learned. It is no longer only blemishes and bruises on fruits and vegetables that customers reject. There is now specialized branding for niche commodities like coffee and chocolate, salt and cheese—where it is clear that you get what you pay for in terms of taste and care, and possibly in terms of ethical practices, sustainability, and nutritional value. As Josef Brinckmann of Traditional Medicinals told me when we interviewed him for *Numen*, "There's a difference between a microbrewery's India Pale Ale and a bottle of Budweiser. There's a difference between a Snickers bar and a Swiss chocolate bar. And it's really the same with herbs. You can get the Snickers bar or the Bud or you can get the microbrew or the Swiss chocolate bar or anything in between." (Josef is considered one of the foremost thinkers and leaders on sustainability and the botanical supply chain. I didn't know it at the time, but this was to be the first of many conversations he and I would have over the next thirteen years.)

Quality standards in the dietary supplement industry are regulated under the Dietary Supplement Health and Education Act of 1994 (DSHEA). The act officially defines dietary supplements, which include herbs as well as vitamins and minerals. Under DSHEA and in particular under the Good Manufacturing Practices that were subsequently implemented by the FDA over ten years later, quality is defined in specific steps to ensure the "identity, purity, strength, and composition" of each ingredient and product.

More rigorous and detailed quality standards are found in recognized pharmacopeias, like the United States Pharmacopeia (USP), the American Herbal Pharmacopoeia, European Pharmacopoeia, and others. Though companies can choose to source only pharmacopeial grade plants, herbal products that are not formally approved as botanical drugs do not need to meet the requirements listed in the USP. These products are regulated as a food category, rather than as drugs. This is the primary reason why there is such variation in quality produced by different companies. More on this below.

Discerning quality with herbal products is more complex than it perhaps seems and has to do with more than regulatory frameworks. For example, I can tell the difference between a good and a bad apple, a field-ripened tomato and one that was grown out of season. But when I first started working with medicinal herbs, the signs that indicated good quality weren't obvious to me. It was self-evident that dried herbs that are still vibrant green are better quality than dried herbs that are brown and lifeless. Beyond that, I had to learn what to look for and how to interpret what I saw. Quality also includes correct identification. That seems obvious but it isn't. When I was a beginning herb student, any two jars of dried herbs looked exactly alike to me, like green pieces of dried leaves. And there was no way I could discern by taste or appearance whether a liquid extract made with a combination of herbs actually included all the plants listed on the label or some others entirely. Nor could I tell whether something potentially harmful was present, such as pathogenic microbes, pesticide residues, arsenic, or lead. Or whether the plants had been harvested at the correct time and handled in the ways that are known to retain the constituents.

What's needed is knowledgeable buyers making sure they are sourcing high-quality raw material. Yet that knowledge about herbs and identification was lost in the US, Steven Foster said. Unlike countries such as Europe, India, China, and Russia—almost every other country where the tradition of using plants as medicine didn't fade—in America the complex grading systems for discerning quality in manufacturing botanical medicine were lost when the Eclectics died out. Without this deeper understanding of how to identify high-quality raw material, buyers have had nothing to go on but price. And so in the 1970s and '80s, the US quickly became known as the price-buying market.

Many European phytomedicine and other botanical companies are at least one hundred years old. Two, three, and four generations of family members are involved, and knowledge about sourcing and processing of medicinal plants is passed through the generations. In the US the leading companies weren't even established until the late 1960s. And the founders of those companies had no strong tradition to turn to for guidance. When botanical medicines died out in the early 1900s in the United States, the traditional networks of trade and manufacturing fell away. The scientific field of pharmacognosy began to die out as well. Plant knowledge was integral to the curriculum in US pharmacy schools from the late 1800s to the 1930s when herbs were part of mainstream care. But by around the 1970s and 1980s, pharmacy schools began dropping medicinal plant study from their curricula and eventually closed their pharmacognosy departments, often subsuming the subject under medicinal chemistry. The USP and the National Formulary dropped most monographs of crude drugs, including echinacea, black cohosh, and other mainstays of botanical medicine, between 1930 and 1950.[9] (Many of these have been or are in the process of being readmitted.)[10] In contrast, European and Australian pharmacopeias continued to list one hundred crude drugs and required companies to follow these pharmacopeial standards. This was not required in the 1950s in the United States. Pharmacists stopped preparing plant medicines, and so they no longer needed the tools to determine the identity and quality of crude drugs purchased from botanical supply houses. Plant medicines "fell away not because they had been shown to be ineffective," Steven Dentali wrote in a 2010 journal article. "They just fell out of fashion."[11]

As the focus of pharmacognosy shifted from the containers (plants) to their contents (chemicals), the "smeckers and leckers" (smellers and tasters)—those who could identify plants organoleptically (with their sense organs) and who knew common adulterants and bad-quality herbs—gave way to the "grinders and finders" who were looking for active compounds to be used to formulate new drugs. "Smellers and tasters" evaluated the plant as a "cultural message," Steven Dentali wrote, and were replaced by those operating under the model of drug discovery.[12]

Though much of the back-to-the-land movement focused on folk remedies and kitchen medicine you could prepare with common weeds, it also helped create a renewed interest in information about plants and botanical identification. Even so, in the early days, the herbal renaissance in the United States lacked the scientific rigor found in the European phytopharmaceutical industry or clinical herb programs. Steven Dentali guessed that few herbalists had the technical knowledge needed to productively read a scientific journal, just as few scientists had heard of the medicinal uses of echinacea. Things had gotten so bad that by the late 1970s, noted pharmacognosist Norman Farnsworth had a stamp made that said, SAVE THE ENDANGERED SPECIES: PHARMACOGNOSY.

Without any knowledge about how to evaluate quality and maintain it through the supply chain, those who were sourcing herbs for herb companies tended to make decisions based on price alone. For US companies that weren't purchasing pharmacopeial-grade herbs, there were no systems for ensuring the quality of the imported herbs. "Few people were testing or tasting. They were just buying," Roy Upton told me. And they were simply ordering plants from a list of names and prices printed on a piece of paper. They were not, as in other countries with established systems of trade, examining samples and setting specifications or, better yet, visiting the sources. This led to many sorts of problems in the supply chain, not just for US companies and consumers, but for the international market sourcing raw materials from the US.[13]

The regulations concerning herbal products proved to be one of the most confounding aspects of my research for this book, especially the implications of these regulations on the practice of herbal medicine. The events leading up to and following passage of the Dietary Supplement Health and Education Act of 1994 (DSHEA) are far beyond the scope of this book. The key point is that before the regulations passed, herbal products were in a regulatory no man's land. In the 1970s, companies that sold herbal products risked being shut down by the FDA because there were no clear standards. Drake recalled a visit by an FDA officer who had a bag of Smooth Move tea and told Drake that the company was selling the tea as a drug, which was illegal.

Peggy Brevoort was president of the American Herbal Products Association at the time that DSHEA was passed. One of her goals as president of AHPA was to work with Congress and with the FDA. "We got a lot of pushback. There were deep disagreements. 'We can't work with them!'" Brevoort said. "There were people who felt if you didn't collect the plants from the woods, your business wasn't legitimate. You had to keep it small and pure. There were those who said if you didn't make it in your kitchen, it didn't count. And there were those who said if you *did* make it in your kitchen, it didn't count."[14] Former Healthnotes, Inc., CEO Skye Lininger, who has been active in the natural products industry for almost forty years, said that organizing around the FDA was the first time the left and right came together in the health food industry. "The left, the old hippies, wanted their natural products, and the right, the libertarians, didn't want anyone telling them what to do. And so that formed an unusual alliance."[15] DSHEA was passed in part as a result of the biggest letter-writing campaign ever by constituents to Congress other than that expressing opposition to the Vietnam War. It was considered an unprecedented victory for a renegade industry and a shocking defeat for the FDA.

Under DSHEA, companies did not have to legally prove that herbs were safe and effective for treating specific diseases, so long as they did not make drug claims (claims of disease prevention, treatment, mitigation, or cure) on product labels. This legal definition meant that companies did not have to go through the lengthy and expensive drug approval process (which typically cost $230 million for each drug even at that time).

Mark explained the regulations to me as follows. Companies are allowed to make so-called structure/function claims—claims on how the product can affect the structure and/or function of the human body—but they cannot make claims related to how the product might be able to prevent or treat a disease. Such claims are limited to FDA-approved drugs. Structure/function claims must be truthful and not misleading and must be supportable or substantiated by a reasonable level of scientific evidence. Also, disease-related claims based on traditional use—no matter how compelling—are not allowed. This prohibition against providing such educational information on product labels separated the products from the traditions from which they arose. "Without being able to say what an herb was used for, we have herbs without herbalism," K. P. Khalsa, then head of the American Herbalists Guild, told herbalist and doctor Anne Dougherty during an interview.[16] Or as David Hoffmann said, "The inherent empowerment of herbal medicine was given away. You are only empowered if you buy a product."

DSHEA was a defensive position against the FDA's efforts to prevent access to herbal medicines and dietary supplements, Roy Upton explained to me. He acknowledged that it wasn't perfect, but given FDA pressure, the regulation was what he and others believed was possible and was considered a victory for both the natural health consumer and the dietary supplement industry.

The impact was immediate. Because companies were no longer threatened by closure, DSHEA opened the floodgates for herbal products. The *Wall Street Journal*, *Boston Globe*, and *Detroit News* all featured articles on echinacea in 1997.[17] Dan Rather visited Nature's Way, a supplement company in Utah, to record a news segment on the use of echinacea to prevent the common cold. The following day Nature's Way—and most companies that made echinacea products—were sold out.[18] The market for botanical medicines was estimated at approximately $1.6 billion in annual retail sales in 1994. In 1998 sales were purported close to $4 billion.[19] Companies that had been averaging $22,000 a year in sales were realizing sales as high as $8 million a year by the late 1990s. In 1994 (the year that DSHEA was passed) roughly four thousand products were on the market. By 2017, twenty-three years later, fifty to eighty thousand products were on the market. That huge increase in production brought a whole host of intended and unintended consequences, especially because many of the products depended on plants collected from the wild.

Many people entered the market to cash in, gathering herbs wherever they could—harvesting echinacea growing wild along roadsides in the Midwest, for example—likely paying little attention to the impact of overharvesting or the guidelines governing the harvest or handling of medicinal plants in systems of traditional medicine. Boom-and-bust cycles always wreak havoc on supply chains, and herbs were no exception. *HerbalGram* columnist Peter Landes reported on the oscillations in supply: "The scramble began. Prices for even low-quality goods skyrocket and companies end up paying high prices for poor material. Next, lots of specious or basically valueless material comes on the market and even that is scooped up by unsophisticated users. Growers/gatherers are encouraged by the extremely high prices and seemingly limitless demand and good material is oversupplied just as consumers move on to the next 'hot' herb. (By the way, is there anyone out there not growing echinacea?)"[20] The following year Landes reported: "In many instances inappropriate, carelessly harvested plant parts have been marketed (the whole damn plant instead of just the rootlets or the flowering tops) or whole fields with delicate ecologies have been decimated."[21]

The market reportedly reached a high of $3.87 billion in 1998. And then it began to drop. Mid-year sales in 2000 were down 12 percent. By 2001, they were down 15 percent. Companies planned their growth based on projections that customers would be repeat buyers. But many first-time customers never returned. Products sat on shelves; herbs sat in warehouses. Peter Landes wrote in *HerbalGram*, "Over-projection of sales was easy and obvious just a few months ago; companies that saw a 30 or 40 or 50 percent increase in sales over a couple of months simply projected a continuation of that happy trend, forgetting that every consumer in America would have to buy their second bottle of St. Johnswort or kava to make the projection prove out. This didn't happen that quickly and companies that have made commitments for property, merchandise, equipment, etc., and planned to finance that expansion from projected sales increases and profits may find problems instead if sales (and collections) don't pick up soon."[22]

Product quality was a key factor. Assays of ginkgo, for example, showed that six of thirty products tested did not meet the specifications on the label. Tests of valerian indicated that some of the products did not contain valerenic acid (which is considered an active constituent) "and therefore were probably a different species or a different plant altogether."[23]

Inconsistent quality wasn't the only problem. Just as knowledge about sourcing and producing botanical medicines had been lost, understanding of how to treat health conditions with herbal medicine had been lost. Consumers who bought and took products without guidance from a skilled practitioner didn't know, for example, what the expected time frame would be for the herbal medicine to work its effect.

As ethnobotanist and herbalist James Duke (who passed away in 2017) explained when we interviewed him in 2007 for *Numen*, "Contrasted with pharmaceuticals, which tend to hit you real hard, I believe that the more gentle herbs give you a whole menu of phytochemicals and your body selects from that menu." Those chemicals have different effects in the body: Some chemicals warm the tissue, others cool the tissue, working together to reestablish a healthy balance. As with most natural remedies, plants don't work fast, but their effect is sustainable as they slowly bring a body back to wellness.

Aspirin, which begins working to ease pain in thirty minutes, conditioned consumers to expect quick results. And so in the 1990s when customers first tried taking St. Johnswort (SJW) for depression and felt no noticeable effect within a few days, they stopped taking it. The bottles of SJW sat on the store shelves. Tons of SJW stored in warehouses around the world in anticipation of repeat orders became moldy. Processing facilities built exclusively to extract SJW sat idle.

This enormous waste is just one example of what can result from the separation of the plants from the source—the human and ecological communities where they grew and were harvested and processed and the systems of medicines that codified their use. All that mattered was selling a product and making a profit, regardless of its impact on the wellness of the individual taking the supplement or of the ecosystem, human and environmental, from which the plant was sourced.

Raising the Bar

Mark Blumenthal of the American Botanical Council, and the editor of *HerbalGram*, has been a key leader in efforts to bring scientific rigor to the industry. Mark has dedicated his life to increasing the quality and quantity of educational information on the safety and benefits of botanical-based ingredients so that they can become the first line of defense and are no longer considered alternative. Like others, Mark became interested in vegetarianism and herbal medicine and organic food as a way of protesting the Vietnam War. He began selling Korean ginseng roots from the back of his car and eventually started a wholesale herb company, Sweethardt Herbs, that focused largely on selling Chinese and Korean ginseng, Chinese patent medicines, and teas. He set up shop in his farmhouse on a three-acre farm outside Austin, Texas, with an organic garden, beehives, and an herb business.

In the 1970s Mark discovered that a company in the southwestern US was selling capsules mislabeled as "Wild Red American Ginseng" that turned out to be canaigre, *Rumex hymenosepalus*. (*Rumex* is the genus of weeds commonly known as dock, and it is unrelated to ginseng.) Mark's company was one of the top sellers of ginseng in the United States, and he knew there was no such thing as wild red American ginseng. These collectors had simply invented the name to give the impression that the canaigre roots were associated with ginseng, a plant with much higher value. Mark was president at that time of an industry group called the Herb Trade Association (HTA). As HTA president, Mark wrote an article deconstructing the marketing claims of the company selling wild red ginseng in the Southwest, and he talked about it at trade conventions, urging retailers and herb companies to stop the sale of this fraudulent product and to call the plant by its correct name. It worked. This experience began his focus on documenting fraudulent claims in the US market. Equally important, it showed him the power of education as a way to bring about change in the industry.

The Herb Trade Association also sponsored a series of symposia held at the University of California–Santa Cruz campus in the late 1970s. These meetings brought together for the first time herbalists—Mark Blumenthal, Steven Foster, Ed Smith, and many others—with some of the top medicinal plant researchers in the country. These included pharmacognosists and ethnobotanists Jim Duke, Norman Farnsworth, and Varro Tyler, along with Walter Lewis and Ara DerMarderosian, among others. Dr. Paul Lee, who had taught philosophy and theology at UC Santa Cruz, organized the symposia with help from Steven Foster (in 1979) and the (now defunct) HTA, then under Mark's leadership. They marked the beginning of what would become a long partnership of scientific research with herbal medicine in an effort to rebuild the rigor of pharmacognosy in the herb industry.

Another important step was Mark's development of a trade and herb community newsletter that eventually became the journal of the American Botanical Council: *HerbalGram*. The goal of the journal was to be the "golden key for unlocking the full spectrum of herbal knowledge for the past, present, and future." At that time the voluminous research conducted in Germany and published in German-language journals was routinely unavailable in the US, except among a few scientists. ABC, which Norman Farnsworth, James Duke, and Mark founded in 1988, sought to bring that scientific body of knowledge to US stakeholders—industry, herbalists, and scientists.

Toward that end, in 1998 ABC published *The Complete German Commission E Monographs: Therapeutic Guide to Herbal Medicines*, the basis for regulating herbal products as nonprescription drugs in Germany. During one of our many phone conversations, Mark told me that he considered the compilation of the Commission E monographs as ABC's signature contribution (since that time, though, ABC has created other programs of note as well). Commission E, an expert panel of German scientists and health professionals convened by the German government, compiled the evaluations of the safety and efficacy of more than three hundred herbs, phytomedicines, and herb combinations. Mark explained that this established a baseline of credibility for the safety and benefits of many herbs and herbal products.[24] In a review of the monographs, Steven Foster wrote that they "provided fixed rules and regulations for all drug categories, including medicinal plant products and medicinal combination teas, which allowed manufacturers to work within a reasonable set of guidelines covering labeling, quality control, usage, and safety."[25]

HerbalGram included a range of peer-reviewed articles on topics ranging from the modern science of European phytomedicine to the modern relevance of the history of botany. There were summaries of recent clinical trials of herbs and information on the traditional medicines of China and Vietnam. The journal included in-depth profiles of plants, incorporating traditional knowledge as well as clinical research and studies. ABC began producing peer-reviewed summaries of herbs; its educational catalog at one point listed three hundred books on herbs. Just reading the catalog, let alone the books, provided a sense of the depth, breadth, and scientific advancements in herbal medicine.

In an early letter to the editor of *HerbalGram*, James Hodgins, then the editor of a Canadian magazine, *Wildflower*, wrote, "For the past 20 years, I have purposely avoided contact with herbalist magazines, as they were always top-heavy with unsubstantiated claims, few reference sources, and woven in with an amalgam of mumbo-jumbo essays on crystal power, astrology, etc. . . . Until now [reading *HerbalGram*], I had thought the entire herbalist movement was living in a time warp; totally unconnected with ecological principles or the scientific methods."[26]

Like Ed Smith, Mark Blumenthal likes to wear short-sleeved Hawaiian shirts. At the Natural Products Expo West trade show in 2019, his staff presented him with not only one, but two identical Hawaiian-style shirts printed with images from issues of *HerbalGram* that celebrated Jim Duke. (Jim had been a close friend, mentor, and colleague of Mark's.) Mark wore those shirts throughout the four days of the trade show.

I asked Mark why he chose to focus his life's work on bringing scientific rigor to herbal medicine. He had pursued a degree in political science and philosophy. This impressed upon him the need to cite sources of information to demonstrate that something is not made up. Citing sources ensures that people aren't "uncritically parroting or ricocheting information from others." He said that the blind acceptance of the traditional use of plants made it too easy to dismiss herbal medicine as the Rodney Dangerfield of medicine. He wanted to show that herbalism was real medicine and to bring it more legitimacy. By communicating the scientific literature, he strove to show that herbs had a use and value beyond folklore.

The other major impact of DSHEA is the Good Manufacturing Practices (GMPs). The cGMPs (the small *c* refers to "current") are guidelines that provide minimum requirements that a manufacturer must meet to ensure that their products are consistently produced and controlled to the quality standards appropriate to their intended use and as required by the product specification. Good manufacturing practices, along with good agricultural practices and other such regulations, are overseen by regulatory agencies like the FDA in the United States or similar bodies in other countries.

Compliance with GMPs requires ingredient and product testing and extensive paperwork to ensure that the manufacturing process for each product is properly designed, controlled, and monitored. GMPs help to ensure that products are consistent from batch to batch and that each product is properly made with all of the correct ingredients in the right amounts and no unwanted or undeclared ingredients, guaranteeing product safety and reliability. As part of GMP compliance, the FDA requires that companies do testing to ensure the "identity, purity, strength, and composition" of each ingredient and product. All of these practices require a significant amount of documentation. As Mitch Coven from Vitality Works told me, "In terms of the requirements for implementing the GMPs, the amount of testing companies has to do has grown. Four and a half years ago, we had five people in Quality Control and Quality Assurance section. Now, in 2016, we have over twenty people. Those people are not making product. They aren't selling product. They are just testing and keeping track and pushing paper." Mark echoed Mitch's viewpoint: "At the end of the day, GMPs are more about paperwork and documentation than they are testing."

The GMPs for dietary supplements were supposed to have been modeled on GMPs for the manufacture of conventional foods. However, when GMP regulations were finally implemented, they contained numerous provisions modeled on GMPs for drug companies, which has made it extremely costly and difficult for smaller herb companies to become compliant.

When I began the Sustainable Herbs Program, I intended to focus on small companies like Urban Moonshine in Burlington, Vermont, or Avena Botanicals in Rockport, Maine. It was at the early years of implementing cGMPs, which were to roll out over three years to give smaller companies time to get systems in place. Yet at the time of my writing, both Avena and Urban Moonshine were undergoing tremendous pressure from the FDA about their failure to comply with the cGMPs.

At the International Herb Symposium in 2015, a panel was organized on the impact of the FDA's cGMP regulations on small- to medium-sized herb companies. The room, a college classroom at Wheaton College, was overflowing. Deb Soule was one of the speakers. Another was Jovial King, founder of Urban Moonshine. Deb and Jovial are the next generation of herbalists trying to navigate the regulatory climate advocated for by their predecessors.

Jovial described the ways in which cGMP record keeping was changing her business. Because testing is done by lot, the pressure is to test larger amounts of herbs, more than many small herb growers can manage to grow, as a way to reduce the overall testing and paperwork expenses. This makes it harder for them to continue to buy herbs from farms like Zack Woods Herb Farm in Vermont. Regulations are forcing smaller business to scale up, she said. Deb said that for Avena, which doesn't want to scale up beyond a certain capacity, it has meant making the choice to drop certain products.

"It is a far walk from the garden," Jovial said. "The FDA has set the bar very high, and to reach it, you need a very tall ladder made out of gold. The implications of this are immense." Jovial continued. She said she has moved beyond the question of *How can I keep my business alive?* and now was focused on *How do I keep the consciousness of the herbal tradition alive?*

Eventually Jovial decided that the way to keep Urban Moonshine alive was to sell the business, and in 2017 she sold it to Traditional Medicinals. Avena has remained an independent company, choosing to scale back production, selling only what they can grow, and thus control from seed to shelf, in their gardens.

The popularity of this panel and the discussion that ensued reminded me that this industry grew out of a very idealistic impulse to find a holistic alternative to conventional medicine. After a somewhat gradual beginning, the industry grew very fast. Some companies adopted very high standards but others didn't, entering only to make a quick profit from the growing popularity of herbal medicine. As companies grew, they sourced increasingly large quantities of raw materials from all around the world, which made the industry even more complex. The government regulations created to monitor the industry have been a mixed blessing, and so nonprofit organizations and trade associations have also sprung up to demand more rigor. Everything I have learned from researching the herb industry reinforces the point that it is too simplistic to paint the industry as all good or bad. As I spoke with more people and visited more companies, I realized I didn't want to write a book that focused on the horror stories or the ways the values of herbal medicine were being compromised by the industry. I wanted to tell stories that show the potential for change, one step, or one plant, at a time. And that often means telling the story not of a particular company, but of particular individuals doing the best they can, given the circumstances in which they find themselves.

CHAPTER FIVE

Pick a Plant

Things aren't things, they are processes.

—JOHN POWELL

*W*hile Drake Sadler's vision has shaped the approach of Traditional Medicinals, the company's success and effectiveness in implementing that vision can be attributed to Josef Brinckmann and other like-minded people at the company. "I'm one of these people who has been amazed for decades that the world makes it from one day to the next with all the things that can go wrong," Josef told me during one of our many conversations. Josef has spent over thirty-five years working in the global herbal products trade, much of that at Traditional Medicinals where he has overseen the sustainability department, the research and development department, and currently serves as a research fellow for medicinal plants and the botanical supply chain. "I'm somebody who heard the alarm bell a long time ago, and I continue to be frustrated by the painfully slow pace of progress in mitigating the continued pollution of our world." Josef has traveled all over the world to meet with suppliers, setting a model that shows it is possible to maintain the connection between people and plants even as a company scales up production.

"People talk about all sorts of problems in the mainstream supply chain, quality problems and regulatory and litigious problems," Josef said. "I think the answer is pretty simply, really. You find out where things come from. You go there. You meet people. You develop relationships. You know what you are buying. Buyers and sellers agree on the quality and quantity of what you are buying and what you are going to test for. And you avoid a lot of problems that so many American companies find themselves facing so much of the time because they do anonymous buying. They do price buying. They don't know where anything comes from and they don't want to invest in the costs of quality assurance and of sustainability. If you invest in quality assurance and sustainability, you can get rid of most of your problems.

"If someone says to me with a big smile on their face how happy they are that they got a shirt they really like on sale for only $7.99, I usually rain on their parade, and say, 'Well, somebody probably got screwed. Are you sure it wasn't made in a sweatshop?'" Josef then told me a story about how he tried to buy a bicycle made in the United States. "I called every bike shop within driving distance to say, 'I want a handmade bike. I want an American bike.' And everybody thought I was crazy. I said, 'Well, I'm going to keep going until I find one.' I couldn't find one in California but finally I found one that everyone assured me was made in Madison, Wisconsin, which is where I'm from. So I was really happy to support that Madison business! And then later on I found out that some parts of that bike *were* made in Taiwan and sent to Madison! Not that I have anything against Taiwan," he added. "But . . . I was really trying to support American-made, American business, high-quality craftsmanship."

Josef grew up in the Midwest in a family that put a high value on quality. His father always told him that if you buy or build a chair, it should be such a good chair you could hand it down to your children and grandchildren. It should still be a chair five hundred years from now. He remembered that in the early 1960s, his father came home depressed after attending a conference. "They just rolled out a new concept called 'planned obsolescence,'" his father told him. "They're going to start making things intentionally cheap so they break within five years. This is where it's going. The age of the craftsperson, of building something that is solid enough to last, or of a machine that is built well enough to repair, those days are numbered."

Josef first got interested "in this stuff," as he put it, when he volunteered at a natural food co-op in Milwaukee as a teenager. He noticed the sign in the front window that read FOOD FOR PEOPLE, NOT FOR PROFIT. And even though he is working in an industry that has too often emphasized profits rather than people, Josef continues to use that motto as his guide.

The Herb Supply Network

Ben Heron, then sustainability director at Pukka Herbs, spent years in India sourcing medicinal plants and developing partnerships with suppliers for Pukka. Ben answered many questions for me as I researched this book, and he explained how the various types of companies fit together in what is more of a network than a linear chain. Here's how Ben described that network.

The journey of herbs from soil to shelf is essentially a journey of getting cleaned up. How much the herbs are cleaned up depends on the care and attention brought to each step of the process. A first step is collection of herbs from the wild. (Or herbs may be grown on small-, medium-, and large-scale farms.) Wild harvesters harvest gentian, nettles, elderberries, and more from eastern Europe, or jatamansi from Nepal, or black cohosh or goldenseal from Appalachia, licorice from Spain or Georgia—the list of herbs and countries is endless. The harvesters toss the herbs into a sack. They carry the full sack from the forest or mountain or meadow on their backs or on a donkey's back or in the back of a pickup. The fresh plants or roots are dried, either in drying racks in temperature-controlled homes or woodshops, or on a mat in the sun or in dusty barns or alongside a highway. Then they're stored in old burlap sacks, reused plastic bags, or whatever is at hand. (If the collector is supplying a company that is certified organic or FairWild, however, the bags must be new.) These are sold to an individual trader or to a business called a producer company or producer group. (And the term *primary processing company* is often used interchangeably with *producer group*, too.)

On my research travels for this book, I had hoped to be able to meet directly with collectors in eastern Europe. But the best connections I could arrange were introductions to producer groups. And because of the way the industry works, that was often as far down the supply chain as I could get.

Processing of herbs into a finished product such as a tea or an encapsulated form is a multistep process. It is always better to leave plant material in as large a size as possible as long as possible to retain the constituents. A primary processing company dries and stores herbs until receiving an order from a secondary processing company further down the supply chain. Such an order would typically include a specification sheet describing, at a minimum, the size the plant parts were to be cut as well as acceptable microbe counts, pesticide levels, and sometimes heavy metal counts. On receiving the order, the processor might send a sample to the secondary processing company or the finished-product company (usually called the brand), whichever places the order, for approval. If that buyer approved the sample, the processor would take the herbs from storage and cut them to the size specified.

Secondary processors are typically located in western Europe or other regions where storage facilities, machinery, and hygiene standards comply to European and US standards. Many secondary processors are located in Germany, which has state-of-the-art processing facilities and some of the highest quality control standards in the world. Most herbs in international trade—especially those from eastern Europe, Africa, and Asia—travel through Germany. Secondary processors invest in more expensive machinery that can handle more specific processing requests, usually the size and type of the cut, from their customers. The size and type of cut is determined by the end use of the herb, whether for a tea bag or a powdered extract, say.

Primary processing facilities usually want to keep the herbs as long as they can to add more value, Ben explained. These facilities are typically close to the region where herbs are harvested or grown, often in developing countries, where drying equipment and storage facilities are more rudimentary. And so finished-product companies want to get the herbs out of those countries as quickly as possible to better control the quality. This finished product is then sold by the brand or company whose label we see on the shelf.

The main requirement of production is to stabilize the product as quickly as possible through drying (dehydration) or extraction, and then to maintain that stable product by storing it in a climate (temperature and humidity) controlled environment until further processing is required. The key to doing this successfully is to ensure that what is *in* the plant, its biochemistry, at the point of harvest stays in the plant through processing and handling. These primary processing steps are the point at which most things in a plant's journey from seed to shelf can go wrong. As Chinese medicinal herb grower Peg Schafer said about drying: "It's simple. If a plant has purple flowers at harvest, those flowers should still be purple after drying. If not, something is wrong." The steps aren't complicated. Yet doing them correctly—keeping the flowers purple, for example—is extremely difficult. You can harvest a beautiful herb from the field, I was told again and again, and wreck it in the drying. If you don't wreck it in the dryer, you can wreck it in storage or handling or shipping or steam sterilization, any of the steps between a flower in a field and a stable product on a shelf. To do it well, someone has to be paying attention.

In my garden in Vermont, I gather baskets of nettles, calendula flowers, lemon balm, and mints to dry for tea. I spread the leaves and flowers on screens and put the screens in a handmade wooden dryer with a lightbulb as heat source. When I am rushed, I just spread them in large bamboo baskets to dry. I promptly forget about them. Ten days later I remember the herbs in the baskets. Or after a day drying them in the dryer, I turn off the dryer because I'm worried about wasting the electricity, little as that is. Then I forget about them until I remember to turn the dryer back on.

I test them for dryness—a clear snap of the stem and a satisfying crunch for leaves is my measure—to see if they are ready to garble and put in jars.[1] If they are, I remove them from the screens to put into glass jars when I have time, but then I may get distracted by the need to make dinner. I end up leaving them in the baskets overnight. The temperature cools, especially on the first floor of our house, or it rains. The plants reabsorb the moisture and, in the morning, no longer have that satisfying crunch. And so I need to begin the process all over. In other words, paying attention sounds like simple advice, but doing it consistently, reliably, is a skill that requires effort.

A processor not only needs to pay attention to the requirements of drying plants in general, but must also pay attention to the varying requirements of individual species and specific parts of individual plants. The drying temperature may be different for leaves than for roots, for example. It also depends on the outside temperature and humidity. Plant material will dry more quickly in a dry environment, more slowly in rainy, humid places. The temperature and drying time must be adjusted accordingly.

To be economically viable, most processing companies must handle more than one hundred species of plants. Each species follows its own mini supply chain, and each has particular criteria that must be attended to. A large company like Traditional Medicinals that sells finished herbal products sources about 120 plants originating from about sixty producer companies, situated in about thirty countries, which are processed through about ten companies. A wholesale ingredient trading company like Mountain Rose Herbs, based in Eugene, Oregon, keeps approximately 340 dried botanicals in its inventory. These botanicals are grown, harvested, and processed in regions of the world that face political instability, drought, heavy rains, urban migration, and/or polluted soils. All of these issues potentially impact the quality and quantity of the material. That is a lot to consider.

Seeking Transparency

In the 1970s, '80s, and '90s, herb companies in the US were at least one step removed from the source, though often at least two steps or more, Josef explained to me. Most finished-product companies in the US bought their herbs through a series of brokers and import-export trading houses. The conventional uncertified herb trade was secretive and resistant to transparency, which made visiting the sites where herbs were grown or collected almost impossible. Brokers might be straight traders who simply consolidated lots, stored those herbs, and shipped them to the next link in the chain. Or a broker might add some value to the herbs, usually some form of cutting and sifting. But brokers typically didn't deal directly with individual farmers or collectors, and most didn't maintain close relationships with producer groups.

From the beginning Drake and Josef felt it was important to work with suppliers as close to the source of the herbs as possible. At the time, Josef said, "There was no transparency, no traceability, and no relationships.

"I realized early on that you couldn't just buy anonymously," he continued. "You can't just follow prices around and buy from this place this week and that place next week if you want to have consistent products and make certain that you'll have access to the quantities and qualities you need. You have to have really good relationships with people to do this work."

Initially simply figuring out the country of origin of a particular herb was difficult. Josef would ask his US suppliers questions about the herbs and quality, but these suppliers would in turn have to ask the exporters in Germany from whom they purchased the herbs. It would take them a week to get back to him with an answer. He began asking for permission to speak directly to the person responsible for procurement at the German companies. These buyers were closer to the primary producers, both geographically and because the supply networks in Germany had not been broken, and so were more likely to have the answers to Josef's questions than brokers based in the US.

At first he didn't make much headway. But then in the early 1990s, the communist systems in eastern Europe began to break up, which created an opportunity. Under communist rule, various regions had quotas for purchasing botanicals. Villagers brought herbs to state-owned collection centers, and the government in turn purchased the botanicals to sell on the national and international market. Between 1989 and 1991 that system fell apart. The collection centers became privatized, often ending up owned by the same people who had managed the former communist cooperatives. For the first time, these businesses needed to find their own buyers, so they began to seek out direct relationships with buyers in Germany, Italy, and France. This shift created an opportunity for Drake and Josef to begin meeting with their German suppliers.

At the same time, in early 2000, USDA regulations for a US certified organic program were put in place. Organic certification required traceability and transparency through a supply chain. Bags of organic herbs had to be tracked to ensure that the herbs were actually grown in designated fields using certified organic practices that could be audited.

THE BUSINESS OF BOTANICALS

Thus certification provided a traceable pathway connecting brands and suppliers all the way to the source. If a problem was detected through quality control tests, the company could trace back those herbs to collectors or farms to identify and address it.[2] Unless a company was vertically integrated (the company controlled the raw material from seed through all stages of production), non-certified organic herbs could rarely be traced to the source.

For Traditional Medicinals, organic certification was important both for the assurance that no non-certified organic pesticides or fertilizers had been used and because it allowed them to know the identity of their suppliers all the way to the source. Traditional Medicinals had worked with some organic herb growers since the 1970s, including Trout Lake Farm in Washington. But in 2000, the company told its other suppliers that it was leaving the conventional non-certified supply chain behind. "We have a crystal ball," Josef remembered saying. "This is the future. We see it." Traditional Medicinals wanted all of the producers to achieve organic certification by 2010 and certification for economic and social sustainability according to fair trade standards by 2020.

Josef remembered thinking, "If you won't go there, we won't work with you. We want direct access to our producers. We want to know everyone involved. We want to do site visits and make our own needs assessments, and we want sustainability standards. We didn't know what that meant," he acknowledged. "But we made a commitment to figuring it out."

One of their suppliers, a large US trader, laughed at them, Josef told me. The supplier told Drake and Josef that it was all just a fad. But a few years later, that supplier came back to Traditional Medicinals, saying, "Well, more of our buyers are asking about this as well, maybe it isn't just a fad."

"This was a new way of walking and a new way of talking. At first people weren't very comfortable with this idea. But in our case, it has worked," Josef said. He paused and added that it worked for them because their size gave them leverage to make these demands. "It takes time to get to a place where you can insist on transparency and direct access to the producer groups, and your supplier trusts that you have no intention of going around them and buying directly from the producer. That takes time. But it also takes quantities. In part, it hinges on becoming big enough that your business can have an impact."

Watching the Scorpion

I flew to eastern Europe in October 2015 to begin my journey following herbs through the supply chain. With Josef's help, I had arranged to visit some FairWild certified producers. The FairWild Standard (which I describe in more detail in chapter 10) is a best practice standard for sustainable wild harvesting and equitable fair trade.[3] I spent the first several days in Budapest visiting the regional office for TRAFFIC, an NGO that is one of the founding partners of the FairWild program, and also visiting some producers outside Budapest. After that, I left on a night train to Warsaw and then took a train to eastern Poland. Anna Charytoniuk, who is in charge of international sales for the producing company Runo Spólka, met me at the train station. She was also one of two people at the company who spoke English. We had only exchanged a few emails, but Anna greeted me with a hug, insisted on carrying my bag, and led me to the car where her husband and son were waiting. We drove an hour to the eastern border of Poland, to the small town of Hajnówka where Anna and her family lived and where Runo is based. The town is near the Białowieża Forest, a UNESCO World Heritage Site protecting what remains of Europe's largest and last primeval forest. I spent the night in a small cottage in a renovated Polish village settlement, seemingly built for tourists, though in cold, rainy October I was the only guest. Anna picked me up the next morning to take me to the factory at Runo. As she drove, she talked about her mother who, it turned out, loved to harvest medicinal plants. "My mother is happiest in the forest," Anna said. "When she is there, she'll gather mushrooms or fruits or plants, it doesn't even matter if she puts them in soup or not. She just wants to be in the forest.

"I love it, too," Anna added. After attaining her dream of getting a full night's sleep (she had a two-year-old son who still nursed), she said, she dreams of living in a village with a garden and chickens and a meadow where she could gather herbs.

Josef first met Eugeniusz Sidoruk, co-founder and CEO of Runo, in 2008 at BioFach, the biggest certified organic trade show in the world, held in Nuremberg each year. Producers from around the world meet with potential new buyers and discuss sales and contracts with existing buyers. Josef asked Eugeniusz whether Runo would be interested in implementing the FairWild Standard. Because the margins for primary producers are tight, Eugeniusz was always looking for new markets for the company's herbs. He was also eager to establish a relationship with Traditional Medicinals.

Runo began working with the FairWild Foundation to identify plants that could potentially be included in the FairWild management plan. In 2009 Runo became Poland's first and only FairWild certified processing company. Runo produces dandelion root and leaves, stinging nettle roots and leaves, elderflower, meadowsweet, and many other certified organic and non-organic herbs for markets around the world. The company has become a flagship for the FairWild certification, and because FairWild's success depends on more companies adopting the standard, the staff of Runo welcomed my visit to tell their story.

Runo's office is a single-story stucco-sided neat white building with tall, narrow windows on the edge of Hajnówka. It was a crowded, busy office. A framed embroidery of a flower made by Anna hung on the wall above one desk. Eugeniusz, whom Anna referred to as her boss, was a sturdy man with a bulbous nose and reddish complexion. Like Anna, he was warm and very kind. He waited patiently while Anna translated. He wanted to make sure I got what I needed during my visit, he said, and to do what he could to help.

Eugeniusz does care about plants, but he especially cares about providing jobs. The company is small, he explained, as we sat in a small room in the back of the office. Trophies crowded the windowsill. Anna later said they were from sports competitions that the company had entered. But now they no longer had time.

After an hour or so, Eugeniusz told me we would speak more later and returned to his work. The processing center—where the machinery was located—was across the parking lot. There were separate warehouses for certified (organic and/or FairWild) and conventionally grown herbs and a collection center where collectors delivered their wild-collected herbs. Next to the processing hall was another warehouse for storing sacks of freshly processed material ready for shipment.

I could smell the plants before entering the processing center, a slightly sweet aromatic scent, minty or lemony or stronger, depending on the plants being processed. I could hear the machines, called Scorpions (Scorpion is a Polish manufacturer of herb cutting, sifting, and cleaning machines), before entering the factory, too. Brown paper sacks lined the edges of the room, along with large screens and racks and odd machine parts. A man in forest-green overalls emptied one of the sacks of dried plants into a rectangular metal bin, helping them into an opening at one side where they dropped down a chute and a blade at the bottom chopped them up. The pieces came out on a foot-wide conveyor belt lined with narrow shelves that carried the now chopped pieces to another, larger bin that was constantly shaking. Screens at the base of this bin separated stems from leaves, large pieces from small. How small depended on specifications provided by Runo's customers; the requirements depended on the final use of the plants.

I watched nettles being processed. Finer-cut pieces dropped through one nozzle into a brown bag; these would be sold at a higher price. Chopped stems poured into another bag. When a sack filled up, the worker removed the sack from under the nozzle, rolled down the top, sealed the bag, and set it off to the side. He attached a clean new bag to the nozzle, and then returned to dump more plants into the bin at the top of the machine, doing his best to never let the machine be idle. Two other operators mirrored this work on the two other Scorpions in this room. Around the edges of the room, smaller machines were busy with other jobs, such as sifting leaves and twigs from berries. Once an order was processed, the workers loaded the sacks onto trucks to be shipped to Runo's customers around the world.

The scale of industrialization in the processing hall at Runo was unfamiliar and disorienting to me—a student of homegrown, make-your-own herbal medicine—and I returned there whenever I had free time during my visit. I stood on the side, out of the way, watching. The men nodded and continued with their work. I wasn't sure what I hoped to learn or discover. It was hard to hear over the noise of the machines, a constant grinding clatter. Despite exhaust tubes in the ceiling, the fine dust of chopped and sifted plant material in the air made it hard to breathe.

As I watched the green-clad workers pour another sack of dried dark green nettle leaves into the Scorpion, I thought of *Nature's Metropolis*, environmental historian William Cronon's account of the changes in the Chicago grain market in the 1850s. Cronon described the system before these changes, which hinged on the "seemingly unremarkable fact that shippers, whether farmers or merchants, loaded their grain into sacks before sending it on its journey to the mill."[4] These sacks of grain kept each farmer's grain "intact, unmixed with grain from other farms."[5] The sacks were well suited to traveling on flatboats in riverfront towns like St. Louis. The system was not so well suited, however, to towns like Chicago that were best accessed by the railroads. Unloading sacks from railcars and into automatic machinery took extra work and time, both of which ate into profits. The introduction of the grain elevator, "the most important yet least acknowledged [invention] in the history of American agriculture," changed this.[6] Grain could now be poured directly from railcars into the elevators. Sacks were no longer needed.

I watched the cut pieces of nettles harvested from different meadows by different collectors mix together as the conveyor belt dropped them into the bin, where the sorting process began, in this case by size. I imagined the stream of golden wheat pouring into the elevator described by Cronon, the grain losing "the characteristic weight, bulk, cleanliness, purity, and flavor that marked it as the product of a particular track of land and a particular farmer's labor."[7]

Because pricing could no longer be attached to a particular farmer's fields, the Chicago Board of Trade then created a grading system to determine the pricing of the grain: #2 winter wheat or #1 winter wheat. In this way, Cronon wrote, grain elevators "severed the link between ownership rights and physical grain," and so between the identity of the farmer and the product of his or her labor. This seemingly simple act had a "host of unanticipated consequences" that shape our world today.[8] Describing a similar unraveling with meat, Cronon said, "In the packers' world, it was easy not to remember that eating was a moral act inextricably bound to killing . . . Forgetfulness was among the least noticed and most important of its by-products."[9] "The world of the marketplace," writer Verlyn Klinkenborg noted in his *New Yorker* review of *Nature's Metropolis*, "where city and country met, was—and remains—a world of such forgetting."[10] In the collection hall at Runo, I came to understand I was witnessing the beginning of yet another unraveling, the point at which something of a particular landscape becomes a product governed by the logic of capital, no longer attached to place.

Is Intention Possible in a Factory?

Those at botanical companies increasingly emphasize the importance of transparency and of knowing the origin of the raw material. Josef estimates that only 5 to 10 percent of plants in the botanical world are certified, either certified organic or organic plus an additional sustainability certification such as fair trade.

In the uncertified world, an end buyer has no way of knowing where the raw material came from or how it was grown or harvested—whether it was dried carefully in a controlled facility, or outside in a courtyard with goats and chickens walking across, or on the side of a road in Bulgaria where car tires act as a thresher. These are the herbs that end up in white plastic containers on grocery store shelves, bought and sold like any other commodity, as placeless as streams of wheat pouring into grain elevators. All bets are off, Josef explained, in the uncertified supply chain.

I thought back to the question that brought me on this journey: Is it possible to find intention in herbs that are sourced from the global market? As I watched the action in Runo's processing hall, I couldn't recognize intention. I didn't know where to look for the spirit of the plants piled high in huge warehouses, moving along worn conveyor belts, and chopped in rusty, run-down machines. Anna told me that replacing parts and buying new machinery takes money the company simply doesn't have.

Although the processing hall at Runo was nothing like the spotless facilities at Naturex or the companies Terry and I later visited in Germany,

I liked it better. Yes, Runo was messier, more haphazard. But people were warm and friendly and helpful. Everyone said it was like family, that the Boss went out of his way to treat the workers well and to help them if they needed it. People had worked there for years. Everyone we talked with told us it was hard work, but good work. And that's how it felt to me. But I didn't sense intention in the same way I'd heard it described at herb conferences. Working with herbs at Runo is work done for a paycheck. Stop the pay and the work will stop.

What do "good intentions" mean in the context of a company like Runo? Certifications offer one way to measure attention and intention and to define the practices and methods companies are willing to invest in. A certification program is a beginning, a first step toward reestablishing links between producer and finished product. Sebastian Pole of Pukka Herbs once described third-party certifications as the "guiding lights as a company gets directors, new members of the leadership team, and new owners"—a tool in keeping that business on track with the values it claims.

But such programs aren't fail-safe. An organic certifier from Hungary I spoke with said she believed that people always take better care of what they feed their family than what they sell. There are always corners to cut. They are easier to cut when we don't know whose lives our shortcuts will impact, or if those impacts are far from our home. And ultimately the value of certification comes down to the people responsible for implementing the standards and the quality and attention of their work.

———

In his book *Gardens: An Essay on the Human Condition*, literary philosopher Robert Pogue Harrison wrote about what he called the laral value of a thing.[11] *Laral* comes from *lares*, the Roman word for the everyday gods who guard the house and hearth, "the spirits who, if propitiated, watched over the house or community to which they belonged."[12] If they aren't tended, the gods abandon the hearth.

The laral value of an object is the quality that arises from being in relationship with the world *behind* the object. It is a quality felt but not seen, a value, Harrison said, we can "live by."[13]

The presence or absence of everyday gods depends on what Harrison called the "lost art of seeing," not on the fact of their existence. What we see depends on history and culture as much as it does on the structure of our eyes, he wrote. Contemporary humans are less and less able to see the plentitude of the world. "Nothing is less cultivated these days in Western societies than the art of seeing."[14] Seeing what *is* takes time, he wrote; it requires a kind of depth perception that is no longer characteristic of this age. The promise of herbal medicine is that it offers products that bring wellness not only to each of us, but also to humanity and the earth. But that is only the case if individuals and companies are truly committed to wellness each step of the journey, not just in the finished product on the shelf. Laral value captures this fuller meaning of tending the whole. Yet is it possible for a complex industry to fully tend to a whole process? The *quality* of our attention to the whole is only as effective as our *capacity* to pay attention. And there are limits on how much any one person can pay attention, which means that everyone's attention matters. The question then becomes: What conditions allow people to pay attention?

The deeper I dug into the supply chain, the more difficult I found it to reach any conclusive insight into what was right or wrong, or into how to fix the problems of the herb supply chain. Any solution seemed to depend on conflicting factors: which species of plant was being collected, in which part of the world, in which type of habitat. Was the country at war, or had it been at war? There was no clear path to action.

When I visited that sparkler factor in India, I realized I didn't want to tell the story of the industry as a whole because I didn't believe that doing so was a path forward to change or improvement. I was not interested in understanding an industry where plants are commodities simply traded for profit. I was interested in the stories of those for whom plants were something more, those who saw the laral value in plants and recognized it as part of what is healing.

The advice Josef Brinckmann gives to those in the industry is simple. "Pick a plant," he tells them. Pick one plant and dive in. Commit to getting to know that plant. Really get inside it. Find out everything you can about it. What part of the plant do you use, the bark, root, or the flowers? Where is it from? What is the history of your company's use of that plant?

"If you're making money off that plant, don't you think you should have a subject matter expert in your organization? Shouldn't every person in that company be able to answer the simple question, *Why is this plant important to us? From where do we get it?* What about the lives of the people who pick, grow, and process that plant? What are we doing to protect that plant?

"Visit the plant at its source, at harvesttime," Josef continued. "Unless you visit, you don't know." Look around and see what people's lives are like. What challenges do they face? What are the conditions like? "I guarantee that when you get there and look around, you'll figure out something needs to be done for them directly and/or for their surrounding environment. And then start doing it at whatever level you can afford. When you finish that, just do the next thing.

"It isn't easy," Josef acknowledged. "The thing is, if you're curious, you're not worried about easy."

CHAPTER SIX

Harvesting the Wild

*The supply chain is a tattered tapestry
that needs to be re-woven.*

—MICHAEL MOORE

*A*nna Charytoniuk led me through a door off the hallway from the Runo administrative offices into what felt like a rabbit warren of passages that eventually ended at a large storage room. Three repurposed tobacco dryers lined one side. There were dried plants in burlap sacks, paper sacks, nylon sacks, brown paper bags. Some were still drying on square screens stacked in a pile until someone had time to transfer them to sacks for proper storage. A roll-up door in the back wall opened onto a paved area where collectors could deliver their herbs.

A short, white-haired, bright-eyed woman with a blue-and-green floral kerchief tied under her chin was talking to a tall man. She wore a bright turquoise coat, buttoned to the top, beige stockings under her gray wool skirt, and well-worn brown lace-up shoes.

The woman, whose name I never learned, was showing Krysztof, the head of the collection unit, an assortment of herbs she had brought in a motley collection of reused bags: two or three 30-gallon plastic bags of nettles, six equally large bags of horsetail. She had also dried some daisies, which are worth more than many other herbs because it is more difficult to dry flowers correctly. The daisies were stuffed into what appeared to be a reused bag—pictures of popcorn pieces adorned the sides, along with yellow and white stripes. Smaller plastic bags of various colors held dried elderberries, coltsfoot, and plantain, which was turning a bit brown at the edges. Her son, who was helping her carry the herbs, pointed out a bag of linden. She had dried the herbs in the rafters of her house, the woman told Anna, who translated into English for me. Each bag took her one day to collect. As she spoke, Krysztof weighed each sack on a large scale. He noted the weight on a sheet of paper, and then checked the price on a list tacked to the wall. Because the plants were non-certified, she received the lowest prices on the list; the total came to the equivalent of $38 US. Though I wasn't exactly sure how many bags and different plants she brought and whether she meant it took one day to harvest one bag of nettles or all three of the bags of nettles, even if she spent six days harvesting this material, $38 meant she earned only around $6 a day for her work.

The woman was not yet a registered collector, Anna explained, but last year she had brought a few bags of herbs to sell to the company. Always on the lookout for more collectors, Krysztof had encouraged her to bring back more this year. He now spoke with the woman about becoming a registered collector for the company. Being a registered collector meant that the company would supply her with new, clean paper sacks, he explained. This was preferable for Runo, too, because when collectors use clean sacks it gives the company more control over the quality of the raw material. And most important, Krysztof told her, as a registered collector she would receive a higher price per kilo of herbs.

Ten years ago the company was having trouble receiving consistently high-quality material, Anna explained. Collectors were bringing herbs to one of twenty-five collection points, sometimes delivering as much as two hundred pounds a day.[1] The heads of those units didn't check the quality of the herbs when they were delivered, and so collectors were careless. Bags of herbs might be stored at Runo several months before being processed and shipped to a buyer. If that buyer then discovered a problem, the head of the warehouse at Runo had no way of knowing whether the problem came from the collectors not correctly identifying the plants or not drying them properly, or if it arose from poor storage or handling at Runo. And even when Runo could ascertain that the problem originated with the collectors, the company had no idea which collector or collecting unit was responsible.

Establishing Traceability

Runo established a system for traceability, in which the head of each collecting unit checks each bag at delivery to ensure it is the correct species and that it has been dried correctly. Each bag is then labeled with the ID number of the registered collector, the name of the herb, the date and time of collection, and the collecting point. If a problem is later discovered, Runo can trace back through the labels to narrow down who might be responsible. The overall head of collection then meets with the heads of the collection points to inform them about the situation. The head does not reveal which collecting unit or units are doing the poor job, Anna said, and so everyone worries they are at fault. That motivates them all to make sure the quality of herbs from their collection point is good. This system works, Anna said, and it has made a difference.

This seems like a simple thing. But it is worth underscoring how important traceability is and how difficult it is to document accurately. Customers who buy FairWild certified plants pay a higher price per pound for the assurance that these plants are actually harvested from FairWild certified areas. These areas were mapped and on display at each of the collection units I visited. Studies are being conducted in these areas to ensure that the harvests fall within the regenerative capacity of the plant, and harvesters are paid a higher rate for the plants collected from these areas. As with many fair trade schemes, there are two sides to the benefits collectors receive under FairWild. First, individual collectors receive a higher price per pound for the raw material that is harvested according to the FairWild Standard. There is also what is called the Fair-Wild Premium, an added amount that the FairWild certified operator charges its customers on top of the ingredient sales price. The premium moneys are put into a fund for social development projects in the collec-tors' community. The collectors then meet as a group to decide how those funds will be spent.

These areas and practices are audited annually. Auditors meet with registered collectors, make sure they have been trained, and ask questions to determine whether, in fact, the plants are harvested from the certified lands. Though there is a lot of checking, ultimately, it comes down to trust—the certifiers have to trust that the collectors are telling the truth and are not simply claiming that the plants have been harvested from a FairWild certified area in order to get the premium prices. And that need for trust extends to the relationship a producer group has with the wild harvesters. There is a wide range in those relationships. Runo is one of the best, in large part because of the rigor of its traceability system.

Krysztof is in his mid-thirties, tall and thin with a very short haircut. He has been at Runo eight years, he told me through Anna's translation, and he liked everything about the job. He learned about plants and their medicinal uses as a child from his grandmother. When collectors bring in herbs, he said, he first checks the quality. If, say, a bag of nettles weighed more than it should, he knew to be suspicious. As he spoke, he reached his hand all the way to the bottom of a sack; he was testing for the dryness of the herbs (which he could tell by feel) as well as for the presence of things that shouldn't be there—like rocks. (It is common in the industry to find extraneous items in sacks of herbs. Many told me about pieces of metal, bricks, batteries and more, added either through carelessness or attempts to increase the weight and so the price of the herbs.) Krysztof pulled out a handful of herbs and smelled them, looked more closely at their color and overall vibrancy, and checked again that they had been dried correctly.

Later, a certified FW collector brought in sacks of nettle. Krysztof again checked each bag, but this time much more quickly. He knew this collector, he said, and he could trust the quality of his herbs.

Anna told me that one time Krysztof had questioned whether a bag of herbs he'd received was the correct species, so he took it to the boss to double-check. Had Krysztof not been knowledgeable about herbs or had he not been paying attention, that incorrectly identified bag of herbs could have slipped into the supply chain. And the mistake might or might not have been caught before the end product reached the consumer. Thus, along with the quality control checks and audits, a knowledgeable and attentive head of collection could be one of the most important control points in the entire supply chain.

Hard Work, Financial Risks

It was a cold, rainy October day, not an easy day to be working with dried plants. Runo's season starts in February when collectors begin harvesting pine buds and needles. It continues through November, finishing up with roots: dandelion, valerian, and angelica, wild-collected from nearby meadows. The company purchases plants from wild collectors or from farms in the region. Its busy season was coming to an end—fewer collectors would be bringing herbs to sell, the storage halls were overflowing, and the processing center would be running round the clock to fulfill orders. Workers wearing raincoats and gloves were moving in and out of the rain, loading chopped apples into the dryers. I felt cold just looking at them. Once again I was struck by how many daily details like this are invisible to the consumer at the end of a supply chain.

I've collected red clover, nettles, burdock, a bit of plantain or elderflower in my home state of Vermont. I collect only enough for my family's use, and it takes me an hour or so at the most. Even that amount can be hard work. Branches scratch. Nettles sting. Digging deeply enough to uncover the entire root of a perennial herb such as burdock requires patience. I get into a rhythm and it can be enjoyable, but I am never sorry when the work is done. For those who do this work for a living, day after day, hauling heavy sacks of roots off the steep slopes of Appalachia or picking saw palmetto berries in the heat of a Florida summer, say, the romance quickly wears off.

I was surprised by how incredibly hard all of the work I observed at Runo was—not only the collecting, growing, sorting, and processing of the plants, but also the tasks of tracking ID information and of keeping the material clean. Anna explained that despite their best efforts, it was hard to deliver the herbs to customers on schedule. "So much is involved in sourcing products from nature," she said. "The weather, the rain can make things take longer. For example, today." She glanced outside. "You can't unload herbs outside in the rain. It is hard to wash roots outside or, say, to chop apples." She pointed to where the workers, all men, stood outside chopping.

Remembering Kryzstof giving the woman in the turquoise coat a handful of Polish zloty, watching the men in their green tunics holding umbrellas and loading apples into the root chopper, I felt embarrassed by the naïveté of the questions that brought me on this journey, my wish to discover whether the aliveness of plants was present at all stages of the supply chain. It seemed ridiculous to even ask such a question here, where everyone was striving so hard, not because the plants were to be used as medicine, but because this was their job and they needed to make a living. Some of them, like Anna, enjoyed the connection their job gave them to plants. But their overriding motivation for doing the work was to put food on their table.

The primary producing companies in countries of origin bear the greatest financial burden—and risk—in the supply chain. They must pay collectors on the spot when herbs are delivered. The producing companies must then store these herbs, typically tens to hundreds of tons of material, depending on the time of year. They need sufficient warehouse space to keep these fluctuating quantities in controlled temperature and humidity conditions. The area must be kept rodent- and insect-free. Buyers who order from producer companies don't pay in advance, however. In fact, buyers sometimes don't pay their bills until three months after the plants have been delivered. That is a tremendous risk for the primary producing companies to bear. If for any reason the herbs don't meet the quality specifications of the buyer, they may be sent back to the producer company. Rejection of lots is becoming a tremendous and increasing problem, because pesticides of unknown origin sometimes show up on plants harvested from certified organic areas. These residues mean the plants can't be sold as certified organic; the producer company must then find another buyer, often one on the conventional supply chain that pays a reduced price.

Everyone invested in reliably sourcing high-quality herbs has told me that maintaining relationships with producer groups is the key. Details matter. Especially money, I learned as I talked with Mike Brook, the founder-director of Organic Herb Trading Company (OHTC), about the price pressure that producing companies are under. I met Mike at OHTC's office and processing center, at the end of a dirt road in southwestern England, on my way home from Poland. His office was a small room with a slanted ceiling on the second floor of the building that houses their GMP (Good Manufacturing Practices) certified processing and storage facilities. The building was surrounded by a soccer-field-sized organic garden filled with vibrant medicinal plants, as different from the Naturex factory off the busy road in New Jersey as you could get.

OHTC buys herbs from companies like Runo, and then sells them wholesale to finished-product companies. Mike mentioned the pressure Runo is under with regard to pricing to avoid being undercut by sellers from Bulgaria and Albania. This means the company can't pay enough to collectors, who may then seek other kinds of work. At the same time, OHTC can only pay Runo so much, because OHTC in turn has to sell at prices that are competitive. If OHTC can't find buyers, it will go out of business, and if it goes out of business, OHTC can't help the producer companies at all. It's a delicate balance.

Mike kept interrupting our conversation to make sure I'd had enough food to eat, especially that I had some protein. More than anyone I met, he was most concerned about my needs. This struck me because that is exactly what he and I were discussing—understanding the needs of others as a business strategy.

Mike said he tries to support producers by not pressing them on price. OHTC gets quotes from several companies, and then Mike and his colleagues settle on one and start working with that company. Mike doesn't try to knock them down on price or to negotiate. "Part of the reason for not bargaining," he explained, "is to try to engender good relations with the supplier." He wanted to be respectful, he continued, but his motive was also selfish. As others told me as well, buyers that treat their suppliers fairly, agreeing to terms that are equitable, are more likely to be treated fairly in turn by suppliers. When there are shortages in raw material, for example, the supplier will make sure those who treat them fairly get what they need.

I later spoke with Josef Brinckmann about the same issue. At Traditional Medicinals, "We started to work on a different model," he told me. "Which had to do with relationship building and trust, and getting to know people. It just became important that the company do whatever it could to help improve the quality of life for everybody involved and move more toward a partnership model rather than the old the buyer-is-always-right model. We worked on creating more of an equal partnership, a we're-in-this-together way of looking at it, and forward planning together."

Finding Good Partners

It is easy to determine whether herbs are good-enough quality, Attila Mihály, the owner of Nagy Mihály, a producer company I visited in Hungary, told me. "What matters more is having people skills." His son, Balázs, who was translating for his father, agreed, adding that much of their work involves managing people. Attila spoke Hungarian for long stretches before Balázs could translate. As he spoke, it occurred to me that more than anyone else in the supply chain, primary processing facilities like Nagy Mihály had to translate between disparate worlds.

"Fact," Attila said, interrupting my thoughts, "FairWild certification requires that collectors wash their hands before working with the plants. But," he continued, "if they happen to have water with them when collecting, which isn't likely, they want to drink it, not wash their hands." He said that he tells them over and over to wash their hands. The collectors receive an annual training as required by the FairWild Standard, but some still don't do it.

"What can you do?" I asked.

"Nothing," he answered. Instead, the company invested in a steam-treatment machine to reduce the microbial load of the plants and lower the risk of bacterial contamination.

The economic vulnerability of wild collectors both drives over-harvesting, as mentioned previously, and affects the quality of the raw material. Early on Josef saw that it was far more likely that people who earned a fair price for the herbs they collected would follow good collection practices and do the work needed to verify sustainability. From a company's perspective, it simply makes good business sense to ensure wild harvesters are able to make a living from their work.

Navigating the cultural differences between wild harvesters and every other stakeholder is perhaps one of the biggest challenges. Quality control regulations make sense from a buyer's point of view, but to those whose communities have harvested roots and leaves for generations, they can be patronizing or worse. These collectors and the processing companies have their own standards for cleanliness, their own practices for drying plants—often outside on woven mats or tarps in the sun—and their own ways of storing the plants, in reused sacks in bedrooms or uncovered in barns. Mike Brook started the company because he was unable to find high-quality certified organic herbs. It isn't always easy for OHTC to work with producer groups like Nagy Mihály. Again, echoing Attila, Mike said the herb trade really came down to navigating cultural differences. The countries from which OHTC buys herbs have been supplying medicinal plants to the international market for generations. Mike works hard not to be paternalistic and to respect the ways producers do things. And yet he also has to meet the standards of his customers, who are finished-product manufacturers in Europe and the US. It is a fine line that OHTC must navigate daily. This presents Mike with dilemmas such as whether to tell collectors in malaria-prone areas that they should not put on insect repellent because that creates a risk of pesticide residues being detected on the herbs.

I asked Mike what he looked for in finding good partners and whether he made mistakes. He shook his head. He said he was always overly optimistic that a company could meet OHTC's standards. And that making mistakes was part of the business.

Matt Richards, the supplier relationships manager for OHTC, also expressed the sentiment that it takes time and energy to build relationships that can be trusted—but without trust there is no way to know whether a supplier is doing what they say they are doing. I met Matt on my second visit to OHTC in 2015. In a phone conversation several years later, he said he thought those relationships worked best when he started by talking with a producer group about what they were doing well. "We ask people's permission. We say how grateful we are that we can work together. We start out being appreciative—a mutual declaration of thankfulness," he said, laughing. "Then we can work together to get things done. That works much better than coming in and saying we aren't happy, that their work isn't good enough and that we need things done in this or that way to meet our specifications. It's a way of getting on with people. It's selfish," he added. "If we get on well, the challenges we face will be easier to navigate." I laughed and told him he had repeated almost verbatim what Mike had told me five years earlier. He laughed, too, and said, "Well, Mike has been a good mentor."

When I asked producer companies what makes some buyers better than others, their answer was more straightforward. Erika Schubert, at that time head of Agrimed Hessen, a cooperative of farmers started by her father to market agricultural produce from southwestern Germany, answered without hesitation, "A good company for us is that they don't only buy for one year and the next year look for a cheaper producer. They work together with us to improve the quality." Anna, from Runo, also didn't hesitate: Paying on time, she said, or even better in advance.

Agreements between producers and buyers are only as good as where the money is. Upon request and as required under fair trade standards, Traditional Medicinals has offered pre-financing to its producer partners so the partners can pay their collectors in cash at the time plants are delivered. Traditional Medicinals has done this because it is a good business practice and also to ensure that collectors don't sell to other buyers who may show up at harvesttime with money in hand. This is a real risk. Even though collectors have been assured a certain price on a certain date, they may well sell at a lower rate to a buyer who shows up sooner with money in hand.

When I was visiting the Runo facility, I kept trying to imagine what Josef Brinckmann, Mike Brook, Matt Richards, and Ben Heron looked out for when they made site visits. What showed them that this might be a good company to work with? What were the red flags that warned them off? When I had visited the warehouse at Schmidt's processing facility in southern Hungary, it was filled with huge piles of what looked like overly dry, brown, and not very vital plants. It seemed to me that was a sign the company wasn't so dependable. I asked about some goldenrod that had been harvested after the flowers had gone to seed, the yellow buds now bits of white fluff. Josef Schmidt, the robust white-haired owner of the processing company, said he had told the collectors to harvest the goldenrod right before it goes to seed rather than after, that the constituents were higher before seed set and he could get a better price. But this is what they brought, he said, gesturing to the fluff. Though he paid them less, he accepted it anyway, he added, because he didn't want to turn them away. He would in turn sell it at a lower price to a buyer who cared less about the quality. Thus, what I had judged as an indicator of bad quality and a careless company was actually a deliberate choice by an owner who wanted to maintain good relationships with collectors. Another lesson that a judgment about whether a situation is good or bad may depend on unseen factors.

I once asked Josef whether small details like the presence of spiderwebs—I was thinking of the thick clumps of spiderwebs I had seen hanging from the rafters over the herbs at Schmidt's factory—made a difference. Yes, he said. But then he acknowledged he had seen much, much worse and that, in the scheme of things, spiderwebs were not that big a concern. Ben Heron told me it was okay for herbs to be placed on cement floors while they were being loaded into a dryer. What mattered then, he pointed out, was what people wore on their feet.

Herbs should not be stored in large piles in barns or warehouses, Mike told me; they should always be enclosed in sacks. As he said this, I thought of the many uncovered piles of herbs I had seen when visiting Hungary and Poland. Open air exposes the herbs to fluctuating temperatures and humidity, which in turn affects the volatile oils and overall quality of the finished product, especially microbiological quality. Like almost everything I observed, quality control seems straightforward from a distance, but implementing the standards involves an incredible attention to details.

Capacity is another aspect of a company to consider, said Marin Anastasov, the raw materials and sourcing manager for Pukka, when I interviewed him during our visit to Pukka's offices in Bristol, U.K. Not only capacity in terms of the facilities and the machinery, but also the capacity of the people who run the company. Do they really understand the challenges of delivering the raw material to Pukka? Companies like Pukka and Traditional Medicinals often spend years working with producer groups to get them to a place where the raw materials they produce meet their specifications. It is in their best interest to help those companies stay in business. I recalled that Josef had mentioned the importance of looking at the ownership structure of the business. How long have they been in business? How many years have they proven they can get the material to market? Is the producer group likely to be able to meet the rigorous quality control specifications and standards that Traditional Medicinals requires? And can they do that with or without help from Traditional Medicinals? I asked Drake Sadler about relationships in the supply chain and some finished-product companies' fears that if they are transparent about their sources, other companies will go behind their back. "If we lose our farmers to another company," he replied, "it's because we are not doing something right. It means we've missed something."

Marin also told me, "Pukka is growing very fast, and so it is important that whomever we work with can take the challenge of growing at the same rate. If they can't keep up with our growth, we will outgrow them very quickly. It's like buying clothes for a growing child. You want to buy them a little bit big, so you will have one or two years of usage." It is a partnership that, like any partnership, requires long-term investment and care. Marin explained that if a producer company repeatedly fails to meet the requirements of the finished-product company, it is best to let it go. (Josef confirmed this point as well in a separate conversation.)

Before visiting these companies, I had thought scale of operations would be the most critical factor that would distinguish "good" from "bad" companies, that smaller companies necessarily produced products with more care. Yet I was beginning to realize that it wasn't such a simple equation. What mattered more than scale was the quality of attention that everyone involved in the journey of a plant from source to shelf brings to their part of that journey. It is one thing when we are attending to something linked to our identity that can be traced back to our land, family, village, or region. Or when quality is connected to our pride, social standing, or economic future. But what happens when that connection is lost? When it is simply a financial transaction and there is no relationship between our attention or inattention to our work and the finished product? Certifications provide a framework.

Yet ultimately certifications are most effective in a context where there is trust. It is harder to cut corners or to cheat on someone with whom you have a relationship.

Scale does matter, not just the scale at which a company can pay attention but the scale, as Marin said, at which a company is growing. If a company is selling products faster than it can source material according to its specifications, company managers face a key decision: Should they allow that product to go out of stock for a time, or should they lower the standards for that product's specifications? Going out of stock has tremendous repercussions that directly impact a company's bottom line. And yet many medicinal herbs are perennials. It takes several years from the time of planting until they will be ready for harvesting. Sourcing high-quality herbs requires either long-term planning and relationship building with the producer groups or buying through brokers and ingredient suppliers who do that work instead. For companies with a big enough network, if one producer is out of stock, raw material from another can be used. Yet what if that substituted material doesn't meet company specifications? Do you lower your standards to stay in stock? Or do you go out of stock and lose potential customers, which impacts your ability to perhaps meet other social and environmental commitments your company has made? It is one thing to talk about transparency, trust, and relationships. It is another altogether to main-tain those relationships in an international market. As David Winston once told me, "No herb company has ever said it doesn't want to get bigger." But these are the kinds of decisions that matter in determining whether a company maintains relationships through the supply network in theory or in practice.

An Endangered Livelihood

Josef once described to me what he looks for when he visits collectors. "It's different in every country," he said. "And it depends on how their beliefs inform the way they interact with their ecosystem. But there is something that is the same. I look for how attentive and aware the collectors are. I notice when they are pointing out indicators, what they are looking at when they're walking around, how they describe that this is the right date to collect or the right time of day to collect."

I returned to Runo in 2015, this time with Terry and Bryce to film for the Sustainable Herbs Program. While there, we retraced the route to a neat white stucco two-story house with a tin roof on a single-lane dirt road, the home of Bazyl and Maria Panasiuk, whom I had previously visited with Eugeniusz. Bazyl, a wiry white-haired man, came out to greet us. He wore a plaid flannel shirt and a camouflage baseball cap. He led us back through the gate and into a tidy yard, a large garden stretched out the back, gradually turning into a meadow. He and his sister-in-law, her hair pulled back in a black scarf with orange and white dots and wearing a black coat with orange and white flowers, picked up handmade collection sacks and headed into the meadow.

The land was flat, stretching as far as I could see, broken only by clusters of alder and birch and an isolated house or two. Runo's collection area covers up to thirty-eight square miles of diverse meadow.[2] Bazyl and his sister-in-law walked quickly, talking the whole time. They carry separate bags for each plant, he explained. It saves work later. Once we reached the collection area, they began to harvest, stopping at clumps of comfrey to chop the dark green, oval leaves with a wooden-handled sickle and toss them into their sacks. They worked quickly, filling the bags in a few minutes.

Bazyl paused and asked what else we would like to see. Not waiting for our answer, he led us in a different direction through the meadow, pointing out meadowsweet, gathered earlier in the summer, and yarrow, collected just the week before, stopping finally at a patch of nettles on the edge of a small grove of birch.

Later Bazyl took us back to his home. The shed where they did most of the work was run-down and well used. A long piece of plywood balanced on sawhorses provided a table for chopping and sorting plants at one end. At the other end the table held a screen of green mesh covered in orange calendula flowers, brightening the otherwise muted room. Leaves drying on screens were stacked on one side of the work table. Brown bags tied at the top and filled with plants in various stages of processing were pushed under the table, against the wall, wherever there was room. Bazyl led us up narrow wooden stairs to the rickety attic of the shed that served as the drying room. Racks and racks of screens filled with leaves in various stages of drying lined the walls, beneath the rafters. Leaves were spread on screens on the floor to dry. Empty racks leaned against the back wall. The room smelled like the earth and like plants. If I closed my eyes and inhaled, I could imagine myself in the drying room at Avena Botanicals in Maine or at Zack Woods Herb Farm in Vermont or at Oshala Farm in Oregon. This is the scale of herbal medicine I love. Close to the earth. Plants just harvested and waiting to be processed.

"It's a lot of work," I said to the collector, gesturing to the plants drying in the racks. "Why do you do it?"

"For the money," he replied without hesitating. "So we can buy things for our daughter, give her money for her children." Bazyl was serious though smiling as he said this, his broken front teeth showing as he spoke. He said exactly the same thing when I had asked him that question a year ago, on my first visit to his home. I had also asked what he liked most about collecting. Flowers, he had said, laughing, because they brought in the most money.

When I told Anna what Bazyl said, she replied, "He always says he just does it for the money. But you can tell he likes it. Look how happy he is walking through the meadow and showing us the plants. How proud he seems about it all. He's always thinking about where to collect and how to collect. You can tell he feels this work in his heart."

Bazyl did seem to love this work, and he would probably continue to collect some plants even if it weren't for the money. But he wouldn't collect so many; nor would he work so hard to do it right. The money makes a difference, though not enough to convince a younger generation to take up collecting wild plants as well. Sixty-five percent of the collectors for Runo are over seventy years old, typically they are unemployed or underemployed and are looking for some extra money. As in many rural areas, the younger generation in eastern Europe is moving to cities where there are more opportunities and more excitement. Roughly 10 percent of the herbs on the international market sold as teas, culinary herbs, and herbal supplements come from plants wild-collected in eastern Europe. These products remain as inexpensive as they are in the West because of the availability of cheap labor in eastern Europe. But as the standard of living improves, even without the allure of urban life, fewer people are willing to do the backbreaking work of traveling to remote areas, harvesting leaves or flowers or digging roots in all kinds of weather, in all kinds of terrain, hauling the material back, and, all the while, taking care to handle it in ways to ensure the quality doesn't deteriorate, only to make pennies for their effort.

Josef, who has probably done more to help wild collectors around the world than anyone else in the herbal products industry, told me, "In the traditional wild collection areas around the world that for the past hundred years have been the main suppliers of medicinal plants for the market, there are ghost towns. Elderly people are the only ones left there doing the work. So that's what I worry and wonder about the most." He paused and then continued, "I'm mostly interested in and concerned about whether traditional knowledge will continue to be transmitted. Many of these are communities in very remote places where traditional knowledge about how to manage the ecosystem for their livelihoods— knowledge about harvesting to make their own food and medicine, or to sell to markets—has been passed through the generations. You can't bring migrant workers into a mountainous forest where they have no under-standing of that ecosystem and expect them to manage it sustainably."

He continued. "There is a mass migration in India and China. In our lifetimes most people will be urban dwellers, not rural. This has never happened in history before, that so many people are on the move."

What will happen when these older generations retire or die? Who will do the work? What will happen to the knowledge they have, knowl-edge about the way plants grow and regenerate, about harvesting times and handling, about how to use these plants, a knowledge that these collectors mostly learned from their parents or grandparents?

This question came up when I talked with David Doty of Mountain Rose Herbs while visiting in the summer of 2015. David, who is in charge of international sourcing for Mountain Rose, asked me whether I saw any young people in Poland wildcrafting. No, he said, answering his own question before I had a chance to respond. "You didn't see them. They're not there. They're going to the city. We've seen this on every continent. Every place I've bought herbs. Not only that. Herbs aren't just being depleted from overharvesting. It's that the areas where these plants grow have been logged. They've been urbanized or gentrified. The little niches where herbs flourish, they just don't exist anymore."

Back at the Runo collection center, there was a steady flow of collectors coming to sell sacks of dried herbs. Most were older women. A man in his fifties came with his mother, who collected the herbs herself. A woman in her forties brought in sacks of herbs on her bicycle. Anna was amazed at the weight of what the woman had transported and wondered how she had managed it. This woman told us she liked to harvest because it helped her feel peaceful. Two young boys rode up on their bicycles as we stood outside and handed Anna some small leaves. Anna laughed and, speaking in Polish, handed the leaves back to them. "I told them those leaves are not on our list of herbs to buy," she explained to us, laughing again as the boys pushed off on their bikes and rode back down the dirt lane.

Eugeniusz told us he is worried that in the future there won't be enough collectors to do the work. He tries to pay the collectors more, he said, but he can't pay too much because then companies like OHTC can't afford them. He thinks perhaps it would help collectors to be able to sell fresh herbs to Runo, so the collectors wouldn't have to invest in a facility for drying. But right now Runo's dryers are always busy. They dry five tons of herbs daily and they simply don't have the capacity for more.

It's all interconnected. It goes far beyond any concerns for the sustainability of medicinal plants, Josef explained. "It ties in with the survival of the whole planet. We need to have intact ecosystems to support biodiversity. Though dandelion isn't threatened, diverse meadows are."

"There is an urgency to protect and preserve the last ecosystems where biological, cultural, and linguistic diversity are still connected, albeit by a thread," Josef said during his acceptance speech for an honorary degree from the California Institute for Integral Studies;[3] "where local people are still the keepers of the knowledge of the ecosystem, of the traditional knowledge that informs the great systems of medicine."

In all of my travels in Europe, India, and North America, a theme that kept coming up was environmental changes, especially climate change.[4] Josef told me, "There are places I go back to every year where harvesttimes are no longer predictable. Ten to fifteen years ago they weren't unpredictable. People tell me about tasks they've always done in the second half of September, but now they do them in the first half of September or the second half of October. Crazy stuff is going on. Local people know it. They see what's going on. They try to organize their households' economics based on when different harvests come in. Their livelihood depends on having those harvests at predictable times, but things are no longer predictable. If, say, mushrooms come in at the same time as roots, people will be tempted to harvest mushrooms because they are higher value. And the roots will stay in the ground."

As I followed Bazyl through the fields, I thought about the differences between the lives of the collectors I was able to meet at Runo and those in Bulgaria, or anywhere else, whom I couldn't. What does it mean when your work is at the far end of a long supply chain? Does the price earned for a few sacks of dried herbs equal the value of a life? What will it take to address the economic, ecological, and cultural challenges involved in the collection of wild plants from around the world? I think of the stacks of reports I had seen the morning I spent in FairWild's office in Budapest, years of reports on wild collection in eastern Europe, articles and conference papers about overharvesting, about breakdowns in supply chains, about the need to develop markets and standards of sustainability. Very little seemed to have changed—if anything, the trends they described had simply gotten worse. More information doesn't seem to be the answer.

There is a fullness and richness to Runo that seems to come from the quality of the relationships. Something similar exists at small tulsi farms in South India, which I visited along with Sebastian Pole, co-founder of Pukka Herbs, in 2016. As Sebastian and I walked through the fields with N. R. Madhuvaraj, an agronomist who worked for Pukka's partner company in South India, Sebastian commented, "You can really feel how this place has been cared for." Madhuvaraj nodded, replying, "Yes, even older people don't feel right if at least once a day they don't go around and walk their fields."

My most powerful memories from Poland and Hungary, and even Bulgaria, were of the people I met, not the plants I was ostensibly following. I kept looking for ways to connect with the plants, but the plants, I realized, were connecting me to the people. I've had many, many conversations with Josef about herbs and the supply chain. And although most herbalists speak easily and frequently about love and emotions, I had never heard Josef do so. Except once. He said, "You fall in love with the local people and you can't wait to see them again after your visit. You want them to be successful. You want the tradition to continue. You want to do whatever you can to help them."

In a way that was both different yet similar to what Josef observed, every collector I met during my travels talked about how harvesting plants was peaceful. They all talked about how digging roots and harvesting plants helped them be well and stay well. That it calmed their mind. How hard it was when they couldn't go out to collect. They all talked about how that work fed something that can't be measured, something more than what is exchanged for coins and faded bills. Yet in a global economy driven by growth, everything is reduced to monetary terms. I wondered, can you talk about the laral value of work?

———

Rick Johnson, a retired coal miner, dug roots his whole life. He can no longer go to the hills because of his heart, he said. He and I were sitting on a narrow slab of cement, the porch on his single-story ranch house on a side road in Harlan County, Kentucky, one of the poorest counties in the state. "I always loved to go to the mountains. It was so peaceful." He paused, "You can't run from trouble. Usually you get in the mountains, if you got some trouble, you get a little peace. Now I can't run from it. I just have to sit and bide it." He paused again, looking up the hill to the woods. His son had planted some ginseng close by so Rick could see it from the stoop. "I miss it real bad."

CHAPTER SEVEN

Tending the Garden

The essence isn't something hidden. It is in the details.

—JOHANN WOLFGANG VON GOETHE

$\mathcal{A}$t the last minute, Jeff Carpenter of Zack Woods Herb Farm had invited me to join the farm crew to harvest milky oats. The farm is an hour drive from my home and I headed out quickly, afraid they might finish before I arrived. I needn't have worried. Even if they had finished, there is always work to be done on an herb farm.

Milky oats refers to oat seeds that are harvested when premature and a milky white liquid is present in the seed. The oat plants had fallen over after a heavy rain earlier in the week. The crew—Kate Clearlight, Brian Hoogervorst, and an intern—were sitting on the ground, harvesting the oats one clump at a time. Jeff handed me a basket. He showed me how to wrap my fingers with duct tape to prevent the sharp stalk from cutting my skin as I worked. Kate showed me how to hold a clump with my left hand and slide my right up the stalk to pull the milky tops off the plants into the basket. The motion made a scraping sound like a paper cutter. The oats were striated with a reddish rust from a fungus, which, Kate told me, meant Jeff wouldn't be able to charge as much for them.

We each sat in our spot, harvesting the oats within reach. It was slow work and the sun was hot. It took a long time to fill a basket. And there were a lot of oats. We talked some but mostly we just pulled off the oats in silence, each lost in our own thoughts. When I'd harvested calendula at the farm earlier that summer—a task that had also seemed slow at the time but now, in comparison, seemed quite fast—Jeff had helped. But today he was busy taking care of duties around the farm. At one point he stopped by and asked Kate, who was also the office and business manager for Zack Woods, whether she'd entered the amounts from the most recent harvest of nettles in the harvest log. She hadn't. "Good," he answered. "That makes me feel better." And then he headed off. Kate mentioned that they had just found out that the skullcap had developed a fungal disease and wouldn't be sellable, which meant they would lose a $4,000 wholesale contract.

Kate commented on how slowly the harvesting was going. Brian, who is the first employee Jeff hired after starting the farm, agreed. "At a certain point," he said, "it is no longer cost-effective."

After a while, Jeff checked in again and told us to head down to a lower field to harvest some more oats. We walked behind the Carpenters' single-story ranch house to a gently sloping field bordered by woods where lemon balm, chamomile, and garlic grew in narrow rows. We began harvesting again. After a few minutes Kate said she had learned that milky oats are ready to harvest when nine out of ten in each clump are milky. To tell if an oat is at the milky stage, you press it between your thumb and index finger. If a white latex substance squirts out, they are milky. She had counted only five out of ten in one handful, and, in another, only two or three. Brian said he would take some of the oats to Jeff and ask for his opinion.

"They'll weigh more anyway if we wait," Kate pointed out. Brian, who doesn't use any medicinal herbs himself, commented, "Plus they're more medicinal then. It isn't all about the profit, you know."

"Oh yeah, the medicine," Kate (who *is* an herbalist) replied, laughing. Brian headed up the hill to find Jeff.

Questions of Scale

Zack Woods is a family-run small farm with six employees on ten acres at the end of a dirt road in northern Vermont. We had been working in a small patch of oats next to Mel and Jeff's house. Neat rows of plants in many shades of green, some with a blush of purple, bright orange, or dark pink, spread out around the house. Straw mulch covered the soil, breaking the bands of green. From afar, the rows looked like strips of colors in a painting, small-scale and to my mind, right-sized, unlike the sameness of a sea of corn growing in fields in the Midwest.

Mel is Rosemary Gladstar's stepdaughter, and she and Jeff previously ran Sage Mountain Herbs, a small herbal products company that made tinctures and salves. Like others who started herbal product businesses, they found it hard to source high-quality herbs. Jeff was working part-time in a nursery at the time. He liked working with plants and so they decided to start growing their own medicinal plants. For the first few years after founding their herb farm, they continued working off-farm jobs—Jeff in a restaurant and Mel as a teacher and then principal of Stowe Middle School. They both now work full-time on the farm. Their goal is to provide the highest-quality certified organic herbal medicine they can.

Mel and Jeff believe passionately in the importance of small, family-run certified organic herbs farms, and their book, *The Organic Medicinal Herb Farmer*, describes how to cultivate medicinal herbs for the market. Writing the book was a remarkably generous act, an herb grower once told me, considering that in doing so, Mel and Jeff were essentially educating their competitors.

Their niche works because there is a strong network of herbalists interested in buying certified organic and domestically grown herbs, especially those grown by small farmers who are also herbalists. Mel and Jeff have succeeded by emphasizing their close involvement with the farm, their understanding of the life cycle of the plants they grow, their knowledge as herbalists about how the plants will be used, and their commitment to caring for the spirit of the plants.

Mel and Jeff's vision of healing is much broader than simply growing nettles and oats and yarrow. They are committed to the whole system of medicinal herb production. As Mel explained, "In order for the system to be sustainable, to be strong, to be well, for wellness for all, we need to make sure the system works on each level. It needs to work from the ground level with the microbes in the soil, to the seeds, to the plants growing on the farm, to the ecosystem of the farm. How are the laborers being paid? How is their lifestyle when they leave the farm? How are they being treated on the farm? How are the plants being handled? When are the plants being harvested and are they respected?

"I am concerned about the herbal industry right now," she continued, "because it seems it's gone from the medicine of the people to big business. That scares me. Not that I don't want the medicine to reach more people, absolutely it should. But when it is done at the expense of the farmer, the plants, the workers, the planet—just so that some big business can make more money and sell more herbs—I have a real problem with that." Yet it is difficult to see how to farm in accordance with these values and still provide the quantities needed to satisfy demand.

A month or so after harvesting those milky oats, I stood at the edge of an immense field of calendula, one of many fields of medicinal plants on a 160-hectare farm south of Frankfurt, Germany. Rather than narrow bands of varying shades of green like those at Zack Woods, solid orange stretched almost to the horizon. The calendula was planted densely for ease of mechanized harvesting. Though the same species as the calendula I had harvested the previous summer at Zack Woods, it seemed like an entirely different plant. The blossoms were smaller. Their orange coloration was less vibrant. Each stalk bore several flowers in different stages—one or two in full bloom, a bud or two just opening, and several already gone to seed, the petals drying out and fading. This crop of calendula would be harvested with a combine, which would mix together buds and flowers in different stages of flowering. At Zack Woods, by contrast, Mel, Jeff, and their field staff harvest daily by hand, selecting the full blossoms, to ensure the flowers are harvested at their peak.

The calendula from this German field would be sold as certified organic, just as Zack Woods calendula is. Beyond that, the two farms seem to have very little in common, and I found myself wondering about how the extreme differences in their scale and methods impact the quality of the plants, in ways that can, and cannot, be measured. Mel and Jeff believe that the intention with which they farm, their attention to what they refer to as the spirit of the plant and to prayer, also impacts the energetics of the plants and their medicine. What did energetics mean when growing herbs on this scale? Even without considering that question, there must also be differences related to soil health, water use, and fairness of labor practices. Wouldn't these impact the quality of the medicine made from the plants grown on these two very different farms?

While in the U.K. after my first trip to eastern Europe, I showed a British herbalist some video footage from my travels. She asked me to stop and replay a video of a man pitchforking stalks of freshly harvested echinacea from the back of a pickup into a mechanized chipper. The chopped material streamed out of the chipper into a pile on a cement floor. Another man shoveled the chopped pieces into the dryer, a garage-like room with a heated floor and cement sides. She was shocked to see how seemingly carelessly the plants were handled. She noted how much more stalk there was compared with the pink flower heads, which contain higher levels of active constituents than the stalks. Like most herbalists, I felt ambivalent about both the fact of that mechanization and the scale of it. I had been surprised by the chopping, too, by the pitchfork, by the bits of pink petals flying onto the cement floor. Yet after a month following herbs through the supply chain, I no longer trusted my surprise. I wasn't sure what part of my reaction was naïveté and what was a reasonable response.

Growing herbs on the scale needed to meet demand and at a price point that allows the farmer to be viable requires some degree of mechanization. Every herb grower I met justified the particular mechanization choices they had settled on. And though those justifications seemed to change as their level of mechanization changed, each rationale made sense to me.

As Jeff Higley, co-owner of Oshala Farm, an organic herb farm in Applegate Valley, Oregon, told me, "It's a question of moving stuff around; the better you are at doing that, the more competitive you will be. At the end of the day we are material handlers. Anything you can do to make that more efficient is good."

Even so, I wondered how mechanization impacted the quality of the plants. Was there a point at which the machines became so large or so numerous that the values at the heart of herbal medicine about reciprocity and relationship were lost? I again thought about attention and scale and how the quality of attention is impacted by the scaling up that mechanization allows. I realized I needed to suspend my assumptions that small-scale, hand-harvested herbal medicine is always better than what can be grown and processed mechanically and to try to discern the differences that mattered.

———

Unlike collectors of wild herbs, the herb farmers I contacted were perfectly willing to meet with me and explain what they did. Terry, Bryce, and I visited small farmers who grew tulsi, lemon balm, turmeric, marshmallow root, plantain, thyme, and other common and uncommon medicinal plants. Many of these plants would otherwise grow unbidden as weeds, but planting them in regularly spaced rows allows the farmer better control of growing, weeding, and harvesting. We also visited huge farms where lemon balm, catnip, echinacea, or artichoke plants grew in undulating rows that extended into the distance. Some of the farms we toured were certified organic or biodynamic certified, but we also visited a few farms where herbs were grown with the use of pesticides and fertilizers. We saw fields of mono-crops and fields so diverse you couldn't tell the "crop" from the weeds. Some farms were completely mechanized. On others every task was done by hand.

Either farmers grow medicinal plants on contract for a buyer who handles the drying and storing of the plant material, or they do that work themselves. We met large landowners in Washington, Oregon, Germany, and India who hired employees to do the planting, weeding, transplanting, and harvesting. Some of the farmers we visited included smallholders who grow specific herbs on contract with a large processing company that handled marketing and distribution in addition to drying and processing. And at the opposite end from the large farms, we visited farmers like Mel and Jeff Carpenter, typically in developed countries, who sold directly to the herb community, either to medicine makers or to wholesale distributors.

Most farms employed a mix of harvesting methods—leaf and root crops harvested by machine, flowers harvested by hand. Some farms had mechanized transplanting as well, but on others, planting was done by hand. I visited Zack Woods several times while working on this book, and each time I returned, Jeff and Mel had mechanized an additional step. Like every other farmer, they were navigating the line between providing the quality they believed was necessary and keeping costs under control.

Learning How to Grow Wild Herbs

Mark Wheeler, founder of Pacific Botanicals, had no particular interest in herbs when he moved to Applegate Valley on the western slopes of the Cascades in southwest Oregon in 1979. He was doing research on aquaculture on the Oregon coast at the time. Like many who turned to herbal medicine, he began thinking about his diet and health. He put in a vegetable garden and soon discovered that he liked working in his garden more than he liked his work in aquaculture.

Applegate Valley is a prime spot for growing medicinal plants. Summers are hot and sunny and the soil is fertile. Because there is little industry in the area, there are few if any potential sources of offsite pollution.

Mark left his previous work to begin raising vegetables and nursery stock for sale. He also began experimenting with growing some medicinal herbs for his own use in the backyard. One afternoon, by happenchance, Ed Smith and Sara Katz stopped to buy some of Mark's vegetables. They saw his herb garden and told Mark they were starting a small herbal extract company called Herb Pharm. They asked if he would like to grow some plants for them.

Mark is soft-spoken and thoughtful. He spent several hours with Terry, Bryce, and me walking through the fields of the farm he built over the past forty years. He pointed out various species of herbs, commented on the growing requirements, and described how he created what was one of the first two farms in the United States to grow certified organic herbs. I asked him about his vision. He walked silently for a few minutes, thinking about my question, and then said, "A lot of people want to change the world with what [they] do." But, he continued, the only way to accomplish that is to do what you believe in and love and not worry about whether other people think you are right or wrong. And so his vision, he concluded, is to just keep on doing what he is doing.

THE BUSINESS OF BOTANICALS

In the early 1900s professor L. E. Sayre warned of the threat of over-harvesting wild populations of *Echinacea angustifolia*, commonly called coneflower, from Kansas if then-current collection rates continued. "About a month ago we had a call from an agent of an Eastern house for the purchase of 40,000 pounds and from another agent, an order of 20,000 pounds," he wrote.[1] Two hundred thousand pounds of root had been collected from Rooks County, Kansas, the previous year, he reported.[2] Forty thousand pounds of roots is a lot of roots. Two hundred thousand pounds is even more, especially at the turn of the twentieth century, when echinacea wasn't grown in rows in farm fields and harvested by machine. Instead various species of coneflowers grew wild in mixed midwestern meadows. Some harvesters used sustainable practices to dig up those plants, removing only a certain percentage of the roots to ensure the plants will persist into the future. Yet others, especially when there was a spike in demand, harvested all the plants they could to cash in on the market while they could.

Demand for echinacea dropped in the middle of the century, and the pressure on wild populations declined. As the market picked up again in the 1980s, so too did overharvesting. In 1984 an herb buyer reported that Missouri was shipping thirty thousand pounds of wild echinacea roots and tops to European markets each year, which had led to a decline of coneflowers growing on Missouri roadsides.[3] In the winter of 1987, seven thousand yellow coneflowers, *E. paradoxa*, were reported stolen from a glade at Missouri's Ha Ha Tonka State Park. Steven Foster also wrote that Ronald McGregor, author of the review article for the University of Kansas science bulletin *The Taxonomy of Echinacea*, told Steven he was unable to find colonies of a species called *Echinacea atrorubens* in prairies where he knew they typically grew, and that landowners had reported that plants were dug without permission.[4]

Cultivating medicinal plants is an obvious way to solve these problems of overharvesting. Even so, early growers of medicinal herbs in the United States began growing medicinal plants like echinacea primarily to control quality. Some sold those plants to companies that

manufactured finished products; others, like Ed and Sara, found growers like Mark to do it for them while they also looked for land to begin
growing some themselves.

"With imported herbs, we aren't getting their number one quality,"
Mark explained, echoing what many others told me. "We're probably
getting their number three quality, which is often the bottom of the
barrel. There is so much contamination in imported herbs. Cigarette
butts, newspapers, nails, dirt, feces, the whole gamut. We can do a much
better job here."

Traditional healing systems including Ayurveda, Traditional Chinese
Medicine, Tibetan medicine, and traditional Western herbalism recognize that the presence of the healing constituents in herbs depends on
how and where the plants grow, including factors such as the type of
soil and the altitude. Just as the plants express the signature of place, as
discussed in chapter 1, the medicines made from those plants are based
on that signature.

The concept of terroir is well known for wines and some food
products. A winery in Tuscany for example, will emphasize how the
qualities of its wines differ depending on the sandiness of the soil,
the slope of the hill, the quality of the light. The finished product is a
product of that unique landscape. A discerning wine drinker can taste
that landscape, the relationship between product and place, in the glass
of wine. The relationship between medicinal plants and where they are
traditionally grown is not straightforward, especially when balanced
with competing trends to cultivate medicinal plants outside their native
area. As Josef Brinckmann pointed out, these include "quality control,
climate change, contamination from polluted air, soil, and water, supply
chain security and traceability, as well as costs of production and price
pressure."[5] In the US there is also a growing interest in bio-regional
and domestically grown herbs. Growers like Mel and Jeff Carpenter
talk about the importance of the relationship between a plant and a
place, yet they grow herbs like astragalus, tulsi, and others that are
traditionally grown in other regions. And so the concept of terroir

does not necessarily translate neatly into medicinal plants sourced for a global market.

The Traditional Chinese Medicine concept *daodi* means that a crude drug has been grown in the places where they were traditionally cultivated or collected and processed according to traditional methods. Geo-authentic botanicals is a standard, based in China, designed to certify that the raw material is a "specific material, cultivated or collected in their traditional production regions, of a specified biological age at maturity, with specific production techniques and processing methods."[6] Wilson Lau, vice president of Nuherbs, a wholesale seller of Chinese herbs to the US market, has developed his company on this concept that the quality of the herbs is directly connected with where they are grown. "Based on that traditional knowledge," he explained when we spoke on the phone, "these herbs work as they do because they grew in specific areas. If we grow the plants in a different area, the plants will be different. It doesn't mean they will be better or worse, just different." The constituents in plants can vary even when they're growing in the same general locale because of differences in microclimate, such as whether they're growing on the north side of a hill or the south side. Wilson also made the analogy to wine, saying that a Cabernet will taste different if it is grown in California rather than in Oregon, even though those places are fairly close geographically speaking. What does that say about the differences between medicinal plants grown in Oregon and China? In numerous articles on this topic, Josef has written that more research is needed to assess and quantify whether geo-authentic herbs are actually higher quality and more effective than the same species grown elsewhere.[7]

For these reasons, some companies have a policy of first sourcing a plant from the region where it is traditionally grown. Yet as a risk management strategy, those same companies also have a policy of trying to maintain at least two different sources for each herb. Thus, some of the plants used in their products inevitably were grown outside their region of traditional use. It is then the responsibility of the company to ensure that the species grown in environments different from those documented in traditional use will, in fact, contain the same constituents and thus stimulate the expected effects in the human body.

Figuring out how to cultivate herbs that have traditionally been wild-harvested isn't always straightforward. The tradition of growing herbs for production, outside of kitchen gardens for home use, had died out in the US when the demand for plant-based medicines dried up in the early 1930s. There were no textbooks or models to guide new herb farmers on how to grow echinacea, goldenseal, or any of the medicinal plants traditionally harvested from the wild.

Lon Johnson is another of the pioneer herb farmers, the first to begin growing organic herbs in the US, at Trout Lake Farm in southwestern Washington in 1973, even before the USDA organic certification existed. Amway/Nutrilite purchased the farm in the late 1990s. Even so, most of the certified organic echinacea sold in the US market still comes from these fields stretched out beneath the snow-covered peaks of the Cascades.

When Lon started Trout Lake Farm, he gathered ideas wherever he could about how to grow herbs and what machinery to use for washing roots, sorting seeds, and drying on a large scale. "Some people willingly shared ideas, others not so much," he told me when we spoke on the phone. You couldn't just walk into a company in Europe, where farmers had been growing and processing herbs for generations, and ask them to share their secrets. Lon figured out how to retrofit used seed-cleaning equipment for cleaning roots and hops dryers for drying herbs.

"I'm asked all the time, is it easy to grow echinacea?" Ed Smith told me as he looked out at his fields of the plant, a sea of pink gently moving in the breeze outside the window of his beautifully designed home which, he had told us, echinacea built. He and Sara purchased the land in the 1980s and began growing a portion of the plants they used in production in addition to continuing to purchase herbs from growers like Mark and harvesters from overseas. "And my pat answer is: It's very easy to grow echinacea. It only took us ten years to figure out how easy it is. It's easy—if you know how.

"Each species is an entity into itself," Ed continued. "You have to grow it according to that particular herb's personality. Some herbs love rich, loamy soil. Others don't. Each one is an individual, just like a human being."

The first echinacea crop Ed and Sara grew at Herb Pharm didn't look good so they plowed it back into the soil. Ed suspected that the soil was malnourished. He contacted herb traders from Kansas where echinacea grew in the wild, who told him that echinacea liked "sweet" soil—soil with an alkaline pH. Ed began working to re-create that type of soil in his field so it would match echinacea's natural habitat in the wild.

Another challenge in cultivating wild plants is balancing quality and quantity. The constituents considered responsible for an herb's medicinal quality often are present in larger amounts when plants are under stress. Remove the stress—by irrigating fields, supplementing the soil, managing pests—and those constituents may not be present to the same extent, which may mean the plants have less medicinal efficacy. And yet if plants are allowed to grow under stressful conditions, the crop might not grow as well or as abundantly.

"We want good yields," Mark said. "The higher the yield, the more money we make. At the same time, we don't want to sell a product that is inferior." Figuring out the balance took a lot of trial and error.

Plantain is a useful example, Mark told me. Plantain has a wide range of uses as medicine, and it is also one of the most common weeds in the US. It grows through cracks in sidewalks, in lawns, in waste ground. But plantain wasn't being grown commercially in the US in the 1980s, and so companies were importing wild plantain from Europe. Mark set out to find the spots where plantain was growing naturally on his farm, and then he tried cultivating it in those areas. He had to figure out how many harvests would be possible per year and how to harvest the crop efficiently. He had to determine the best way to dry the crop, which meant deciding how much plant material to put in the dryer at a time, how many times to turn the material, and what temperature to use. Once it was dried, he had to figure out the milling—which, he explained, was the most difficult thing to nail down. Plantain grows low to the ground, and the leaves end up covered with a lot of dirt. Mark needed to devise an efficient method to clean off the dirt. The milling process also had to remove the flower spikes and the one hard rib on the back of the leaves, since neither was part of the specifications for the finished product.[8] So half the material milled was thrown out.

"If you pull two thousand pounds out of the dryer, you'll only end up with one thousand pounds of product. It's a very expensive crop to produce," Mark said. When he sent samples to Pacific Botanicals customers, who typically bought plantain wild-harvested from eastern Europe, they said it was the best sample they had ever seen. But then, Mark said, they would ask, "The price is pretty high, is it worth it?"

I asked how he would respond.

"It's a learning curve," Mark said. "Companies have to be educated. They often don't understand why herbs grown here cost so much. Labor is the biggest cost in producing herbs—we pay in one day what people in Asia make in a month." Companies understand this disparity in labor costs, Mark said. "But as with everything, it depends on what price the market can bear."

Michaël Friedman, who manufactures a line of medicines for doctors and naturopaths and has sourced herbs from Pacific Botanicals for years, told me that Mark was especially good at figuring out how to grow good-quality medicinal plants that hadn't been cultivated before. He recalled that Mark once told him that with forty hours and a computer, he could figure out how to grow anything.

Figuring out how to grow the herbs is only the first step. Michaël also said he has contracted with farmers who agreed to grow new plants for him but then didn't deliver because they had planted the wrong variety of the herb or overestimated their yields or had problems with high microbial counts. In one case, Michaël said, the farmers simply forgot to plant the seed for the crop Michaël wanted, because they had so much else to take care of on their farm.

Labor Challenges

I first met Jeff Higley of Oshala Farm and his wife, Elise, at the Medicinal Herb Growing & Marketing Conference in 2016 in Port Townsend, Washington. At the time, they sold contracts of bulk herbs wholesale to herb companies, which then sold these herbs directly to consumers. The wholesale prices were too low to cover the costs on their farm. "We're hard workers," Jeff said. Elise continued his thought: "We work fourteen hours a day. In the morning with headlamps and at night with headlamps, always checking on the water, checking on the plants, checking the greenhouse, checking the dryer. You invest all that time, and then you have to bargain over how much something is valued. Obviously, there isn't that connection [with that work]. And so how do we build that connection? We invite people to help on the farm. After one afternoon handpicking calendula, they say they will never question our prices again."

At the conference I attended a discussion among herb growers about the challenges and realities of trying to grow medicinal plants in the United States. It was an interesting gathering of competitors sharing their strategies and tricks of the trade with one another and with potential new competitors. The farmers sat in a circle and took turns speaking about a variety of topics: labor costs, machinery, suppressing weeds, building soil fertility, and more. Matt Dybala, the farm manager for Herb Pharm, talked about the importance of being efficient, especially with weeding. Eighty percent of their farm budget is devoted to labor costs, he said. Sixty percent of the labor budget, in turn, is spent on weeding. Anything they can do to reduce weeding costs pays off. Herb Pharm has eight full-time workers and twelve pickers hired in season. If the crew weeds in the morning and picks red clover in the afternoon, Matt's goal is to make enough money on the harvest of red clover to cover the cost of weeding in the morning. As others began to share their approach to labor, weeding, and mechanization, I thought about our visit to Trout Lake Farm the previous summer. Danielle Hawkins, the farm manager there, spoke in a similarly specific way about the hours of weeding and the cost of labor.

As Danielle, who rose to her current position after starting out as an intern, drove me, Terry, and Bryce around the farm, she reeled off facts and figures: how many workers it would take to weed a ten-acre field of skullcap, how many seconds it takes a root to pass through the root-washing machine. She double-tasked as she answered my questions, figuring out when she could move the weeding crew from the skullcap to another field and taking phone calls from the head of production to discuss delivering the catnip harvest from the fields to the dryer. I was impressed by the breadth of her knowledge. Danielle could describe the growing conditions needed to increase the medicinal properties of every species on the farm. She understood how the timing of harvest could impact the levels of chemical constituents in a crop. She knew how to operate the threshing machine so that it removed as much of the crop stems as possible. She pointed to a field of skullcap where a row of twenty-five blue-clad workers were weeding. The men and women were from Mexico, working at the farm as part of the H-2A temporary worker program, which allows a foreign national worker into the US for temporary agricultural work.

The H-2A program helps employers who anticipate a lack of available domestic workers to bring foreign workers to the US to perform temporary or seasonal agricultural work including, but not limited to, planting, cultivating, or harvesting. Danielle explained that Trout Lake pays the H-2A workers $12.42 an hour, which per day is equivalent to what workers would earn in six days in Mexico.

Danielle explained the program, how the wages were set, and that Trout Lake provided housing and transportation to town for groceries. The pale blue tunics were required by the Good Agricultural and Collection Practices for Medicinal Plants (GACP)—a set of guidelines developed in 2003 by the World Health Organization (WHO) aimed at improving the safety, efficacy, and sustainability of medicinal plant material being used in herbal medicines in the market. "Two dollars apiece," Danielle said, pointing to the uniforms, again demonstrating her comprehensive knowledge of the logistics of running the farm.

At the end of the tour, Danielle said she loves her job. Between equipment breakdowns, interactions with people, planning the production strategy for an herb that has suddenly become popular, and learning the nuances in harvesting one herb compared with another, her job is always new. "No day is ever the same," she told me.

All the farmers I interviewed told me that labor is their biggest challenge. A large amount of labor is devoted to weeding on any organic farm that doesn't use pesticides to kill unwanted plants, but precision in weeding is especially important on herb farms. On organic vegetable farms, weeding is important so that the crops don't have to compete for nutrients and sunlight, yet there is little risk of confusing the vegetables and weeds at harvesttime. A tomato is a tomato. And there is no danger to the consumer if a little lamb's-quarter ends up mixed into a harvest of tomatoes or cucumbers. However, harvesting herbs is another matter altogether. Fields of tulsi, peppermint, lemon balm, and catnip are easy to distinguish if you know what you are looking for, but if you don't, they all look like a sea of green, leafy aromatic plants. It is difficult—and labor-intensive—to sort out weeds after the harvest. Thus, the most efficient way to ensure a clean crop—meaning that no other species that would be considered accidental adulterants are mixed in—is to control weeds in the field in every way possible. At Trout Lake Farm, Danielle showed us the farm's most recent acquisition: a GPS tractor that could cultivate the soil to within an inch of the valerian seedlings that had just germinated. Juan Cortez oversees machinery at Trout Lake and is one of the tractor drivers. We spoke in the field when he took a break from harvesting catnip. He jokingly said that he can sleep while the GPS tractor drives through the fields; the tractor does all the work. Except, Danielle pointed out, turning around at the end of the crop row. "Yes," he agreed, laughing. "I have to wake up and turn it around and then go back to sleep!"

With the previous equipment, Juan weeded at the painfully slow speed of one to one and a half miles per hour. Now, with the GPS tractor, he covers four to four and a half miles an hour. That degree of improvement makes it easy to believe that investing in machinery is worth the cost. One young farmer once told me that given the choice he will always invest in equipment. For example, he was thinking about buying a better weeding attachment that would remove 99 percent of the weeds in a field. He'd rather spend $20,000 on equipment and $20,000 on his crew than $40,000 on labor, because if he got stuck, he could always sell his equipment.

The cost of hand labor is daunting, but availability of labor is also a concern. "The labor just isn't there anymore," Danielle said. Many farmers told me that Americans don't want to do farmwork. Elise Higley of Oshala Farm said they had lost labor to the growing cannabis industry in southwestern Oregon—there is no way she and Jeff can compete with the prices workers are paid to trim cannabis buds. She is also concerned about whether workers from Mexico that they have employed over the years will continue to return because of the US crackdown on undocumented immigrants. *This* year they did, Elise said with relief. That was in 2017. Her emphasis suggested that, as with most things related to farming, she didn't assume that meant she could count on it in the future.

Living with Uncertainty

During my visits to established farms and businesses like Herb Pharm, Trout Lake, and Pacific Botanicals, I found it hard to imagine the uncertainty they faced in the early days of their operations. A primary question for farmers each year is which crops to plant, and how much of each. Mark said he decides what to plant based on previous demand. Pacific Botanicals has contracts with some buyers, but Mark and his farm manager speculate quite a bit. Seventy percent of what they grow hasn't yet been sold at the time they plant in the spring. And in the case of perennials, they have to gamble on what demand will be years down the line. "We put them in the ground hoping they will sell." It may be as long as three years until first harvest. "I often tell people if they like to gamble, they'll love growing herbs," Mark quipped.

Because farmers grow medicinal plants to make a livelihood, ultimately what matters is that they produce crops of sufficient quality at a price point that allows them to stay in business. Mitch Coven of Vitality Works told me that he often hears the claim from growers that their herbs are the best around. "Herbalists tell me they are growing organic licorice that is better than anyone else's and they are selling it for $20 a pound," Mitch said. In response, he tells them, "I can buy organic licorice for $4 to $5 a pound, and it has been tested for lead and microbiological level." Mitch then presses his point. "I ask them about the microbiological level of their licorice. I ask about heavy metal content and if they knew what was being done on their sites thirty or forty years ago? A full heavy metal profile costs $160. A microbiological test is $100; that's $260 plus shipping to find out what I already know from the grower who sells his licorice for $4 to $5 a pound." And, Mitch concluded, even if he were considering working with the herbalist whose licorice is $20 a pound, once he tells them the quantity he needs—in the range of a thousand pounds—the conversation is over.

The question of scale and quality is also on the minds of growers who are new to the business, such as Vermont herb grower Aaron Locker. When I visited his farm on a rainy late-October day, Aaron talked about the challenge of finding the right scale. If you are too small, you can't produce things efficiently enough to keep your costs low enough for wholesale buyers to afford them. If you are too big, you have too many herbs to sell. Aaron said he has also been pondering how good is *too* good—so good he might price himself out of the market.

———

Farmer Randy Buresh started talking as soon as Terry, Bryce, and I climbed out of our car. Randy and his wife and their sons run Oregon's Wild Harvest on the eastern slopes of Oregon's Cascade Range. He led us to a row of biodynamically grown ashwagandha without a weed in sight, but even so, weeds were what he was worried about. He dug a root, knocked off the dirt, and broke off a piece to taste. Unlike the root from the warehouse I visited in South India, I was happy to taste this ashwagandha. "The weeds grow faster than the herbs," he said. They use a flame machine to kill the weed seedlings that emerge just before the crop seedlings do. This helps reduce the weeds, but weeding still requires a lot of hand labor. That is their biggest expense on the farm. At $100 per person per day, when there are ten workers in the field, your profit margin shrinks fast, Randy said.

"But it's not about the profit margin," he continued. "It is about growing things in the US, and that it is sustainable, and that it is here for future generations. You protect the soil and you save the seeds. Nothing is more important. You do that and you've done your job. That's all there is to it."

Randy and his family moved to this farm three years ago from farther east. They were still establishing their new farm and weren't yet as mechanized as they hoped to be. They had dryers to build, fields to plant, and there was always the ongoing work of weeding and harvesting, planting and transplanting, managing pests and irrigation, planning crop rotations, ordering seeds and saving seeds, mechanical failures, and the many other tasks that growing herbs organically demands. Randy said he became interested in traditional herbal medicine as he saw society losing a connection to the plant world. He read all of medicinal herbalist Michael Moore's books as well as Rudolf Steiner's, he said. "There is a deep connection between us, the plants and the universe. Whole plants work if the quality is there.

"We're gonna make it if it kills us," he told me. "I worry about it every day. I wake early in the morning, thinking, *What do we have to do today to pull this off?* I figure if I can even come close to breaking even on the farm, we've done our part."

"What do you do when you wake up worrying?" I asked.

"Get up and go to work, pretty much," he said. "Just get up and go to work."

CHAPTER EIGHT

Viriditas

For centuries people have spoken of the Greek myths as of something to be rediscovered, reawakened. The truth is it is the myths that are still out there waiting to wake us and be seen by us, like a tree waiting to greet our newly opened eyes.

—ROBERTO CALASSO

*J*eff Bodony questioned what to my eye were vibrant fields of *Echinacea purpurea* growing beneath the snow-covered Cascade mountains at Trout Lake Farm, which we had visited earlier that week. Jeff is heavyset, with a graying beard and unkempt hair tucked under a straw hat cinched beneath his chin. He wore a worn United Plant Savers T-shirt and green khaki shorts. Jeff and his wife, Lizzie Matteson, own thirty-six acres of land at the end of a long, winding dirt road in the mountains between Applegate Valley and Eugene. They tend half of those thirty-six acres, which they call a forest garden, as polyculture, a mix of trees, vegetables, and medicinal plants. They grow the medicinal plants for Heron Botanicals, a botanical company that produces extracts for naturopaths, which they jointly own with the company's manager, naturopath Eric Yarnell. They call their forest garden farm Viriditas Wild Gardens, named after Hildegard von Bingen's concept of the "greening power of nature." Von Bingen was a German Benedictine abbess of the twelfth century, and *viriditas* reflects her idea that the healing power of God resides in everything green. Healing is achieved by tending that aliveness, an aliveness that is most directly experienced in the natural world.

There wasn't a cloud in the sky on the day Terry, Bryce, and I visited Viriditas, and that, it seemed, was how conditions had been most days of that hot, dry summer. Jeff and Lizzie were concerned about the lack of rain. They pointed out plants they were trying to keep alive by irrigating with the limited water available on their hill because of the drought, and other plants left to struggle on their own. They especially talked about soil—about how the quality of the soil affects the quality of the plants and, so, the medicine. They also explained that the methods used to grow plants, in turn, have an impact on the soil. It's a relationship, Jeff said. Neither can be considered in isolation. He and Lizzie are trying to grow medicinal plants in ways that imitate how those plants grow in the wild, while still allowing for harvesting in a semi-efficient manner, at least efficient enough to make farming economically viable. This was the most biodiverse farm Terry and I had visited, and as Jeff and Lizzie showed us around, they acknowledged that much of their approach to forest gardening is experimental.

Jeff turned the conversation back to my comments about Trout Lake's echinacea. "In what ways is the echinacea grown in the middle of a ten-acre field different from echinacea growing in the prairie of Kansas or Oklahoma? The species is the same, but what does that really mean?" Jeff asked. In nature plants connect with one another through their root systems and the mycorrhizal networks in soil, in intricate relationships confirmed by recent scientific findings.[1] But those kinds of relationships can't be maintained in a monoculture. "A ten-acre plot of echinacea is no different than a one-thousand-acre field of corn," he said. In both cases, there is only one species present. But diversity is important, because each species of plant feeds a different part of the soil biology. "Where you grow a diversity of species, you have all these organisms being fed," he said, "and this amazing dance of life forms underground." That dance provides vitality and energy and power to the plants. "So you're raising a different quality of plant material." I understood Jeff to mean these plants were healthier, more vibrant, more filled with viriditas. Their approach to growing herbs is about feeding and tending that aliveness, which calls, first of all, for recognizing the value of that aliveness and being able to sense its presence.

Jeff is opinionated and confident. He has covered the wall above the desk in their living room, which also serves as their office, with quotations printed in large type, by everyone from former CIA director

William Casey to Edward Abbey to James Hansen and Marcel Proust: "The real voyage of discovery consists not in seeking new landscapes but in having new eyes." There are several by Wendell Berry. One from Krishnamurti: "It is no measure of health to be deemed sane in an insane society." And one by D. H. Lawrence: "This is what is the matter with us. We are bleeding at the roots. We are cut off from the earth and the sun and the stars."

"We have all of our relations around here," Jeff said. "That's another piece of it, when you talk about the energetics of the land. Trout Lake Farm is great. They grow all that great stuff. But here—it's like everyone is here. The eagles are here. They come to eat the bass out of the pond. The ground squirrels and the skunks and foxes, some coyotes, bears, cougars are here. The plants know this is a more intact, integrated ecosystem. I'm sure they know it. Because you can just walk around and see how happy they are." It is possible to measure marker compounds in medicinal herbs, and this provides some indication of the quality of a plant. But a chemical assay can't measure the qualities Jeff and Lizzie are planting for—vibrancy, vitality, the aliveness of the plants, the greenness of God.

Once an object becomes an item of commerce, Jeff added, "There is a shift in consciousness. You lose the viriditas piece. And losing that is probably the most dangerous part, because it allows our egos to believe we are the ones running the show." Most I met in the industry didn't agree with this conclusion. In any case Jeff and Lizzie were trying to show that it is possible to grow plants for the herbal industry that still hold the aliveness at the heart of herbal medicine.

Herbs are wild by nature. We know many of them as weeds—dandelion, chickweed, mullein, burdock—that most gardeners try to remove from their gardens. A dozen or so different species might grow intermingled in a ten-foot-square patch of ground. The biggest challenge to growing them in this way, as Jeff and Lizzie have found, is the cost of production. Ultimately, herbs must be carefully separated by species so that the end consumer can trust that the plant they purchase is, in fact, the correct medicine. No one wants lobelia, an herb that induces vomiting, mixed in with their peppermint. So the question becomes, how can one grow medicinal herbs in a diverse permaculture model and then harvest them in a way that guards against contamination? Is the cost of doing that justifiable? And, as importantly, will consumers be willing to pay? The answer hinges in part on whether the difference in quality between herbs grown via permaculture and herbs grown in a monoculture is something real or is just a matter of opinion.

"The medicine of plants is also the medicine of place," Lizzie said as we walked through their forest garden. I have heard this said before by others, but at Viriditas Gardens I grasped more deeply what it meant in practice, how in the act of taking a remedy concocted from a plant harvested on that land, I was ingesting that entire web of connections. Was it possible to taste or sense the medicine of a place? I wondered. What would it take to be able to do so? The priests and shamans in Hedangna also have the ability to see *charawa*, which is an essence in grain imbued by the ancestors that makes the grain last much longer than the physical substance otherwise should. Charawa echoes what Lizzie describes as the medicine of place, that unseen web that when enlivened through prayer translates into the material world. Like the laral value of an object, this unseen quality is strengthened by the offerings we make, offerings expressed in our care and attention. This first requires that we deem this web of relationships, from mycorrhizal networks to Hildegard's viriditas, worthy and recognize that it needs our care. Not seeing this invisible dimension, the priests and shamans say, makes humans selfish. Because we cannot see this web of reciprocity on which our life depends, we do not understand our role in that web and our responsibility for the part we play. As Jeff said, we begin to believe we are in charge.

"We are all here," Jeff said, gesturing across the landscape. The web of life in the field vibrates with aliveness, and that is the essence of viriditas. It isn't magic. It is simply paying attention.

Poisoning Pests, Poisoning Ourselves

During my travels as a Fulbright scholar, I visited a farm that grew *Gloriosa superba*, commonly known as flame lily or gloriosa lily, with Dr. B. Meena (referred to as Meena), an agronomist from Tamil Nadu Agricultural University, with which I was affiliated. The university is in Coimbatore, a busy manufacturing town in South India. Gloriosa seeds are extracted and the extract is exported to Europe, where it is used to treat gout.

Bala Kumarn, a farmer and trader, dressed in a short-sleeved white button-down shirt and dark slacks, greeted us and offered us each a coconut with a straw, a welcome drink after the hot drive in the university jeep with no air-conditioning. Dark crimson gloriosa berries were spread out in a large cement-drying yard in front of his two-story, pale yellow home, also made of cement. We finished our drinks and Bala led us into a small, separate building next to his house. Metal shelves filled with plastic containers lined one side of the room. The container labels were printed in Hindi but the skull and crossbones signs didn't need translation. Scattered across the floor on the other side of the room were various attachments and sprayers for applying the contents of these containers on the fields.

Bala was unique, Meena had explained on our drive out, which is why they had arranged this visit. Most farmers just ask the shopkeepers for instructions on how much and how often to use the pesticides, the agronomist said, but this farmer worked closely with the agricultural university for guidance so that he applied only the amounts needed and at the proper times. He didn't trust those selling pesticides to give good advice, he told Meena., because they benefited from selling more of any product and so they recommended using far more than was necessary. Watching him looking closely at his plants with Meena, I was impressed with the questions he asked and the ways he listened to Meena's answers.

He led us across the gravel driveway to the fields where he grew gloriosa behind a chain-link fence. The flowers had to be hand-pollinated because, I was told, the butterflies that had pollinated them naturally had left the region because of spraying chemicals on other crops. I couldn't find other confirmation of this, however. In any case, Bala hires 550 women to artificially pollinate the flowers. The women collect the pollen with a brush and dust it on the just-opened flowers to ensure maximum seed set over a period of three months. As we admired the stunning crimson and yellow flowers, staked to make pollination easier, my thoughts were haunted by the shelves full of chemicals. How could anything emblazoned with skulls and crossbones be considered acceptable to use on plants that would be sold as medicine? I asked Bala if any of the gloriosa he grew was certified organic. He became animated, gesturing with his hands, and asked, "What is the meaning of organic? I'm not against it. I just don't know what it is." He added that they now have developed pesticides and fertilizers that are very focused and specific and so not as damaging as they had been. And, he said, "So many people are into organic blindly. They don't know the research." He explained that they had done studies to see that the pesticides and fungicides used on gloriosa plants aren't found in the seeds and that, in any case, repeating what Meena had said, he only applies what is needed.

Later on the car ride back, I asked Meena what she thought. She shrugged. "It depends on the mindset of individual farmers. Bala is a businessman and so his focus is on increasing his income, not on the public. If we heard from organic farmers, though, we would be convinced by what they said. Because for them, consumer safety is more important."

"Pesticides are designed to kill," film director and author Josh Tickell wrote in *Kiss the Ground*.[2] In fact, Tickell pointed out, some pesticides contain chemicals originally created to kill humans. Tickell gives the example of IG Farben, the chemical company that produced the chemical weapons used in warfare and at Auschwitz (and owner of the patents for, among other products, Bayer Aspirin). After the war IG Farben repurposed its deadliest chemicals, "right down to the use of Zyklon B—the deadly gas used to kill at least one million Jews," as an insecticide on American farm fields.[3] This bears repeating. The chemicals used in the gas chambers at Auschwitz have been repurposed to spray on fields where food is grown.

During the time I was writing my dissertation, one of my closest friends in graduate school discovered she had breast cancer. Julie had surgery and then began a brutal cycle of chemotherapy. I often drove her across Boston to the medical center for her treatments. The nurses would hook up Julie to an IV in a room filled with men and women twice her age. We sat while her body was filled with chemicals to attack the cancer and, the theory went, allow her to live. As we left the infusion center, the nurses warned

Julie not to let her urine splash on her body because the chemicals from the chemotherapy make the urine toxic. I thought I had misunderstood, so I asked Julie about it. She explained that I had heard correctly; the nurses were warning her to minimize her skin exposure to the same chemicals they deemed safe enough to inject directly into her blood.

I understood that, in this case, chemotherapy was the best tool at hand to try to keep Julie alive. That it failed to do so—Julie died from metastasized breast cancer at the age of thirty-seven—makes it easier to criticize in retrospect. At the time, it did seem like the best alternative.

Yet I still don't understand *why* that was the best alternative available to her. I don't understand how we have come to design medicines using chemicals that create the very conditions those medicines were created to heal. As with the farmer who sprayed pesticides on his medicinal herb crops, what prevents us from seeing that the means *are* the end? What twist of perception allows us to believe that, in poisoning the world, we are not also poisoning ourselves, poisoning the people and places we love?

"In our complex dealings with the physical world, we find it very difficult to recognize all the products of our activities," literary theorist Raymond Williams wrote in *The Country and the City*. "We recognize some of the products, and call others by-products; but the slag heap is as real a product as the coal, just as the river stinking with sewage and detergent is as much our product as the reservoir."[4] Side effects of medicine aren't side effects, pediatric neurologist Dr. Martha Herbert told us when we interviewed her for *Numen*. They are just not the effects we want, but that makes them no less important or worthy of our concern. Seeing those effects is simply another way of seeing double.

Organic India, a certified organic tea and supplement company, was founded because an Ayurvedic doctor was concerned that the medicine he was providing to patients was formulated from plants grown with chemicals, and that those medicines were doing more harm than good, Kyle Garner, then CEO of Organic India USA, told me during a phone interview.[5] So the doctor decided to start growing medicinal herbs organically. Kyle added that drinking non-organic tea or, as he called it, herbs "steeped in pesticides," gave him the chills. In his usual understated way, Mark Wheeler of Pacific Botanicals echoed the sentiment:

"It doesn't make sense to use herbs for health reasons when those herbs have been sprayed with chemicals. It just doesn't wash."

Looking at the issue of chemicals from yet another perspective, Organic India wants to ensure they are not destroying the planet just to source some extra turmeric. In other words, the impact of their methods for growing turmeric on the health of the ecosystem is as important as the quality and quantity of the turmeric in the teas and capsules they produce. Both impacts, as Raymond Williams would say, are products, not just the bottles we see on the grocery store shelf.

Growing herbs for an expanding market brings questions about process and product to the forefront. Agricultural consultants and government agency staff may justify the use of pesticides in terms of economics and output—that they are necessary in order to allow farming enterprises to achieve reasonable profits. Framed in these terms, conventional farming can be hard to dispute, especially in countries with limited resources.

Shortly after my trip to the gloriosa fields, I attended the stakeholder conference in Tamil Nadu where I met Mohan, the trader whom I had visited outside Madurai. Farmers and researchers came together at the conference to discuss cultivation as a way to develop reliable supplies of medicinal plants for the national and international market and generate incomes for farmers in the region. They discussed viable species for cultivation, marketing opportunities, technical research, seed supplies, and more. I spoke with people interested in growing herbs organically, but they all said there was no market for certified organic material in India. The cost of certification and the price of the organic material was simply too high. Plus, they said, no one was asking for certified organic materials, neither the Ayurvedic companies that were the primary market for farmers nor the consumers of those finished products.

I later learned that India is a leader in certified organic production of food. In 2018 India had the largest number of organic producers in the world—and with a reported 1,149,000 producers, significantly more producers than anywhere else in the world. The next three countries were Uganda (210,000 producers), Mexico (210,000) and Ethiopia (203,000).[6]

Only India's producers increased, up from 835,000 in 2016. The others all stayed the same or decreased. In 2018 there were 2.8 million organic farmers worldwide, a drop from a reported 2.9 million in 2017. It isn't clear what caused this shift, and it requires more information to understand whether this is a trend or not.

According to Dr. Shailinder Sodhi, president of Ayush Herbs, Inc., there has been a dramatic increase of the number of producers growing certified organic medicinal plants in India in the last two years—at least for the export market. Ayush Herbs produces herbal products based on the principles of Ayurveda and sourced from their own farms in Himachal Pradesh in Northwest India. Sodhi predicts India will become the area of fastest expansion of certified organic farming in the world.

Yet while the number of organic producers was increasing, from 1999 to 2017 the amount of agricultural land in the world designated as organic has increased only slightly, rising from 0.3 percent to 1.4 percent, or from 11 million hectares to nearly 70 million hectares.[7] That is roughly 98.5 percent that is not certified. Even in the United States, the organic herb market is hardly large enough to have an impact in increasing the land in organic cultivation. I asked several people in the industry what they could tell me about the size of the organic herb market in the United States. Everyone qualified their answer by saying the percentages they mentioned were just a best guess. Kyle Garner told me that the herbal supplement industry is an $8 *billion* business and that organically certified companies make up around $100 *million* of that business. Mark Wheeler guessed that 15 to 20 percent of all herbs used as medicine in the US might be organic. Sebastian Pole said he thought certified organic herbs represent perhaps 1 percent of the overall international market.

Others were hesitant to hazard a guess. Rupa Das is in charge of quality control and sourcing for BI Nutraceuticals, a leading herb processor and distributor providing raw material for all the major players in the US. In 2019, BI was purchased by the Martin Bauer Group, a family-owned German company with a long history as a manufacturer and supplier of botanical ingredients and products. Rupa told me that out of fifty companies she works with, only one requires certified organic materials. It depends on a company's customers, she said. If their customers aren't demanding organic ingredients, the company won't source organic herbs.

Here's how I translate these statistics: Most of the medicinal plants cultivated worldwide have been sprayed with an input that can cause deleterious health effects that people may be seeking to avoid by buying and ingesting products made with those plants. There are maximum levels of pesticide residue allowed on herbal products that reputable companies adhere to. While these levels address concerns about the safety of the finished product, they do not consider the impacts of the practices on the whole system, on the health of the farmers and farmworkers handling the fertilizers and pesticides, on the pollinators, on the water, the air, and the web of relations that Jeff and Lizzie nurture on their land. What blind spots prevent us from realizing that this disconnect makes no sense?

The deliberate use of pesticides in agricultural production produces an additional unintended consequence that has become one of the biggest threats to organically grown crops around the world: residues of pesticides of unknown origin. We produced a video for the Sustainable Herbs Program focused specifically on non-point contamination. Peter Schmid, general manager for Worlée, a German supplier of botanical raw materials to the international market, brought up the topic when I spoke with him at the BioFach trade show in 2019. Peter said that in quality control tests, his company is detecting pesticide contamination as a result of spray drift, which has become worse since farmers have begun using new tools that produce a spray mist with finer droplet size. Using these tools allows farmers to cut down on the quantities of pesticides they apply, because the spray application covers plant surfaces more efficiently. But the spray particles are so fine that they rise high in the air, especially when temperatures are hot, and they drift extensively, traveling as far as twenty-five kilometers from the spray site. Eventually, though, those spray droplets land somewhere, possibly on the fields of a certified organic farm.

This problem of pesticides of unknown origin has become so serious in Bulgaria that the country is no longer a reliable source of certified organic herbs. Josef Brinckmann told me that at BioFach 2019, producer groups from every continent reported having problems with pesticides of unknown origin showing up on herbs, even wild-collected herbs from remote places and certified organic crops that were never sprayed. "In many cases, consumers have an unrealistic notion that certified organic things should be pesticide-free," Josef said. "Which hasn't been true in decades. The problem is we are living on a contaminated planet. So certified organic products are the best you can do. You should still support it. But you are still going to find pesticide residue at the level of parts per billion. Who knows where it came from—from drift, from irrigation water or melt coming down from mountains. That's just the reality. The whole planet is polluted. That's where we're at. People should be alarmed."

Every batch of certified organic herbs must be tested for residues, and the level allowed is minute, usually 0.02 part per million in Europe. In the United States, the tolerance level is zero for many herbs. But as Josef explained, this brings in additional problems. Because of non-point contamination, certified organic plants often can't pass the zero tolerance level. For example, he said, "A small producer in Eastern Europe is doing everything right, investing in sustainable production and equality. They're in a remote area. It's as clean as it gets. And yet 0.005 part per million of something from who knows where is detected on their material in the port coming into the US. FDA tests it and says, that's illegal, ship it back." Josef described a stakeholder meeting where he found himself in the unexpected role of arguing for the US to follow the EEU framework of minimum pesticide levels (which he described as a more rational framework) rather than the zero-tolerance framework in the US. Zero tolerance, he said, was the least rational framework for contaminants in the world. He hoped this recommendation would wake people up to see "the problem isn't necessarily the pesticide residues on the stinging nettle leaves. It's that there are pesticide residues on everything all over the planet. Let's clean the place up," Josef said emphatically. "That's what Earth Day forty years ago was about. We need to start cleaning the air and the rivers and the soil. The problem hasn't gotten better. It's gotten worse."

Scientific investigations of organic and non-organic produce do not show one to be consistently superior to the other based on the nutrients analyzed, claims Steven Dentali of the AHPA. Sebastian Pole strongly disagrees, citing in particular a study by Newcastle University that found higher levels of antioxidants and lower levels of pesticides in organic crops versus conventional crops.[8] Either way, I understood Steven to be making a larger point, that the comparison takes too narrow a view. "You need to ask: What kind of world are you supporting? What system of health? If you are interested in the health of the soil, the health of the communities and economies where the plants are from, you need to ask a different set of questions. Capitalism leads us in a certain direction," Steven said. "It is up to us to ask whether that direction is the one we want to take." Questioning the prerogatives of capitalism requires that we see beyond what the market wants us to see, and it requires that companies make decisions based on deeper considerations, not just what makes sense financially.

Hope in Relationship

The western half of Karnataka state in south-central India includes the steep, tree-covered Western Ghats, a UNESCO World Heritage Site and one of the eight hot spots of biodiversity in the world, stretching from the states of Kerala to the south to Gujarat to the north.[9] Terry and I had come to visit producers with Sebastian Pole and Ben Heron of Pukka Herbs. Sebastian had started the company with co-founder Tim Westwell in 2002 as a way to source certified organic herbs from India for a line of medicinal tea formulations.

I'd first met Ben in the U.K. after visiting Runo in Poland. He and Sebastian then invited us to join them the following winter when they visited some of their suppliers in Karnataka state, in and around the South Western Ghats. Ben is tall and thoughtful with a shock of dirty-blond hair parted in the middle. He carries a small spiral notebook in his baggy jeans that he pulls out to take notes in during conversations with farmers. He wore a mauve button-down shirt when we traveled with him in India—he was wearing the same shirt a year later when we spoke by Skype on the phone. He laughed when he saw the video and said maybe he should buy some new clothes. Ben consistently applies his principles in his actions. At one point in our stay in India, we were offered a beer. Ben asked where the cans would be deposited afterward. He didn't like the answer. So he didn't have a beer. And Seb later told me that once on the morning after New Year's Eve when they were in Goa, Ben went out to the beach to pick up the trash left from fireworks set off the night before.

One morning, the four of us headed out for a three-hour drive to a community of farmers that Sebastian and Ben hoped would begin to grow certified organic field mint. As we approached the community, the driver turned down a narrow dirt road past fields of sugarcane. Though only ten minutes from a busy town, the community's atmosphere was peaceful. A crowd of men and a few women greeted us with garlands of tulsi leaves. We posed for a photo beneath a banner announcing our arrival and Pukka's partnership with Phalada Agro Research Foundation. Phalada is a primary processing company that works with herb farmers, grows its own certified organic herbs at its farm in Hosagunda, and has a processing facility outside Bangalore.

Ben, Terry, and I followed the crowd of men down an even narrower dirt road. We walked past a large group of motorcycles, left our shoes in a pile of black plastic flip-flops, and climbed the steps to the unfinished second story of yet another cement building. A deep purple canopy had been set up to shade rows of red plastic chairs. Men milled about outside and upstairs, talking or smoking. After some time, thirty or more men came and sat down. Seb, his shoulder-length curly brown hair tucked behind his ears, dressed in a slightly rumpled long-sleeved dark blue shirt, black jeans, and Birkenstocks, stood to make a short speech. He paused frequently so that N. R. Madhuvaraj, the agronomist for Phalada, could translate. Ben and Seb, both of whom lived in India for many years, speak Hindi, and they converse directly with farmers in Hindi when they visit the north of India. But in southern India a different language is spoken in each state; English is often the common language. This made it challenging to speak directly with the farmers. Ben and Seb had worked with Phalada since Pukka began, and the two companies had a close relationship. Thus while language differences were a very real challenge in sourcing medicinal plants from around the world, this arrangement worked.

"We've been on a big journey with Phalada," Seb said to the farmers, "exploring and growing high-quality organic medicinal herbs. We've worked together fifteen years, and our intention is to work together for the next fifteen and the next fifteen after that." He talked about the importance of understanding the character of the plant, "to study the nature of field mint as you understand the character of your children. You have to understand field mint that same way," he said. His speech was short and to the point. He touched on the key points—Pukka was there for the long haul. There would be a market for field mint if the farmers were ready to grow it.

Mr. Shastry, the head of Phalada, followed with a speech in Kannada, the primary language of Karnataka, but this speech wasn't translated for us. After that, huge vats of rice were brought around for a lunch of vegetables, curry, and chapatis. These lunches are a formality, and Seb tends to take the lead on them, he told me as we began to eat. He is the big-picture thinker and speaker for Pukka. Ben and sourcing specialist Marin Anastasov will return at another time for more detailed work with farmers, checking their diaries, doing farm audits, and troubleshooting problems. "They're the experts," Sebastian said.

After eating, Ben and Seb went outside to the fields to speak directly with the farmers. About fifteen farmers gathered around. Ben stood next to Mr. Shivarayappa, the farmer who had hosted the lunch, and who had pioneered growing field mint in this region, where most other farmers grew chilies or mangoes to sell on the open market. More men crowded around to listen. Mr. Shivarayappa explained that he began growing mint two years ago. At first, he wasn't that keen to do so, but he took it as a challenge.

With Shastry translating on his behalf, Ben asked how the income compared with that from other crops.

"If the market is good," Mr. Shivarayappa said, per acre of chili or mango, he could get about 65,000 rupees. He earned double that— 130,000 rupees—last year growing field mint for Phalada. Looking around at the crowd, Seb remarked in English, "So that's why so many farmers are here today."

Shastry nodded in agreement. He asked the farmer whether that sum was more than he expected and whether he thought he could get the same yield every year. Mr. Shivarayappa said that yes, he was confident he could double it.

Shastry asked whether it was reasonable for all the other farmers to expect to make 80,000 to 100,000 rupees by growing field mint. "If the farmers' expectations are too high, they might be disappointed," he added.

Mr. Shivarayappa replied that he thought that level of yield was reasonable.

Ben asked about the flooding of fields during the previous growing season. Mr. Shivarayappa explained that the flooding was the result of runoff from the neighboring fields during the heavy rains. Ben looked surprised. He asked where the boundaries of the neighboring land were. The farmer pointed to fields where cotton, a highly intensive conventional crop, was growing. There was no buffer zone between those fields and Mr. Shivarayappa's fields. I knew this was not the answer Ben wanted to hear, but his expression did not change. He simply turned to Shastry and asked him to talk about the importance of buffer zones.

There are two sources of contamination that organic farmers need to be concerned about, Shastry explained to the farmers, direct spraying of a field and a lack of buffer zones to minimize the risk of contamination from a neighboring conventional grower. "For us and for the customer, there is a certain amount of risk with growing certified organic plants. Phalada buys the herbs from the farmers out of trust. We test it at Phalada. If the material doesn't pass, it's gone," Shastry said, gesturing with his hand the waste and the loss. "It's the same for Pukka," he continued. "When it arrives there, they test it. If it doesn't pass, it's gone. Phalada doesn't get any money. Those are the rules. You have to have buffer zones."

The men nodded. Ben then spoke up about the importance of hygienic drying. "We're not boiling this like rice," he said. "This is a medicine. We have to treat it in the most hygienic way possible." He paused to let

Shastry translate his words. I could tell it was a point he repeated often,
especially in India.

———

Later we drove on to see fields where ashwagandha had been hit hard by
a drought, reducing the expected crop by half. In the car Ben took out his
notebook to go over his notes. He asked the field director for Phalada, a
young man who lived in the area and visited the farmers regularly, to follow up with Mr. Shivarayappa to make sure he implemented the changes
they had discussed. Ben listed the changes. The field director jotted a
note to himself in his own pocket notebook. Keeping track of everything
that had been discussed seemed like the most challenging part of these
site visits. Ben added reminders to himself in his notebook. He later
said it took days to copy over his field notes to ensure nothing would
be forgotten. An entire supply chain for Pukka's products depended on
his thoroughness in following up. If Mr. Shivarayappa's field mint didn't
pass the organic inspection—or if any of the products Ben oversaw came
up short—Pukka would face shortages of the ingredients for some of
their most popular tea. If they face shortages, they either risk going out
of stock, which I was repeatedly told no company wants to do, or they
need to find new suppliers, which is not easy to do on short notice for
companies like Pukka that adhere to rigorous quality control standards.
These are the kind of details and interactions that require incredible
attention to detail. How they are handled determines the quality of the
relationships on which those supplies ultimately depend.

We drove a short way to the next farm and climbed out of the car by
the ashwagandha fields to observe the condition of the crop. The earth
was hard, with deep cracks from the lack of rain. Ashwagandha has been
a good crop for farmers who aren't set up to irrigate crops, but, Ben
explained, it needs good rain during at least one of the months when
the seed is germinating, June, July, or August. This year the monsoon
didn't come until September. Three-quarters of the farmers with whom
Phalada and Pukka had contracted had lost three-quarters of their crop.

"It's pretty bad when a drought-resistant crop suffers from a drought,"
Seb said as he knelt next to a plant that was only a quarter the size it

should have been at that time of year. Three years later, in the winter of 2020, farmers lost even more of the crop to flooding.

Sebastian and Ben make sourcing decisions plant by plant, depending on the opportunities and the options. Just as a field of organically grown crops requires a lot more labor to weed, it takes a greater amount of time and effort to find growers willing to grow certified organic herbs and to develop relationships with them. You need to stay long enough to get beyond the presentations and meetings like the one at the Shivarayappa farm to the real work, Seb told me as we drove. Plus, it is helpful to see the crop at different stages. They try to visit several times a year. They had visited in November, just two months earlier, and there was too much rain. Now there wasn't enough rain.

The work of building relationships, especially with the small farmers, is never finished, though Ben and Seb don't visit their trusted suppliers, such as larger certified organic farms in the United States, as often, Ben said. But they try to balance sourcing from US farms, where it is easier to control quality, with smaller projects where they work with farmers like Mr. Shivarayappa who own only two or three acres. Those projects require more investment of time, resources, and money, Ben explained, but they had a greater social impact by providing what they believe is a good livelihood for small farmers in economically insecure regions of the world.

Years ago I read the essay "The Star Thrower" by Loren Eiseley before it became a popular classic. The image in the story has stayed with me over the years: The narrator walks the beaches of Australia, passing collectors picking up starfish washed ashore by the tide, destined to be grilled for resort guests to consume. In the distance the narrator sees a figure bending down and throwing something out to sea, then bending down and repeating the motion again. The narrator discovers that this man is picking up the stranded starfish and flinging them back to the ocean. The next morning the narrator returns and passes the collectors again. He sees the star thrower ahead of him, picking up a starfish, and throwing it into the ocean. The narrator pauses and then bends and does

THE BUSINESS OF BOTANICALS

the same. They continue, not stopping to speak. The work before them is too great. "The task was not to be assumed lightly, for it was men as well as starfish that we sought to save . . ."[10] They will never fully accomplish their goal. Yet the two men keep at the work, tossing the starfish one by one into the sea.

"From Darwin's tangled bank of unceasing struggle, selfishness, and death, had risen, incomprehensibly, the thrower who loved not man, but life," Eiseley wrote. And in this way he revealed "that there looms, inexplicably, in nature something above the role men give her."[11]

Much of Jeff and Lizzie's vision for Viriditas Wild Gardens was not realistic in economic terms; nor did it offer a viable alternative in the current model of sourcing herbs on an international scale. The weeds in their gardens were out of control, and production was lower than they hoped. They were struggling to find a grower or farm manager to help share the work and the vision. The last I heard, they were trying to sell their farm. But the vision that inspired them, the importance of rebuilding and supporting the broader web of relations as a key part of healthy farming systems, is gaining traction in the regenerative agricultural movement that has flourished in the four years since I began the Sustainable Herbs Program. Regenerative agriculture is essentially the kind of organic farming that the early organic farmers have done from the outset, "a practice of agriculture that improves soil, plant, water, human and planetary health," Tickell wrote in *Kiss the Ground*, his book that helped galvanize and give focus to efforts to build soils.[12] Even though no one I met is able to completely apply the principles Jeff and Lizzie espouse, the herb farmers I visited in the US as well as Ben, Josef, Sebastian, and others sourcing herbs from around the world are all doing the best they can to balance the aliveness of plants at the heart of herbal medicine with the challenges of shepherding a viable business in a globalized world. They are working with the intelligence of nature, showing up and paying attention to what is called for, using business in the service of life, not the other way around.

Collecting calamus from organically certified meadows outside Hajnówka, Poland, for Runo Spólka.

Anna Charytoniuk of Runo and her mother standing in the fields behind Anna's home where they collect herbs for their personal use.

An example of the uncertified supply chain: weighing wild-collected medicinal plants outside a collection unit near Madurai, India.

An example of the uncertified supply chain: the collection unit outside Madurai, India.

Plowing brahmi fields for transplanting, Hosagunda, India.

Transplanting certified organic brahmi at Hosagunda, India. Because brahmi typically grows in wet areas in the wild, fields are flooded before transplanting.

Harvesting certified organic brahmi, Hosagunda, India.

Washing freshly harvested brahmi, Hosagunda, India.

A landowner uses a mechanical cultivator to clear weeds from lemon balm fields outside Plovdiv, Bulgaria.

Taking freshly harvested lemon balm to the nearby processing center for drying, outside Plovdiv, Bulgaria. Immediately drying freshly harvested plants helps preserve the quality.

Harvesting lemon balm outside Plovdiv, Bulgaria.

Removing weeds from comfrey fields in southern Bulgaria. Photo courtesy of Willow Fortunoff.

Sebastian Pole, co-founder of Pukka Herbs, speaking at a farmers' meeting in Karnataka state, India. Mr. Shastry is to his immediate right. Ben Heron is second to Sebastian's left.

Organic calendula fields at Zack Woods Herb Farm, Vermont. Photo courtesy of Jeff and Melanie Carpenter.

Conventionally grown calendula on a farm south of Frankfurt, Germany. Photo courtesy of Willow Fortunoff.

Danielle Hawkins, farm manager of Trout Lake Farm, one of the largest organic herb farms in the US and the source of much of the organic echinacea on the market.

H-2A workers weed a field at Trout Lake Farm, Washington.

Weeding with a GPS tractor at Trout Lake Farm, Washington.

Harvesting certified organic valerian at Oregon's Wild Harvest, Sandy, Oregon.

Chopping freshly harvested valerian root before washing and processing at Oregon's Wild Harvest, Sandy, Oregon.

Harvesting the leaves of conventionally grown Jerusalem artichoke outside Frankfurt, Germany.

Unloading a truck of certified organic ginger at Phalada Agro, Bangalore, India.

Washing organic ginger at Phalada, India.

Drying organic ginger at Phalada, India.

Sorting organic ginger by quality before processing at a primary processing facility in Bangalore, India.

Removing organic tulsi from drying racks at Zack Woods Herb Farm for garbling (garbling may be mechanized but can also be done by hand).

Drying organic calendula at Oshala Farm, a thirty-acre organic medicinal herb farm in Applegate Valley, Oregon.

Drying Jerusalem artichoke leaves at a three-story drying machine outside Frankfurt, Germany.

Garbling or separating the leaves and stalks of organic tulsi at Zack Woods Herb Farm, Vermont.

Processing (cutting and sifting) dried roots at Runo.

The processing center at Runo, Poland. Freshly chopped plants are sifted through screens in the large bin in the background. The chopped plants travel through the hoses and into bags.

Processing certified organic turmeric at Phalada, India.

Processing at Agrimed's processing facility, which had been completed shortly before our visit in 2016, Germany.

A certified organic storage facility at Runo, Poland. Certified raw materials (organic, FairWild) must be kept in a separate warehouse with a document trail tracing the plants to the source.

A wholesale distributor of medicinal plants in Bangalore, India. An example of bad handling practices.

Storage of certified organic herbs at Trout Lake Farm, Washington.

Storage of dried medicinal plants in the uncertified supply chain, Madurai, India.

Transporting dried medicinal plants at an Ayurvedic company in Kerala, India.

Processing companies send samples to finished-product companies to ensure that the herbs have been prepared to a company's specifications. Photo courtesy of Willow Fortunoff.

A sparkler factory outside Madurai, India.

Different sizes of processed nettles, Dary Natury, Poland.

A senna farmer walking in Rajasthan. Senna plants can thrive in these arid conditions.

Drake Sadler, co-founder of Traditional Medicinals, meeting with villagers to decide the design of a new school that the Revive Project and Traditional Medicinals Foundation plan to build in this community.

Nioma Sadler, co-founder of the Traditional Medicinals Foundation, with village women in western Rajasthan.

The author trying to make chapatis while visiting the Traditional Medicinals Foundation's Revive Project in the villages that grow senna for their Smooth Move tea. Photo courtesy of Amelia Ahl.

Jayant Sarnaik in the sacred grove of bibhitaki trees where great hornbills nest.

Sorting out the bibhitaki husk from the fruit.

Drying bibhitaki fruit at the Nature Connect processing center.

Training for FairWild certification for haritaki, Nature Connect, and the Applied Environmental Research Foundation, Western Ghats, India.

Haritaki fruits wild-collected in the Western Ghats, India. Photo by Ben Heron.

The author and Ben Heron visiting the GMP certified manufacturing center where Pukka's tea bags are produced, Bristol, U.K. Photo courtesy of Willow Fortunoff.

CHAPTER NINE

Supporting Supply Communities

It is important that awake people be awake.
The darkness around us is deep.

—WILLIAM STAFFORD

*T*he heat hit me like an oven as I climbed off the airplane in Jodhpur. It was late April 2017, one of the hottest times of year, and the rains were late. Emily Davydov, the director of strategy and partnerships at the Traditional Medicinals Foundation (TMF), was there to greet me, and as we rode to a hotel to pick up some fellow visitors, she began telling me about TMF's Revive Project. I'd watched the brief videos about the project on the foundation's website, but I didn't have a full understanding of the issues, except that water scarcity was a significant problem in this region. I had only to look out the jeep's window to confirm that was the case.

The Traditional Medicinals Foundation works in partnership with Traditional Medicinals, the company, to support education and community development (such as building schools, training village health workers, and helping to improve food and water security) in the communities from which TM sources botanicals. When I visited OHTC, I'd asked Mike Brook what made a good company. Without hesitating, he responded, "Being invested in serious issues that matter for the industry as a whole." He added, "Which Traditional Medicinals has done from the start."

In 2007 Drake Sadler stepped aside as CEO of Traditional Medicinals to focus on social initiatives through the foundation, which he co-founded with his wife, Nioma Sadler. Nioma is also the founder of

WomenServe, which works worldwide to empower women and girls. Drake, Nioma, Emily, and Amelia Ahl, program manager, were in Rajasthan for ongoing meetings with partners. They were also introducing the project to Steve Demos, an adviser for Traditional Medicinals, and his girlfriend, Julia, whose last name I didn't catch. Nioma was introducing a new WomenServe employee from California to the region and their work. They invited me to join them. Originally the visit was to include filming for the Sustainable Herbs Program, but subsequently we were asked not to film, so I ended up coming on my own while Terry and Bryce stayed in South India.

Emily was the foundation's first employee, and she explained that TMF's work with producer communities is not a feel-good side enterprise of the Traditional Medicinals company. Rather, the foundation undertakes its work because community resilience leads to a more sustainable supply chain. Encouraging sustainable farm methods is important, Emily said, but so is community development, because tired, underpaid workers are more likely to cut corners. And on top of their farmwork, women in the villages in this area used to spend eight to ten hours a day walking to fetch water (some women still do, though through the work of TMF these numbers are decreasing). "Stressed workers are not good for the quality of the senna," Emily said. Freeing women from that drudgery by investing in water security was a way to ensure agricultural quality.

Although the origin of senna's use as a laxative is not precisely known, Arab physicians were the first to introduce it into European medicine. Senna is now accepted as an "essential, safe, and effective medicine for the relief of constipation."[1] It is the main ingredient in Smooth Move tea, one of TM's top-selling products. As such, the company realized that it was critical to find a reliable source of organic pharmacopeial-grade senna leaf.[2] India is the largest senna-producing and -exporting region in the world. The plant, with its silvery green leaves and small pale yellow flowers, thrives in the harsh conditions of the Thar Desert of Rajasthan. (Senna also grows in the Sudan and Egypt, where it is wild-harvested and cultivated in what have lately been conflict zones.[3])

At the hotel, we picked up Steve and Julia and headed off for a three-and-a-half-hour journey northwest of Jodhpur to Phalodi, which is near the border with Pakistan.[4]

Rajasthan is a state in northwestern India, and Jodhpur is on the northwestern edge of the state. The city is one of the most widely photographed in India: forts and minarets made of dusky pink sandstone and marble set against a sea of rolling sand. It is hot and, like all of India, crowded. We drove out of town on a flat two-lane road past the ramshackle single-story, one-room shops selling bottles of soda, potato chips, single cigarettes, and other sundry items that spill out of every Indian town into the countryside, in this case into the desert. I'd been in deserts before, but never one like this. Even from the comfort of our air-conditioned jeep, I was intimidated by the landscape—heat shimmering above the flat sand as far as I could see, heat shimmering above women walking beside the road with shawls over their heads, shielding themselves from the heat. Isolated trees grew here and there, but once we passed through the sprawl, there seemed to be nothing but sand as far as we could see.

As we rode through the desert, my thoughts wandered back to my graduate research work on the Makalu-Barun Conservation Project (MBCP), a large-scale conservation and development project in eastern Nepal. The MBCP was a smart project based on exciting, in-depth research by some of the brightest Nepali researchers in the country at the time. My research was independent of MBCP, but it focused on issues of land tenure and access to natural resources that were related to the project's ongoing work in the region. I had imagined that upon completing my PhD, I would make a career working for a project like MBCP. Eighteen months later, though, I had left Nepal disillusioned with the project and with international development in general. In the end MBCP did not seem that different from most development projects scattered across the mountains of Nepal, leaving behind a wake of abandoned buildings, broken irrigation pipes, empty water tanks, disillusioned villagers, and thick reports (one of which I had produced) locked away, unread, in metal file cabinets. This trip to see TMF's work was my first encounter with a development project since that time. I couldn't help being skeptical.

Water as Empowerment

We arrived late in the afternoon at Hotel Barsingha Villa, a luxurious renovated fort off a back road in Phalodi, an otherwise nondescript town. The fort had been renovated as a hotel about ten to fifteen years ago when German consultants were regularly traveling to the region to implement a solar project. Now that the project was completed, few Germans or other tourists visit. The hotel stands empty much of the year and is a perfect place for TMF staff and visitors to stay, especially ones not used to traveling in the desert and in India.

I dropped my bag in my room, the most elegant of my accommodations in India, tastefully designed, large, and airy despite the heat. I went down to the courtyard to meet with Amelia. We sat at a small table and ordered a beer. Strings of lights and large paper lanterns lit the area in the growing dusk. Like Emily, Amelia was young, articulate, and confident. She had been at TMF for a little over a year at the time of my visit, taking Emily's job as program manager when Emily was promoted.

After a bit Drake joined us. Amelia said he and Nioma had attended a long and somewhat tense meeting with village leaders to negotiate a land donation for a new village school that Traditional Medicinals Foundation hopes to build. As he sat, he gestured around the hotel. It hadn't always been this easy, he said. Although TM had developed good relationships and transparency through most of its supply chain, it had not yet found a senna supply partner that met those requirements.[5] And so beginning in 2004, they began to search for a partner in India with the capacity to produce a high-quality, more reliable, and more consistent source of certified organic senna. The company began site visits in 2006.

At the time, farmers were growing senna by hand, broadcasting seed on marginal lands not suitable for growing millet and other grains, which were their primary crops. Whatever senna seeds sprouted, the farmers would allow to grow and then would harvest the plants to sell on the open market. Although senna has been incorporated in the Ayurvedic system of medicine, the herb was not used traditionally in the Thar Desert. Farmers were growing it purely as a commodity crop, Drake explained, and since traders bought it by volume, farmers didn't focus on ensuring the medicinal quality; their aim was to maximize biomass of the plants. Like herb growers and collectors everywhere, the farmers often added gravel and stones to the sacks of senna to increase the weight and thus their income. TM's goal was to find farmers who were willing to work with the company to grow senna of consistently high medicinal quality to sell for a premium rate.

Drake and Nioma made their first trip to the Thar Desert in April and May 2006, before the rains had come—the hottest time of the year. Everyone they encountered, Drake said, especially the women, talked about water. Drake and Nioma learned that, beginning at age five, young girls in these villages became responsible for retrieving water, which usually involved a thirty-minute walk each way, five times a day. Yes, these girls spent up to five hours a day, every day, doing nothing but carrying water. They never went to school, and female illiteracy in the villages was above 90 percent.

It was dark in the courtyard now, and the lanterns cast shadows across the courtyard of the old Rajasthani fort. Drake continued his story. A few weeks after they had returned to Northern California in the summer of 2006, he came home from work one day and called out to Nioma as he entered their house. She didn't reply. He paused, then resumed speaking, reflecting that he still becomes emotional when he remembers that day. Drake called out to Nioma again, and then he saw her standing in their garden with the hose in her hand, watering plants. She didn't turn around or even seem to hear him. As he walked up, he realized she was sobbing. "Her whole body was heaving with tears," Drake said. He embraced her while she continued to sob. "We can't go back there again," she said, when she could finally speak, "unless we do something about the women and their lack of water."

The next morning we headed out in two jeeps to visit a school. I rode with Drake and Steve. This was Steve's first trip to Rajasthan, and so Drake told us about the challenges involved in producing high-quality senna. The traditional way of growing senna, he explained, is to harvest after the plants flower, because the leaves are larger then, and so the farmers, who are paid by weight of harvested material, make more money. But the levels of sennosides, the active ingredient in senna, reach their peak just *before* the plants flower. The leaflets are smaller then, but they are more potent medicinally. Most finished-product drug companies would buy semi-purified senna extracts with high sennoside content from the extraction companies that supply active drug ingredients. If the raw material (senna biomass) purchased from farmers had low sennoside levels, the extraction houses simply purchased more biomass and made repeated extractions in order to reach the sennoside levels needed. There were no senna buyers asking for raw material with high sennoside content, and thus farmers had no incentive to change agricultural practices.

In 2010 TM sponsored a multiyear agricultural study to determine best practices for cultivating pharmacopeial-quality organic senna with higher sennosides in the Thar Desert. Until this goal was accomplished, TM would, when necessary, add extract of senna to its Smooth Move tea mixture in order to standardize the sennoside content in each cup of tea. Once farmers could reliably supply higher-sennoside-content senna leaf, use of the expensive extract would no longer be necessary, which would be a significant cost savings for the company.

In addition, the company would be able to use less senna in the tea blend (without changing the blend's effectiveness), which would allow for increasing the amount of other herbs in the formula that balance undesirable digestive effects that senna can produce, such as gas and bloating. An additional benefit is that these other herbs cost less than senna. Thus, in addition to making a more consistent tea, the overall cost of the blend would be lower. In all ways, improving the quality of senna made good business sense.

In 2010 Eleanor Kuntz traveled to Rajasthan, where she spent two years conducting the research to develop the agricultural protocol that TM would then recommend to the senna farmers. Eleanor had studied herbal medicine with Rosemary Gladstar, but her professional background was in the population biology of plants.

Eleanor organized a series of tests with the farmers to demonstrate how weeding could improve yield and, in turn, bring the farmers more money. She also studied the effect of shifting the harvesting time. She directed some farmers to harvest senna before flowering, and others after flowering. Together they measured the weight differences. She calculated the extra amount of money the farmers would make from harvesting after flowering, when the volumes were greater but the sennocides were lower, compared with harvesting before flowering. TM would pay a premium price to cover that difference. After seeing the results, the farmers agreed to harvest the senna earlier. There was a double benefit. Not only would they receive a higher price per pound, but by harvesting a month earlier, they reduced the risk of losing the plants in the event of drought, disease, or other problems.

TM made other changes as well. To make weeding and harvesting easier, they convinced the farmers to begin planting seeds at consistent spacing in rows, rather than simply casting the seeds into the fields by hand. The TM staff developed a system for sorting and selecting seeds from plants with consistently higher sennosides. "This seems like very simple agricultural practices to implement," Drake told me. "But it is very hard to get people to change old habits."

At the time of this writing, about eight years after Eleanor started her research, the senna that farmers are growing for Traditional Medicinals is two and a half times more potent than when they started. The farmers are meeting Good Agricultural and Collection Practice (GACP) standards and teaching these practices to other farmers. TM pays a 15 to 20 percent premium above the open market prices because producing senna to the company's specifications takes more work on the farmers' part.

Because of the work TM has done with farmers, the company with which TM works in Germany now also reaps the benefits of raw material with higher sennocides than can be found on the open market. The company thus needs less raw material to produce the level of sennocides desired in finished products. This means less raw material needs to be stored, shipped, and processed. Less raw material passes through the company's processing equipment, which reduces production costs and wear and tear on machinery. Lower production costs have in turn increased profits, a portion of which both companies, TM and their German partner, invest back into the senna communities. And lower production costs mean that the company can pay more to the farmers without increasing the price of the finished product.[6]

In their initial meetings with senna farmers, Nioma and Drake committed to work with the farmers to improve their senna, to pay a premium for high-quality material, and to make social investments in their communities. But they would do this only if the male farmers agreed to implement women's empowerment measures and allow girls to attend school. While working in Nepal and studying anthropology, I had always been hesitant to impose my own perspective, believing instead that it was better to respect cultural diversity. Yet I was impressed with Nioma and Drake's clarity and directness and I wondered if whether *how* an opinion was expressed—whether it was done with respect—in fact mattered as much as the content.

By this time we had arrived at the school, a one-story structure that looked like rural schools in developing countries around the world: an L-shaped building that contained a series of fifteen-by-fifteen-foot classrooms. Boys and girls dressed in tunics of the same tan color as the walls of the school stood arm's length from one another in the courtyard of packed red sand. Through a translator Drake and Nioma introduced Steve, Julia, and me to the group, and then the children began their morning prayers, a series of chants they sang by heart.

Following the prayers, the children went to class. In each classroom thirty to forty children crammed shoulder-to-shoulder on long, flat cushions on the floor. I watched as Nioma stood in front of the class, smiling, and said, "Remember the game I taught you yesterday?" She began to play rock paper scissors with individual children. Drake and Steve joined in. I stood to the side, unsure what to do. The children were transfixed by Nioma. I was, too. This visit was the first time I had met her, and I was immediately struck by how at home and present she was, not only with these students, but with everyone I had seen her greet.

Finishing a few games of rock paper scissors, Drake, Nioma, and Steve moved on to the next classroom, where they repeated their performance.

Later, as we stood outside in the school courtyard, Drake told me they needed to expand the school. It had been built based on the number of children expected to attend, but once the school had been built, more children showed up, and then even more after that. One class has to meet outside in the courtyard until an additional room is added on. And thus the meeting Drake and Nioma had attended the previous evening—to continue the process of acquiring more land for classrooms.

Good for People, Good for Business

As we traveled to the next stop, Drake told me how he became involved in what was essentially rural development work in the communities where he was sourcing botanicals from around the world. After his first visit to the lemongrass fields in Guatemala, he began visiting additional supply communities. If a village had schools and teachers but no books, Traditional Medicinals itself supplied books or whatever was needed. In the early days they didn't know whether their efforts would be effective; they just felt they had to do something.

As I listened, I looked out the jeep window at all the shades of brown in the landscape. I'm used to New England and its lush, green trees. I wasn't prepared for this landscape—the sun radiated off the brick houses made of a combination of sand and mud with cow dung, which faded into the brown earth. The leaves on the few trees were covered in dust, adding texture rather than color to the overall landscape of brown. I later found out that the previous May, in 2016, Phalodi held the record for the highest verified temperature recorded in India (124 degrees Fahrenheit).

Drake continued talking, bringing my attention back inside the jeep. "Herb supply communities are in some of the poorest areas of the world. It makes good business sense that we do something to address that, not just for the sustainability of the supply chain but also because it is the right thing to do."

While in his twenties, Drake came across Paramahansa Yogananda's book *Autobiography of a Yogi*. He told me, "I began to study Yogananda's teaching, which is all about right living—practical advice like *Do it this way, organize your life like this*." He began to think about the concept of right livelihood. "Yogananda also wrote about right living and conduct of business and how business should follow a righteous spiritual path. I became inspired by this notion of connecting business with right livelihood, right discipline, and right thinking using business as a vehicle for social change. Herbalism was secondary for me. Primary was using business as a way to do social good. That's what I was interested in, and in creating jobs," Drake said. "Solving social issues in supply communities was important," he added, "because it made good business sense."

Most commodity networks are called supply chains, a phrase that evokes an image of metal chains, each link connected to the link immediately above or below but not to any others. It's not a very resilient model, nor does it represent the reality very accurately. The difference is not only a matter of language. How we describe the flow of commodities shapes what we see and value and what we ignore. We see the product, senna in this case, and not the context or webs of relationships in which the senna is grown and processed. A chain cannot convey viriditas, the aliveness of plants. Jeff Bodony and Lizzie Matteson's work as herb growers at Viriditas Gardens was not to feed a supply chain but rather to nurture the conditions that allow the ecosystem's greenness to thrive. The output of herbs to sell was only part of their reckoning; they produced enough to meet Heron Botanicals' orders. But they focused first on feeding and stewarding aliveness, which they believed ultimately created better medicine. In the same way, Drake and Nioma focused on doing what they could to support the aliveness of the community—and to do so by supporting the lives of women. By paying attention to the process, they believed they would produce a better product.

The work done by Traditional Medicinals Foundation differs from community to community. In Rajasthan they focus on providing water and education. In Bosnia they work with women who are still impacted by the lingering trauma of the Bosnian War. In Poland they are working to find solutions to the challenge of aging collectors. In Hungary they are working to support the social well-being of the Roma communities who suffer up to 70 percent unemployment. The key, Drake said, is to be adaptable to the situation.

My visit to Rajasthan was packed from the moment I arrived, with encounters intentionally created to offer insight into the lives of men, women, and children in the desert villages. The quality of these encounters was possible only because of the quality of the relationships Drake, the Revive staff, and especially Nioma had developed with these communities.

Later that afternoon I visited the home of Pushpa, the head of a self-help group, with Nioma, Emily, Amelia, and the new staff member of WomenServe. From the project's beginning, Nioma insisted that Revive focus on empowering women in the communities. Women's self-help groups, a model popular in micro-credit community development, are key to this. Several women gathered in the mud-floored room of Pushpa's house. They wore bright-colored shirts and floor-length skirts—pinks and reds, with gauzy dark pink or red scarves on their heads, which they would occasionally pull over their face, especially, it seemed to me, when they felt shy. The land was so flat and brown. The pinks and reds of the women's clothing were a welcome respite.

Pushpa was lovely and tiny, half hidden behind her veil as we sat cross-legged on the mud floor. She is a village health worker who distributes medicines, assists in births, and helps with vaccines and hygiene and at the schools. As a self-help group leader, she motivates women—mothers, daughters, and daughters-in-law—to come to meetings. Each woman who wishes to attend must contribute 100 rupees a month. The women then take turns receiving a loan from their shared savings. Pushpa has organized two groups so far. Manali, the local fieldworker for Revive, TMF's partner organization in Rajasthan, told me that everyone trusted Pushpa, and that she was a real leader. If people don't come to the meeting, she'll call them to come. Two women in her group had taken loans for 18,000 rupees that they then paid back with 1 percent interest. One had used the money to buy a breeding goat. One goat will lead to fifty goats, Pushpa explained. The other woman used it for a flour mill.

At the monthly meetings, women talk about hygiene and how to use their savings. But mostly they gossip. The other women in the room, sitting shoulder-to-shoulder along one side of the room, nodded in agreement and said that was their favorite part of the meetings.

"We hardly get a chance to get together," they said, laughing. "We have to gossip."

Through the translator, I asked Pushpa what difference being involved with the Revive Project made for her. Without hesitating she said, "Confidence."

Younger girls, dressed in skirts and white shirts rather than traditional Rajasthani dress, gathered in the room to listen. Nioma asked what they thought of their mothers going to the self-help group meetings. One replied that she was happy her mother was working. The others nodded.

I asked the young girls sitting around the edges of the room what difference the self-help groups made for their mothers, "They are more confident," they said in unison. Nioma said that the biggest changes she has seen since her first visit to this village is that the girls speak up with louder voices. They have more confidence as well.

We went into another room with a cook fire on the floor in the corner. Women and younger girls crowded into the room to watch Pushpa demonstrate chapati making. As the guest, Pushpa told me, I should be the first to learn. She quickly showed me how to knead and roll out the dough on a round board and then drop it onto the steel chapati pan. She moved it around with her fingers, flipped it a few times, and was done. Then it was my turn. Surrounded by a crowd of women and girls who had grown up making this simple dish, I self-consciously started kneading. What looked so easy, wasn't at all. I kneaded it too thickly and then too thinly. Pushpa reprimanded me each time with a "tsk tsk" and a quick demonstration about how to do it correctly. Finally rolling the dough to her satisfaction, I put it on the pan and then flipped it too soon or too late. Pushpa, who had seemed so meek and shy behind her scarf, tsk tsk'd again. After a few more attempts, I gave up, gratefully relinquishing my spot to Nioma, who made a chapati perfectly, with no instructions. When we all praised her, she said, simply, "That's because I lived here in a past life."

Following the Heart

Drake told me that Rajasthan felt like a second home to him. He added that it felt like a first home to Nioma. Nioma later told me that she loves the landscape of Rajasthan. When she is old, she wants to live in an apartment in Jodhpur, she added.

While Emily, Amelia and I wore kurtas over lightweight pants (the typical attire worn by foreign women who wished to be respectful of social norms in rural India), Nioma wore the traditional rural Rajasthan dress. The clothing looked cumbersome and hot, but she didn't seem to mind. Each time we arrived at a school, farm, home, or community center, Nioma walked directly to the women, gripped their hands, and looked them in the eye as she said hello. An interpreter translated, but Nioma spoke directly to the women, not to the translator. If the interpreter hesitated, Nioma would say firmly, "Tell them. Translate that."

I later commented on her directness. "I am direct," she agreed. "That's how I get my way."

As we rode back to the hotel after our visit to Pushpa's home, I asked Nioma how she'd started doing this work. She explained that her parents were nomadic isolationists, a term I'd never heard before. Her family had moved house more than six times before she reached age twelve. She hadn't attended school as a child, even though that was what she wanted to do more than anything. That was why she identified with the illiterate women and girls in the farming villages and wanted to do everything she could to help them have the chance to go to school.

Once TM had decided to work in the region, Nioma said, TMF hired Emily to do a baseline survey of community needs. What she found simply confirmed what Nioma and Drake saw on that first trip—they had to provide water security first. Only then could they begin trying to improve agricultural practices. TMF addressed water issues by reclaiming *naadis*, the traditional watering holes, which had filled up with silt. Like many development projects, TMF requires a village contribution, typically in the form of labor, to make sure the community is invested in the project. But as was the case in Phalodi, it can be challenging to get people to participate at first when they have no evidence of the benefits. "This is a poor part of rural India," Emily explained. NGOs had come before with plans and then not followed through, and so villagers didn't trust that TM was any different. Yet as a few individuals stepped forward to participate, others began to see the differences TMF and the Revive Project were making, and they came forward to participate, too.

The second afternoon of my visit, I joined Nioma and the interpreter to meet with a woman, Goga Udavan, who had received a *taanka* (an underground rainwater catchment for individual households) a year ago. We were led inside a small mud house to a bare, mud-floored room with one open window. We sat cross-legged on mats on the floor with Goga and her five children (three girls and two boys), ages nine to fifteen. Nioma asked her when her children had started school and what grade they were in. Goga said she realized it would be good for them to go to school and they'd all just started this past year. They were shy because they are older than others in their class, but she said they were all treated equally.

Before the taanka was installed, the closest water source was a half-hour trek. Goga said she would take five trips a day, one hour for a round trip. She made the trips with her oldest daughter, who was sitting quietly by her mother. She and her daughter would wake at 4 AM for the first trip. Her days went like this, she said: wake, get water, eat, get water, cook, get water, clean, get water, and finally go to sleep at 9 PM before beginning the day again, waking before dawn, worrying about getting water. Her body ached, she said, but she had had no choice. That was her life, every day for twenty years.

Goga now wakes at 7 AM and goes to sleep at 7 PM. She takes a daily bath. And she works eight months of the year in the fields for hire, making 300 rupees a day.

As Nioma continued talking with Goga, it came out that most of that money was handed over to her husband, who was addicted to opium.

Nioma asked whether Goga's husband wanted to stop using opium.

"No," Goga answered.

"It must be so hard for you," Nioma said, leaning forward, looking Goga in the eye.

She nodded. She said her husband gets angry when he doesn't have opium.

"So it is better when he has it?" Nioma asked.

"Yes," Goga said.

Her daughter, just as lovely as her mother, sat quietly, not saying anything. She married a year ago but often comes back to see her mother. She stays for fifteen days or so; her in-laws don't mind, Goga said.

Nioma encouraged her to join a self-help group. Then she would have the resources for herself. She would need to bring 100 rupees a month as dues, Nioma said. Could she do that? Goga nodded and said that yes, she'd fight to get the money. She said she didn't have family close by, but she did have friends. Nioma asked who her best friend was. Her daughter, Goga said. Goga's daughter smiled and nodded slightly.

Later in the day I asked Nioma how she decided what projects to support and focus on and how to implement them when she did. We were now sitting on the edge of a circle of about fifteen women who were learning how to embroider a turquoise blue design on a square of white muslin. This was one of two pilot groups to teach traditional handicrafts, both to keep the practices alive and to impart marketable skills to the women and young girls. The session was being held at the community center, which had been built with funds provided by TM's German partner. No one except me seemed bothered by the temperature. The women focused on their work. This session was part of the beginning stages of the training. A woman trainer with experience selling crafts to an international market had come to the village from the capital city, Jaipur (340 miles away). The trainer taught groups of three women the embroidery pattern, which had been made by a designer in Delhi. They worked in small groups to ensure the women understood what to do. When the program first began, the women would take the squares home to finish, Nioma said, but the fabric often ended up dirty or was eaten by goats. The Revive Project has since set up a room in this building with sewing machines where the women come to do the work, which probably makes it more enjoyable and also keeps the squares clean.

Watching the women intently stitching, Nioma answered my question. "I guess I mostly follow my heart. I didn't have an education. I don't have a PhD, or even a GED. I wasn't trained in this work. I just follow my heart."

I've never seen a development worker interact with villagers the way Nioma does—holding their hands, asking them questions directly, looking in their eyes, and listening to their answers. She is determined and focused and very caring. She follows up on what she learns, and she makes things happen. The interpreter later told me that Nioma cares for everyone as a mother. If someone is sick, she brings them medicine. "She shows up and she follows up."

I was especially struck by how the young girls watched Nioma. They followed every move she made. Their faces lit up when she turned to speak to them—even more so when she reached for their hands and gazed into their eyes. Nioma understands the power of her charisma and she uses it to accomplish the things she believes are important.

As our conversation with Goga came to an end, Goga lay down on the mat. She wasn't feeling well, she said. Nioma commented to me in English that Goga's willingness to lie down was a sign of how comfortable she felt talking to us. Goga exclaimed that she was so thankful for Nioma: She now can have water from a taanka and stay here at home.

Nioma said she was glad about that and that she just had one thing to ask of her. She wanted Goga to do something for herself and join the self-help group. Goga nodded and said she would.

As we walked out of the compound, I saw her husband, squatting against the mud wall, looking vacantly into the desert.

Driving back to the hotel in the jeep, windows opened because the air conditioner in this jeep wasn't working, hot desert air blowing in, I asked Nioma what kinds of things she worries about. "When I go to sleep, I see the faces of the girls," she said. "Especially the girls who had to drop out of school. And I feel like I failed them. And then I think, *I need to get to the next group, need to do what I can to keep them in school.*"

The interpreter commented, "The project is so successful because people consider Nioma like family. She is a very observant person and what she doesn't understand, she asks."

I asked Nioma what most satisfied her about the project. She shook her head. "I'm not satisfied with anything," she answered. She said that

Drake encourages her to see what she has accomplished, but she instead only sees how much more there is to do.

––––––––––

Eleanor, who had worked closely with Nioma while in India, said this: "The project is successful because of Nioma. It's her vision—she can see beyond what is right there, she creates a heart connection with people. We should all be able to do that, but we can't. She creates that and she goes back and then she does it again.

"There are a lot of difficult men," Eleanor added. "And Nioma still manages to have real conversations with them. She'll say, 'You think this way and I think that way and we can still walk down this road together and go on this journey.'"

To illustrate her point, Eleanor described one man in the community who had a very strong sense of, as she put it, *Why should I water my neighbor's garden?* Which meant, Eleanor explained, *Why should I care about my daughter's education if I am giving her away in marriage?*

"But through the Revive Project, his daughter got a bike and began going to school," Eleanor said. "And then as he saw the changes in his daughter, he slowly changed his mind, which brought him around to the whole project. And Nioma made that happen.

"The Revive Project shows the importance of addressing the human dimensions of this work," Eleanor continued. She went on to say that Nioma and the Revive or WomenServe staff take the time to meet with the villagers and talk with them about their lives and challenges. "The message of these conversations is: *You matter to me. Your troubles matter. If your troubles are less, my troubles will also be less as the buyer of your senna.* It isn't about doing the projects to meet some metrics or to tell a good story on their website or to put it on their label. They are doing it because of this human connection."

––––––––––

In 2000 TM set a twenty-five-year goal to establish a sustainable supply chain. They picked twenty-five years, Josef Brinckmann explained to me, as a way to acknowledge how hard that will be. "It was our way of saying, this is hard work, but we are going to do it. And we are interested in *really* doing it. We really wanted to ask—what does it mean to have a sustainable supply chain? It's not something that can be done quickly."

The company recognized that unless they took action to invest in sourcing and source communities, at some point the crops their business depends on would run out. Rather than continuing to search for new suppliers, TM decided to invest in the places where they were already sourcing their materials to ensure that the supply doesn't give out— because on the most basic level, that kind of investment makes good business sense. But it has never been only about business.

Nioma and Drake set up the Traditional Medicinals Foundation to demonstrate that working in the communities where they source herbs is a valuable and necessary risk mitigation strategy. The more resilient the communities are that supply the herbs, the healthier their supply chains. This is a fundamentally different approach to thinking about sourcing and supply chains. Rather than only focusing on improving the constituents in a crop or even more broadly improving the quality of the field, they start with the belief that that field is only as healthy as the overall community within which the farm is located. "If TM wants a sustainable supply of senna in ten years," Drake told me, "the whole community needs to be thriving. If they don't have water, if girls aren't in schools, what kind of sustainable community health is that?"

TMF conceives of its work as a path to ensuring a supply of better-quality senna, Emily added, "But sometimes you don't even really know the outcome until later."

I asked for an example.

Drake told a story about a small school in a remote region. They needed a school for 140 children. TM offered to build the school if the community donated the land. In response two neighbors agreed to each contribute some property for the school. Two years later during his speech at the opening ceremony, Drake had recognized the families for donating the land. Later, one of the members of the community approached Drake. "He said, you think that the most important thing that happened is that we have a school now and education is happening for children," Drake recalled, "but something much more important than that occurred."

The man then explained that the two men who had donated the land were from two very different castes and this was a divided caste community. Though the men were neighbors, they never spoke or cooperated on anything. Their decision to come together to help build a community school marked the beginning of a new era of community collaboration and cooperation. Because two children of these landowners attended school, each of a different caste, other children began attending as well. The man explained that people of both castes also dug out the *naadi* together. Now mixed castes are taking water from the same source. The school and water security are significant benefits to the community, but what really happened was a breakthrough in the caste system.

"That's how it goes," Drake said. "There are often unintended consequences that happen with this work. Things happen as the result of something we didn't intend, or outcomes that are much greater than our intentions."

I asked Drake what he looked for when he first arrived in a community—how he found people he could rely on and trust. He said, "Over time, the appropriate leaders emerge, the kinds of people who are not just there for themselves. You just have to be patient, not be too quick to make decisions about things, and let the game unfold and come to you."

On the last day we attended a celebration at the new storage center and community hall where we had met the previous day for the sewing project. A teacher stepped to the microphone and said, "Before the Revive Project, we didn't know what social responsibility was. We only thought about ourselves. We didn't think about our community or anything beyond our own needs and family. But then you came, and we saw what social responsibility means. Without society, we are zero." He paused and then ended, "I assure you that from now on we will do our best for our community."

The speech led me to think about how plants are more effective at helping to retain soil moisture when they have larger leaves that provide more cover. This in turn can change the conditions for the better for plants that grow in that soil in the future. Emily and the other TMF staff would be the first to admit their work isn't perfect and that much more needs to be done. But they have made a start. Beyond the beneficial changes in the communities themselves, TMF's actions are changing the conversation about how companies source raw materials. They are demonstrating that investments in supply communities in the herb industry are good for business. Their actions have repercussions far beyond producing a high-quality cup of Smooth Move tea—though that cup of tea can be the vehicle for those transformations.

Radical Engagement and Trust

Storytelling has been one of the engines of capitalism from the start. Cinnamon, cloves, pepper, and nutmeg were desirable in the Age of Discovery in part because sellers convinced buyers that those spices *were* desirable. In the current era of global capitalism, so-called socially responsible companies construct the images of their good work as carefully as any conventional company plans its advertising campaign. Companies that advocate transparency don't provide complete transparency. Only certain stories make the cut—of happy farmers, healthy soils, earnest stewardship of the land, traceability of every product, and, increasingly, of carbon sequestration and climate change mitigation. It can sound too good to be true, and so usually I believe that the claims *are* too good to be true. The stories that corporate marketing departments tend to tell, like the Neuralgine placards hanging from the side of Weiss and Diebold's horse-drawn wagons, typically skip over the exceptions and the complexity that are inevitably part of global supply networks.

I set out on this journey to make visible the invisible relations behind the finished products, to see behind the marketing claims on a product label. While on my visit to Rajasthan, I perhaps saw more deeply into the broader community than anywhere I visited. And yet during that trip, what I saw and didn't see, what I heard and didn't hear, was more managed than it had been during any other site visit. Nevertheless, as I flew back to southern India to rejoin Terry and Bryce, I realized that my experience observing the TMF project had far exceeded my expectations, despite the structuring of the experience, in contrast with many others that had fallen short of my hopes. Which made me reflect on transparency and on my own expectations.

Like much of conscious capitalism, the premise is that buying a product produced by a so-called ethical company is a way to support the commitments of that company and avoid being complicit in the negative impacts of a capitalist economic system. Yet purchasing the products of an economic system based on growth can never be a complete and effective way to solve the problems created by growth. It is disingenuous as a company to make that promise and naive as a consumer to expect it is possible. Even so, as I saw in Rajasthan, sometimes buying products can provide resources that make possible encounters that are the seeds of transformation. In other words, buying the product isn't necessarily the significant act that companies may claim it to be. It may be one way of beginning, but for our purchase to lead to more actions and have a greater meaning, companies need to let us see more than a nicely packaged story.

Yet framing it this way—that we either buy or not—limits the actions we can take. What if we reframe the question to consider the political and economic structures that shape those choices in the first place? And to ask whether it is possible for a company to be socially and ecologically responsible in an economic system that is not? Put another way, can a company be ethical in an economic structure that is unethical? And is it possible to change that structure from within? If so, we can ask what a company is doing to change those larger economic structures to be truly in service of humanity and the earth. We can then ask how we can support these efforts, through our purchasing power but in other ways as well. It is not enough for a company simply to wish to change the world; that company has to commit to the hard work of actually trying to change that world, which unfolds in its day-to-day decision making.

Of all the companies I visited while filming for the Sustainable Herbs Program, only Sebastian Pole allowed us to attend a sourcing visit with cameras rolling. He wasn't worried about what our footage would show, he said. "If you look in someone's refrigerator, or around the sink, I doubt everyone has got that perfect. We're very idealistic in our expectations. And that's potentially a reflection of our distance from—not our closeness to—nature." The closer you are, the more complications become apparent, the more difficult it is to distinguish things as either right or wrong, black or white.

What if companies were to share more about the behind-the-scenes decision making, to trust their customers, as Sebastian trusted Terry and me with our camera, to see those complications, sharing stories that offer the depth and nuance needed to grasp the challenges company managers must cope with day after day? And what, in turn, would be our responsibility as their customers in return for that trust?

It seems reasonable to expect companies to reveal the sources of the raw materials in the products they sell, as well as the impacts that our purchases have on the communities that grow and collect those raw materials. But it also seems reasonable that consumers should not rush to judgment or have unrealistically high expectations if they are unwilling to learn about and accept the real complexities of sourcing botanicals. If we consumers could instead see ourselves as partners with herbal product companies—working together to solve really tough problems—could that deeper level of engagement offer some of the very healing we seek to experience by using herbal medicines? And in turn, what if companies treat the buyers of their products as citizens of a shared world, not simply as consumers to whom they hope to sell another product? Such a shift requires a significant, even radical, level of engagement and trust between consumers and business. It requires understanding that buying may be one way to bring about change, but it will never be enough to expect buying to be the *only* engagement necessary to bring about change. It is not an admonishment not to buy. It is a charge to take responsibility to learn and understand the ways our purchases do and do not make a difference. And not stopping there.

CHAPTER TEN

Conservation as Livelihood

If we choose to use plants as our medicine, we then become
accountable for the wild gardens, their health, and their upkeep.

—ROSEMARY GLADSTAR

*J*ayant Sarnaik picked up Terry, Bryce, and me one morning at a
guesthouse on a busy side street in Pune, Maharashtra. Jayant
is co-founder of the Applied Environmental Research Foundation
(AERF), a stakeholder in a FairWild implementation project. His turquoise T-shirt read CONSERVATION LEADERSHIP PROGRAMME, an award
he had received in 2016 for his conservation work in the North Western
Ghats. Jayant has dedicated his life to protecting the biodiverse forests
of the Western Ghats. He grew up in Pune, Jayant told us as we sat
in a massive traffic jam of cars, trucks, jeeps, and motorcycles on the
single-lane road heading out of town.

"It wasn't the same city then. It was a wonderful place when I grew
up. Now it is a mess," he said, shaking his head and gesturing out the
front window to the chaos on the road and the shabby buildings crowded
on the roadsides. Pune, which is near the western coast, is one of the few
cities in India that does not have a water problem, he told us, and so
everyone is moving there.

Jayant answered questions with a full stop, closing the conversation
until I asked another, which he would then answer, again with a full stop.
Serious and focused, he often wore an expression that seemed to convey
dissatisfaction or disapproval. But as I came to learn over the next five
days, Jayant lives immersed in questions of the environment—and he
lives in India, where there is no distance between human actions and

the devastation of the plants and ecosystems he has dedicated his life to protecting. It's easy to understand why he has an intense focus on his work and an unremitting sense of urgency.

We had come to Pune to film two flagship FairWild projects introduced in the state of Maharashtra related to collection of haritaki and bibhitaki fruit. Haritaki and bibhitaki are two of the three fruits used in triphala, one of the most well-known Ayurvedic formulas, popular for its ability to cleanse and balance the systems of the body. Bibhitaki and haritaki trees are being widely cut down for use as lumber, and the goal of the projects is to make the standing trees more valuable than the lumber and, thus, to protect the biodiversity of the Western Ghats.

Earlier that month I had interviewed an elderly botanist at an office at the botanical garden for Arya Vaidya Pharmacy (AVP), one of the oldest and leading Ayurvedic companies. While most people I met on this project were introduced to me by their first name only, this botanist was universally referred to as Dr. Vasuduran. He had retired from teaching and now advised AVP on quality control, particularly in ensuring that raw material was correctly identified. He was soft-spoken and kind. We spoke in English. After speaking for a few minutes about how he found both Ayurveda and biomedicine to be useful, he paused and said, "I am in a delicate position now, because I cannot open my heart before you." I wasn't sure how to respond, so I stayed quiet. After a moment, he continued, and he did open his heart. "Really, I feel sorry for the fate of Ayurveda. For hundreds and hundreds and hundreds of years, we have been protected by Ayurveda. It is a system based not on experiments but on experience and we have used it to our benefit. But now the future is not very bright." He spoke so quietly, I had to lean close to hear his words.

"Ayurveda has been commercialized. And that should not have been done," he said. "What is the main aim of the industry?" he asked, rhetorically.

I answered, tentatively, "Money?"

He nodded. "That tells you everything. The aim of an industry is always to make money."

Many medicinal plant species have almost disappeared from India, he said. He didn't provide a more specific number, likely because no one really knows. "Simply disappeared," he repeated. The land along the west coast of India in the North Western Ghats, where I later traveled with Jayant, is classified as forest. "But if you want to see a natural forest, you would have to search for days," Dr. Vasuduran said, noting that the total forested area of the region is now only 10 to 12 percent. The same forces destroying forests throughout the world—population growth, agricultural encroachment, road construction, urban sprawl, as well as the voracious appetite of the Ayurveda industry—were destroying the forests in the Western Ghats.

"What we have lost is lost forever," he said. He looked out through the smudged window to the jungle of medicinal plants in the botanical garden, the plants wizened and covered in dust from the lack of rain.

"So now people are learning to live without contact with the earth or the sky. They are constructing multistory apartment buildings thirty to forty stories high and living inside. They aren't touching the soil. They aren't seeing the sky. No wonder they are getting diseases."

As much as 80 percent, or even more, of Indian medicinal plants on the market are sourced from the wild. By volume, around 72 percent of the herbs used in commerce are harvested from meadows, forests, riverbanks, and roadsides, but there is very little accounting of population density or quantities harvested.[1] "Why haven't these large companies done more about conservation?" medical anthropologist Unnikrishnan Payyappalli asked when I met with him in his small apartment in downtown Chennai, the capital city of Tamil Nadu. "The success of their business depends on it. Yet very few have done anything to address or ensure that their businesses have the resources they need to survive." Unni's wife, agro-economist M. S. Suneetha, took part in our discussion, too. Her research has also focused on medicinal plant supply networks in India, and she commented that many companies could no longer make certain products because those plants are no longer available. "They always just thought, *Oh we will find the plants somewhere else*. And now they can't find them. No one has been paying attention to the signs."

Ben Heron first came to India in 2000 to study woodcarving and painting in the state of Himachal Pradesh in Western Himalaya. He gradually became involved in environmental conservation initiatives and organic farming, because he realized those issues were more pressing than learning to paint. He focused especially on medicinal plants, many of which were threatened or endangered, but were still being dug and sold to the industry. With a group of Indians from the area, he developed a program to cultivate some of these plants. Through this work, he met Sebastian Pole. Seb asked Ben whether he would to try to cultivate medicinal species. It took Ben several years to even find some of those species, let alone figure out how to grow them. At the same time, Ben also began visiting Pukka's suppliers to work on training them in WHO's Good Agricultural and Collection Practices (GACP). After a few years, Seb hired him as Pukka's sustainable herbs manager.

Ultimately, Ben came to realize that conservation has to be driven by financial incentives. And for there to be financial incentives, he said, there needs to be enterprise. "When Pukka sells teas in supermarkets, we're really raising funds for conservation. And that's an exciting conservation strategy. It's not just about doing business. It is about merging the two worlds. I came into business from conservation, and the business [Pukka] has also come into conservation from the same ethics, the same values."

Once Ben changed from working through a nonprofit model funded by grants to an enterprise model at Pukka, he found that his relationship with villagers in Himachal Pradesh shifted. "Before, people would ask me, 'How much money have you eaten?' and accuse me and other program staff of 'lining our bellies with money,'" he recalled. When he came in as an employee of Pukka, though, "We were no longer seen as eating money," Ben said. "We were seen as *investing* money. Our relationship with the community changed overnight. It was a massive shift. They trusted us far more when we were operating as a for-profit company because that's how everyone operates in a day-to-day business, whether selling a bottle of milk or medicinal plants."

Balancing Growth and Drain

Overharvesting of wild-collected plants has become a significant problem for some medicinal species. One way to protect wild plants is to bring them into cultivation, and most herbal companies prefer to source cultivated material to ensure a continuous and uniform supply of a particular species.[2] But cultivated plants require significant investments and inputs and must still compete on the market with wild-harvested plants, which require little more than a collector's labor and so can be sold at much lower prices. Thus companies must find long-term solutions for sustainably sourcing wild-harvested plants.

Ben and Josef Brinckmann and others who work directly with wild collectors around the world also recognize that cultivation doesn't address the problem of livelihood for the collectors. Shifting to cultivation is only one solution to the problem of overharvesting. It isn't *the* solution, Ben told me. Those who harvest wild plants typically live on the margins of society. They don't have access to land to grow their own crops, and they also lack other economic opportunities. Unless collectors are presented with another source of income, they will continue to collect wild plants, which means that the problem of overharvesting from the wild may continue, even though those species are now also in cultivation. "If people can be provided with financial incentives to preserve biodiversity, well, that's the ultimate answer, because the need for income is their ultimate concern," Ben said.

Germany is one of the larger importers of medicinal plants worldwide. In the early 2000s the head of the plant conservation division of the German Federal Agency for Nature Conservation, Uwe Schippmann, decided that Germany had a unique responsibility to measure and verify the sustainability of the plants it used. But he wasn't sure what the most effective approach might be. The German Federal Agency for Nature Conservation decided to provide funding to develop sustainability standards. In conjunction with the World Wildlife Fund, TRAFFIC, and International Union for Conservation of Nature, a group of conservationists, academics, herbalists, and industry representatives set out to design those standards.[3]

The challenge of making wild collection sustainable is twofold, Uwe explained to me when we met at the BioFach trade show in Germany in 2019. First you need a method to determine how much can be harvested from the wild without damaging populations in the long run.[4] "It takes work and resources, but it is possible to figure this out," Uwe said.

Then, once a quota is set, the second challenge is how to enforce the quota; ease of enforcement depends on whether a country has effective control bodies. Ease of enforcement also depends on whether collectors have legal rights to the resource. In many regions of the world, resource rights are not clearly spelled out and so they are difficult to enforce.

"A question that has followed me through my career is when to start to be worried," Uwe said. "We start to worry when there is a boom in trade." Uwe gave the example of pelargonium, a species that grows primarily in South Africa. A product on the market using pelargonium became popular in Germany in the early 2000s. Researchers knew the pelargonium was from wild sources. "As a biologist you start asking, is that good for the species?" Uwe told me. As they studied the plant, though, they discovered that it grows in very dense, limy soil, and it is very difficult to dig the roots, which are quite brittle, out of the ground. When the roots are hacked at and pulled, the rhizomes break. "When I understood that that is the case," Uwe said, "I immediately relaxed, because that is an in-built sustainability element—nobody can dig out the whole plant all the time. Some part will always remain and regrow."

For species that don't regenerate so readily, determining the impact of harvesting on trade is more complicated. To do so, you need to understand what foresters call growth and drain. How much biomass is being taken out of the forest relative to how much is regrowing? To determine how much is growing back, you need information on species populations, density, and rate of regeneration. This kind of detailed information about wild populations of medicinal herbs simply isn't available, and neither is information on what quantities are already being harvested. Also, as Uwe pointed out, the amount of plant materials that can be safely harvested varies by species. In the case of pelargonium, harvesting the root is not necessarily a problem. But for plants such as goldenseal, which doesn't easily regenerate on its own, there is a greater risk from overharvesting.

In the early 2000s, companies were claiming that the herbs in their products were "ethically wildcrafted," but without supporting data on plant populations, distribution, and regeneration rate, those claims didn't mean much. The certified organic standards for wild products did require that the plants are harvested from designated, certified areas where chemicals have not been applied. But these organic regulations were vague about the requirements for collection methods (in terms of site requirements, traceability, and resource management protocols to ensure sustainability), and thus there was variation in how reliably the standards ensured that wild plants were not being overharvested.

"I was tired of seeing products in the market that said 'ethically wildcrafted,'" Josef once told me. "When I'd ask how they verified that, by what standards, companies couldn't answer. Had they done a full survey of the collection area over many years? Do they have statistics on regrowth? Do they know how much has been taken out? Or the effect of harvest on related species? No one had any evidence. It's as if I was supposed to trust the claims because ethical wildcrafting was cool."

Josef was invited to join the group called the International Standard for Sustainable Wild Collection of Medicinal and Aromatic Plants (ISSC-MAP) as a representative from industry; this was the group that rose out of the work that Uwe and others began in Germany. At first they focused primarily on biodiversity and sustainable harvesting. Yet, the members recognized that cultural diversity and ecological diversity are interconnected. And so in 2008, ISSC-MAP merged with an initiative led by the Swiss in cooperation with other NGOs to develop a standard that addressed fair trade and accountability in the collection of wild species for the herbal supply chain. The new initiative was called the FairWild Standard, which combines the essential elements of both standards, covering ecological, social, and economic issues.[5] The FairWild Foundation was established to promote and implement the Standard.

The FairWild Standard forces companies to ask—and answer—questions such as: What is the population of the target species? What are the amounts of destructive harvesting? What is the rate of reproduction if harvesting sustainably? Will a stand of the target species be able to regenerate if 20 percent is harvested, or 40 percent, or 80 percent? It also asks how collectors are treated. Are they paid a fair wage? FairWild certified plants are sold to traders for a higher base price than plants from the open market. Also, as described earlier, FairWild certified collectors receive a premium fund, which they jointly then decide how to allocate.

Because of the complexity of the certification, companies began by figuring out how to certify well-studied species that weren't threatened. As with certifying dandelion at Runo, the idea of protecting bibhitaki and haritaki trees is to provide a financial incentive to promote biodiversity more broadly, in this case in the Western Ghats. That's the theory, in any case, Josef said, but "there is always a market for easier standards." The thoroughness required for FairWild certification means it is also a very challenging standard. Pukka and Traditional Medicinals are the two biggest champions of FairWild; few other companies have taken it on.

Sebastian told me that the difficulties aren't simply because of what the standards demand, but because documenting the sustainability of wild plants is extremely challenging. And then auditing those practices is difficult as well. It hasn't been done before. For Pukka, the input of time, staff resources, and finances is worth it, Sebastian concluded.

The human race is on permanent overdraft, Sebastian said. "We think we can spend what we don't have. But that's not how most of us manage our finances. We decide we don't have enough money to go out and so we don't . . . With FairWild, there are checks," he continued. "We check ourselves and our auditors check us. There are controls through the system. You need that because we are a big old population, over seven billion of us, using a lot of the earth's resources.

"As Pukka becomes more successful, the last thing I want is for us to damage the source that we were trying to support and care for in the first place, whether that be the planet or the collector or the herbal tradition. With FairWild, we know that anything we source from the wild is being looked after."

———

Along the route to the FairWild project in the North Western Ghats, even after we had passed through the worst traffic, the road was still crowded with cars, buses, and black auto rickshaws. Horns honked.

Jayant picked up our conversation, saying, "The field of conservation is becoming very challenging. Especially in an open access landscape where no one has clear legal rights to the resources. People have their forest and their aspirations are changing and their value structure is no longer in line with their tradition. That is when you see the rapid degradation of their resources."

The Ayurveda industry isn't concerned about the sustainability of raw materials; their only interest is selling medicine to make money, Jayant said, echoing Dr. Vasuduran's words. "What is going to work to keep the pressure on the forests low and to address people's needs? We have only one common denominator to deal with. That's money," he continued in his somber tone. "Unless there is a monetary gain, people won't be motivated to do anything. We should use that for conservation."

Protecting a Precious Resource

In partnership with the Durrell Institute of Conservation and Ecology (DICE), part of the University of Kent, AERF applied for a Darwin Initiative grant in around 2008 to work to protect sacred groves of giant trees in the Western Ghats, some of the few remaining places with primary old growth. Their proposal was rejected because it lacked a plan for supporting rural livelihoods in the area, and so Jayant contacted the FairWild Foundation, which in turn put him in touch with Ben. The two began to discuss medicinal plant species that might be appropriate for including under FairWild certification. They identified haritaki and bibhitaki.

Triphala is one of the oldest Ayurvedic medicines, Jayant said, and yet few of the users or the manufacturers were aware of where the fruits came from. "They don't know the fruits are borne on large trees that support the nesting sites of giant hornbills, and biodiversity in general, even though this is right here in the Western Ghats. This is in our backyard. That is the level of ignorance we are talking about."

The great hornbill, also called the great pied hornbill, builds nests in natural cavities in the trunks of the bibhitaki trees, many of which grew in the sacred groves AERF was working to protect. Once a pair of hornbills has found a nesting site, they return to the same tree year after year. Yet, these trees were being chopped down to meet the high demand for their valuable timber.

The female hornbill closes herself in the tree cavity for five months to sit on the eggs, Jayant explained. The male hornbill travels in a thirty-kilometer radius from the nest tree to find food, which he then brings to the sequestered female. Known as a forest maker, the male bird eats only the center part of the bibhitaki fruit and then disperses the seeds through his droppings as he travels.

"What is the tiger's role in forest conservation?" Jayant asked rhetorically, and then answered his own question: The tiger likely plays an important role in controlling herbivores, which in turn allows saplings to grow. "Compared to the tiger, the hornbill does much more to save the forest and biodiversity, which is in turn a way to save human life," Jayant said. Protecting the bibhitaki tree by providing a market for its fruit is a crucial way to save the nesting sites of giant hornbills. And so this project is, at its heart, a way to support the natural regeneration of rare and threatened plant species growing in the Western Ghats.

It was important that Jayant had approached FairWild for help, rather than the other way around, Ben said. Although everyone talks about relationships all the time in the herb industry, most of those relationships are top down. "We as a company come in and say, 'This is what we are going to do, this is what the market demands,'" Ben said. Producer groups often look to certification standards such as FairWild as a way to generate more business, he added. This isn't necessarily a bad thing. It becomes problematic, though, when the people behind the project don't have their heart in rising to meet the eco/ethical credentials FairWild requires, when the "promise" of conservation is used simply to attract buyers. In the case of the bibhitaki project, Jayant's passion for conservation provided the energy to fuel the work.

Ben and Jayant spent a year developing plans for a FairWild project that would change the paradigm and make the trees more valuable left standing than they were if cut down. Under their plan, Pukka would buy the FairWild certified bibhitaki fruit and FairWild haritaki fruit from the Bhimashankar region, to provide a financial incentive to protect the trees and support the communities. In partnership with DICE and Pukka, AERF submitted a second Darwin grant application that included plans for FairWild certification of the fruit. This time they received the funding. Then began the long process of launching not just one, but two FairWild projects in some of the most challenging conditions in the world. The project areas were remote with little infrastructure, and many in the community lacked the training to manage complex projects.

The scenery changed as we rode west and began climbing out of the plains. The land began to feel more forgiving. There were more trees and shrubs, fewer buildings. Best of all, it became cooler. The haze from pollution that hangs over so many urban and semi-urban areas in India lifted. The dirty, dusty landscape gradually became golden as we arrived at dusk at the guesthouses that would be our home base for the next few days.

The next morning we woke early to drive to a sacred grove where a particularly active pair of hornbills were nesting. We drove down a dirt road lined by shrubs and tall trees and parked by a gate at the forest entrance. Walking past the gate we came to a pale mauve, single-story temple surrounded by trees. Large signs described the fifty-five giant trees, including bibhtaki, being preserved in this eight-acre grove. The signs also shared information on the history of the temple and the rules for visiting: Keep peace. Don't shout. Don't give material or anything to the birds.

This land was a certified sacred grove, which is why so many large trees were still standing. The trees are more slender than I expected a so-called giant tree would be, not as large as some old-growth trees in the US. But compared with other trees I saw in India, which were typically much younger and smaller, the bibhitakis did seem giant. The light green walnut-sized bibhitaki fruits grow in clusters on the branches. The leaves are thick and oval-shaped. A single bibhitaki tree has as many as thirty-five plant species associated with it; they are ecosystems unto themselves, Jayant explained.

In all, we made three trips to this grove to observe the birds. The temple was an active shrine. Worshippers came and went during our stay, including a group of thirty or forty who were celebrating a political victory by making offerings at the shrine. It could be a long wait to see the hornbills, Jayant warned us, and so we settled in. Bryce pulled out his book and lay down on the packed red earth. I wandered into the temple, cool with the pungent smell of melted candles and incense. The temple was open to the outside, with arching doors and windows that led into a spacious, cement-floored room. At the far end, arched openings in the wall held statues of deities covered in tikka powder and wax from the many candles burned as offerings. Garlands of marigolds hung on trees at the entrance.

I came back out and joined the others. The sky was overcast. "Patience is most important," Akash Patil, a field assistant for AERF who joined us during our visit, told us. Akash's work was to monitor nests, keeping track of how often the male bird visits and how long it stays away. He was used to the wait.

After an uneventful hour, Terry suggested we begin to interview Jayant on camera. We set up the equipment and I asked Jayant about the history of the project and its significance. Around ten minutes into the interview, we all sensed a large bird flying in. Terry started to point. Jayant, clearly aware of the bird even though he hadn't turned around to see it, gestured for Terry to stay still.

The hornbill began to feed the female, regurgitating the fruit he had collected for her to eat. Jayant now stepped closer for a better view, gesturing for us to follow. The female was hidden in the cavity of the tree. We could see only the male bird feeding her from his huge yellow bill. I'd never seen anything like it before. The hornbill is roughly the size of a heron, in terms of height and wing span, and the casque, or horn, on top of the massive bill is the most surprising feature. It looked prehistoric. It had a presence, an otherness. We stood, rapt, while it finished feeding. Next, the birds cleaned out the nest—the female passing her waste in her bill to the male, who spat it onto the forest floor. Work complete, the giant bird turned and flew off again across the sky, on another two-to-three-hour search for food, the only sound was its great wings flapping.

During midday, when we were unlikely to see a hornbill, we visited the center where employees of NatureServe, the production company that AERF created, were drying, dehusking, and sorting the bibhitaki fruits in preparation to ship to Phalada. At the processing center at Phalada, the dried husks are ground to powder before being exported to the U.K. A group from an NGO in the South Western Ghats was also visiting, to learn whether they might adopt some of the practices for non-timber forest products villagers harvested in their region, especially amla, the third of the three fruits used in making triphala. Jayant told us he hopes this project will have a ripple effect with other companies, especially Indian companies in the Ayurveda industry. Meeting with this NGO was a step in that direction.

Later that evening we went to a small, outdoor bar. Jayant ordered two Kingfisher beers and some salty snacks. He began to relax more than he had during our whole visit. Companies can buy bibhitaki anywhere, Jayant told us. But these birds have no other options. The project is about the survival of these trees, which can ensure the survival of these birds. Jayant added that AERF is involved in so many different projects, and some people accuse them of being spread too thin. He paused, taking a sip of his beer and reaching for some snacks. But, he said, "the opportunity is not going to return. We have to try sowing lots of different seeds. Some will do better than others. Too much is at stake to not do all we can do."

Establishing Traceability

After three days of interviews and filming about the bibhitaki project, we drove five hours north to the region of Bhimashankar to visit the haritaki project. Unlike the bibhitaki project, where we had very little interaction with anyone from the community, our visit to Bhimashankar focused on the villagers and the economic impacts of the project. In fact, we didn't even see the haritaki trees until the end of our visit, when we walked down a dirt road past the village to where they grew in a mixed forest. I was unfamiliar with the species of trees growing in this region of the world, and to my untrained eye it was difficult to distinguish the haritaki trees from any others.

Another difference was that while the bibhitaki project was designed to develop a new source of fruits that hadn't been previously harvested at scale from that region, villagers in Bhimashankar have been collecting haritaki fruit for generations. They used some for their own consumption, but most they sold to traders in the regional market or to the State Tribal Development Corporation. This corporation was established by the state government in 1972 to prevent the exploitation of tribal members and to provide services, one of which is purchasing wild harvested plants.[6] AERF began to purchase haritaki fruit from the villagers during the 2014–15 collection season. They opened a processing factory during the same season. Like the bibhitaki project, the objective was to provide a financial incentive to protect the haritaki trees and thus the biodiversity of the forest. Because this community historically had a trade of haritaki, the focus was on improving the fruit quality and providing increased value for the villagers involved in the trade, through higher prices and through employment opportunities in the processing factory. The project included plans for studying the impacts of harvesting practices on the sustainability of the harvest, looking in particular at the impact that harvesting fruit at different stages of maturity had on regeneration.

We arrived late in the day. The driver pulled over beside three tin-sided single-story buildings. Just beyond the buildings, a small village of mud houses, some with thatched roofs, some with tin, was clustered around a small temple and a large dirt playing field. A group of boys and men were playing cricket.

We followed Jayant into the first of the buildings, where four men sat cross-legged on a clean blue tarp, leafing through papers and reports. Stacks of neatly tagged burlap sacks filled with hard walnut-sized dried haritaki fruit ready for shipment were piled against one side of the room. Tables and desks were pushed against the wall on the other. The center of the room was empty, likely because the space was frequently used for delivering, sorting, and bagging the haritaki fruit. The men hardly looked up when we entered. Jayant introduced us to Amol Nirban, a business development manager for Ecocert, an inspection and certification body established in France with offices in Maharashtra state. Jayant explained that Amol was there to provide a training with villagers on FairWild practices. He was also there to do a trial run-through with AERF staff in preparation for the actual FairWild recertification in a few weeks. Another man, Umesh Hiremath, worked for AERF, and the two others were villagers who worked in the processing center.

I had come to understand that FairWild certification involved lots of tracking and reporting, but I hadn't realized how much until I saw the many piles of papers spread out on the floor. While the men continued speaking, Jayant explained to us that the certifiers would be looking to see whether the staff of Nature Connect, which bought the haritaki fruits from collectors in the village, could manage the record keeping on their own. The certifiers would also be checking whether working conditions meet the standards and whether the traceability systems actually provided the information needed to trace the fruit back to specific certified trees—that it wasn't just lip service. They would ask questions like whether children worked, if villagers were paid a higher rate for overtime work, and how the community set the price for haritaki. They need to learn to relay this information by heart, Jayant explained as we stood at the side of the room watching them work. This meant making sure that the amounts of fruit purchased and recorded were consistent with how much could be sustainably harvested from the designated collection areas. The certifiers would look for any inconsistencies that might indicate that collectors were either overharvesting or buying cheaper haritaki husk harvested from non-FairWild-certified trees and trying to sell it for the higher certified price. Each collector's trees are registered with a GPS tracking code; labels on each sack of dried husks indicated the trees from which the fruits had been harvested and by whom. This represents an unprecedented level of traceability, especially in the supply chain of wild-collected plants. "That's why I value FairWild so much," Jayant said. "I don't know any other program that can trace the finished product back to one specific tree."

The conversation then turned to bags; along with labels, these are a key issue in most supply chain conversations, especially ones about quality control. The trainer talked about the importance of making sure the bags would not be used for any purpose other than collecting fruit. Jayant interjected, saying that if the villagers are using the bags for other purposes, rather than trying to restrict them, AERF or Nature Connect should provide them with enough bags to meet all of their needs.

As Amol stood up to go, he switched to speaking in English and told me that consumer awareness is essential. Unless customers in the US, Europe, and India are made aware of what FairWild represents and start asking companies to carry FairWild products, then the certification program will not succeed. "It is important not to just buy the cheapest things." Amol then added, "Environmental catastrophes affect the earth as a whole. Buying certified products from another country can be a way to help the whole earth."

So-called conscious capitalism is built on the premise that our buying choices are a political statement and a way to change the world. Scholars, especially geographers and anthropologists, are quick to criticize these solutions, pointing out that such certification programs fail to improve rural livelihoods, especially because they do not address the root problems, both that too little money actually reaches farmers and collectors, and that political and economic structures keep such inequities in place.[7]

Capitalism is a major contributor to many of the problems that socially and environmentally responsible companies hope to address. And it remains to be seen whether conscious capitalism can be used as a way to address those very problems. Yet as I read critiques of certification programs, I wondered if they are taking too narrow a view, focusing on specific measurable outcomes that outsiders have decided are important, in part because they can be measured. What other changes might be happening that we, as outsiders, may fail to see? Ben, who has spent years working to help Indian farmers and producer groups meet the rigorous standards for certification, acknowledges their imperfection. But having gone through the process, Ben also has enormous respect for what they do accomplish, and he believes they are an important tool, though not the only one. The haritaki project in Bhimashankar illustrates the many other impacts certifications have on communities, beyond providing more income. Conscious capitalism falls short when we rely on it as the only step needed, rather than as a first step along the much longer and more challenging journey of addressing the social and ecological consequences of our ways of living.[8]

Amol got into his car to return to his home in Pune. Our driver took Jayant, Terry, Bryce, and me to the guesthouse where we were to stay—a collection of run-down, uninviting pale yellow cement cabins scattered on a hillside. It felt abandoned, but we were told it was busy during the pilgrimage season because it was on the route to one of the most important pilgrimage destinations in India. I was surprised to discover that the one other guest at the time was Rie Makita, a geographer from Gakushuin University in Japan, who was finishing a short-term research project about the FairWild project. Rie had also visited three months ago and was here for a two-week follow-up visit. Her interpreter had had to leave early. Without her interpreter, she was unable to speak with anyone in the community and she had been waiting at the hotel until Jayant arrived and she could finish her research.

Rie joined Jayant and me in the restaurant while Terry and Bryce went to our cabin. We sat and drank sweet tea in a large, high-ceilinged room with windows that let in the hot sun. She had a list of questions for Jayant and jumped right in. Listening in on their conversation gave me an interesting perspective both on the challenges of the project and on understanding those challenges as an outsider. She said that the collectors were complaining about why it was taking so long to start up the premium account.

Jayant let her finish and then shook his head in disagreement. "No, that isn't how it is."

She commented that there were divisions in the community about the project. "What divides them?" she asked.

"That is the question," Jayant answered. "It is simple political groups," he continued. "They don't like the secretary." After a few minutes of discussion about the political dynamics and the premium fund, she switched to asking about the differences between the baby fruits and the adult fruits and the tensions in the community created around harvesting the different sizes of fruits.

I was having a hard time following which group was which or the significance of the baby and adult fruits. More interesting to me was being able to learn Jayant's perspective by hearing him explain it to someone else, especially someone who was skeptical.

"I think it is normal," he continued. "When more money starts coming into a community, there will be dissatisfaction."

"They've lost interest in the project," the ethnographer said, not seeming to grasp his point. "And they have no clue about the premium."

Later I asked Ben about Jayant's comments about the conflicts. The original secretary for the project had, as Ben put it, "too much influence on matters that benefited himself." So AERF had selected another individual to be in charge of the premium fund because he was more reliable and trustworthy. That had created some tension between the different factions.

I recalled that when I visited the FairWild projects in Hungary and Poland, I had heard lots of rumblings about the premium fund, how it wasn't enough or being done in the right way. When I shared this feedback with Anastasiya Timoshyna, who worked with TRAFFIC and oversaw FairWild certification, she said in exasperation, "I'm tired of hearing about what is wrong with the premium fund!" I realized that at that time, my attitude had been rather like that of this geographer. Like Rie, I focused on the perspectives of collectors and producer groups, championing their cause without balancing their views with the challenges that the community was facing, and also that the country—and world—is facing.

"I'm not going to defend it," Jayant replied to Rie. "I'm trying to tell you, there are limitations. Yes, some things are not being taken care of. But compared to *what?* Things are terrible elsewhere. Compared to that, this project is not that bad." He finished his tea and added that she shouldn't put this in black-and-white terms. As the company makes more money, more people take an interest, especially people close to power.

"When something isn't doing well, people don't pay much attention," he said. "People are happy. But when the money and profits increase, there is always more discontent."

Rie persisted. She said that the project seemed successful in terms of fair trade, but she wasn't so sure it was successful in terms of the ecological issues.

Jayant explained that you can't understand the ecological impact through interviews. You gain that understanding only through conducting regeneration studies and monitoring harvest rates in different plots. Only then can you know the impact. You have to visit all of the plots in all of the certified areas three times: when the fruit sets, when people start to harvest, and when the harvest is over. Auditors do random sampling. The FairWild protocol, he explained, requires data. Only when they have that data can they discuss the impact in ecological terms.

He then added, "The local indigenous community members here are getting experience in setting up and running a transparent supply chain. That is the goal. And that is a huge accomplishment. You need to put it in perspective."

He then talked about how the project has created a new supply chain for the villagers. Haritaki is the backbone of this economy. He said that roughly fifty tons of haritaki fruit are harvested from Bhimashankar (I was not able to confirm this figure). It has been big business, but only traders and others with money and connections have benefited. FairWild is changing that on the most basic level, he said. The entire community now knows the true value and price of the resource. Moreover, FairWild is important because it is registering trees in the names of owners. Though these trees were owned by villagers before, because they were not registered as private property, the haritaki fruit was considered to be a wild resource collected from forest department land, and so could only be legally sold to the tribal society, which offered a fixed price and other restrictions. Not only can villagers now sell the fruits to whomever they want, their ownership rights to their trees are legally recognized.

FairWild is changing the political situation, Jayant explained. It is shifting power away from the traders and the marketplace to the collectors and the place where the fruits are collected. So far the volumes are quite small. Jayant estimated that three thousand kilograms of FairWild certified haritaki fruit were harvested in 2015–16, and they hoped to harvest five thousand in the third year.[9] "But," he added, "the seeds are now in place. Who knows what the long-term impacts of those seeds might be? This is how people become empowered. It is invaluable in the long term."

———

Rie later told me that Jayant was biased. I wondered why anyone would assume that the head of a conservation organization wouldn't see things in a particular way. I also wondered why Rie, who seemingly favored the voice of the collectors over everyone else, couldn't perceive that as bias as well. Jayant sounded defensive during their conversation, but since she seemed to be challenging everything he said, that wasn't surprising. Regardless, their encounter gave me pause. It illustrated how difficult it can be for outsiders to understand the dynamics of a community. Who do you listen to? And who do you trust? I thought back to what Drake, Mike, and so many others sourcing herbs from around the world had said about learning who and who not to trust. And that mistakes were part of the process.

As the conversation drew to a close, Jayant asked Rie how long she would take to write her article. Two years, she answered. "Then you should take that long to research it," he said.

———

The next morning Terry and Bryce and I met with Umesh, who has worked with AERF since 2011. He told us he had originally done research on tigers but came to see that conservation work was more important than research, and he had been at AERF ever since. We accompanied Umesh to speak with some villagers in the hamlet of thirty-five households about their experience in the FairWild project.

Unlike my visits to villages with Nioma and Drake, in Bhimashankar we were alone as outsiders. The villagers' presentation was inevitably filtered through their assumptions about what a presentation for an outsider should be. What we learned from the villagers was thus limited, but everyone with whom we spoke raised the same topic: economics. In each interview, whomever we spoke with listed the different prices offered by the traders, the tribal collection center, or FairWild. They also made it clear that one of the biggest benefits has been employment at the processing center. We spoke with the two men who worked in the center, and both mentioned the new skills they had learned. In addition to these jobs, Nature Connect also employs seasonal workers (fifty in 2015 and ninety-three in 2016). Based on the positive role of the processing center for the community, in the paper she wrote in 2018, Rie concluded that the project could be judged a success "in terms of its ability to sustain the community's attention, at least for the initial three years."[10]

I also was struck by the comments of several men and women about the difference it made to them to know how the fruit would be used. "Previously, we thought the haritaki went to the tanning industry," the wife of one of the two employees of the processing center said. (Haritaki fruit is also used in the making of leather.) "Now we have come to know that the haritaki fruit is used as a medicine and that someone is going to consume it. And so now, knowing that, we will take utmost care."

Umesh is training the center workers to take full responsibility so that they eventually can run the project without his or AERF's help. Umesh would smile as he translated the things that the collectors said during their interview, adding, "Oh, that's very good," when they expressed points he had made to us as well. Even if some of this was presented to us to simply make a good impression, everyone with whom we spoke did seem to express pride. They recognized that they were part of a bigger effort to export a traditional medicine to the world rather than being a cog at the bottom of a very long supply chain, with no idea how the product would eventually be used.

Umesh expressed the value of the project this way: "FairWild is so important because human beings and ecology are at the center of trade. Trade for human beings and for nature. Sustainable harvest on one side and biodiversity on the other." He smiled, pleased with this succinct summary.

Building the capacity of AERF staff on the ground was an enormous undertaking, Ben told me. Even though he was used to the slow pace of getting anything done in India, the pace of the project was, at times, snail-like. It was frustrating, for example, that field staff seemed unwilling or unable to complete the resource assessments accurately. Conversely, Ben said, the field staff sometimes went way beyond the level of duty. As an example, he described his interaction with Umesh about record keeping. From past experience, Ben had low expectations. Yet Umesh didn't just

THE BUSINESS OF BOTANICALS

keep records, Ben said. He redefined them. Umesh summarized the records on large posters to explain to villagers how much money they made at the current rate of processing and how much they would need to increase production to continue to increase the money they made. Ben said Umesh's level of detail and his ability to communicate it so that the community could understand and provide input was mind blowing.

Overall, he added, AERF was very skilled at understanding the community's perspective and their needs.

"I would come in from Bristol with my time scales and charts," Ben told me. "I'd be there for one to two days and I'd say, okay, we have to accomplish this all in six months. And the AERF staff would reply, 'We need to proceed at the community pace. If we push it, it will fall over. And if we communicate it wrong, we'll just cause more long-term problems.'

"Given that this was a community that would walk a ten-mile round trip to sell 70 rupees of milk, they aren't in a hurry." Ben laughed and then reflected, "For many people, it's hard to comprehend the pace of India. There are reasons for that pace. And I respect those reasons."

This project wasn't without its problems. As with many of the Fair-Wild projects, these tended to revolve around the premium fund. And with each FairWild certified project I visited, I found myself wondering whether the project was truly accomplishing its stated goal, and whether or not it would succeed over time. From what I observed, it seemed that the amount of staff time required might not make good business sense. And certification required the producer groups to assemble so much documentation, they often had to hire additional staff just to handle the paperwork involved. Despite that, in every conversation I had with the men and women implementing FairWild projects in communities, I was impressed with their commitment to managing a complex network of stakeholders to address what Josef Brinckmann described as the "existential threat of the loss of biological diversity." FairWild broadens the definition of whom the botanical industry is serving to include the plants themselves, as well as the communities and ecosystems from which those plants are sourced. I mentioned to Seb that it was, albeit slowly, including new stakeholders in the decision making. He nodded and added that it was like building not a democracy, but more equality, opening decision making to more members of the community than before. "And that can be tough to sort out."

———

I asked Ben and Sebastian if there are many projects that haven't worked out. We were sitting on the edge of a field in southern India at the time. They both laughed, saying they'd gone on plenty of wild goose chases, on many a long, bumpy road. "We've traveled all over the world," Ben observed. "Some projects work to a certain scale, and it can be hard for them to grow beyond that capacity. It is especially challenging to maintain the quality of herbs and relationships with a company like Pukka that is growing so fast." Ultimately, projects succeed only if the plants produced meet the quality standard. Ben described a project he was exploring growing turmeric in South America aimed at restoring soil fertility and biodiversity in degraded areas of rain forest. "It was brilliant," he said, "Conservation through commerce." Everything was in place. Then it turned out the turmeric had very low levels of active ingredients, and so they couldn't continue, making the point that unless a project works from a business sense, companies are unlikely to be able to go forward.

FairWild requires a tremendous investment on everyone's part. Marin Anastasov of Pukka Herbs summed it up during my interview with him: "Do you follow the demand from your customers, or do you do something you actually believe in? We didn't know whether FairWild would increase our sales, whether our customers would really understand it. We did it because we believe it is the right thing to do. We think it is very, very important to ensure that wild-harvested species are collected and managed properly."

Ben estimated that he has visited the AERF projects twelve to fourteen times, staying anywhere from one day to one week each time, far more than for almost any other sourcing project. He and Jayant have spent many hours together. "We really got to know each other, way beyond other supplier relationships. We found common ground in our love of nature and we had a lot of good laughs." When frustrations arose, Ben and Jayant had their personal relationship to fall back on. "That isn't always the case in sourcing," Ben said. Many of his best memories arose from the times between the work when more informal connections could happen. "And those connections, the work and the quality of relationships, are not unconnected.

"Inevitably, there are tough times," Ben continued. He has worked with Phalada in India for years to establish systems so that the plants Phalada processes meet the quality requirements for imports to the U.K. "We often joke it is like a marriage. It is rocky, not always easy. Lots of strong personalities that can clash. But ultimately, we have a long-term relationship and when we are in rocky patches, we always make it through. There is a lot of love there."

Ben said that nothing has touched him as much as the first time he and Seb witnessed the hornbills, especially watching the male feeding the female. In that instant, he saw what a difference Pukka's work could make by their choice to buy the fruit of these trees, preserving the homes for these amazing birds that depend on the trees throughout their lifelong pair bond. "Seeing those hornbills fed the inspiration for the project. And we needed to feed it. Otherwise the project would have starved," he added, "because it was a very hungry beast."

CHAPTER ELEVEN

Medicine of Place

The universe is full of magical things
patiently waiting for our wits to grow sharper.

—EDEN PHILLPOTTS

*I*n 2017 I received a Fulbright-Nehru Senior Research Fellowship to spend six months in India following herbs through the supply chain. This sounded fairly straightforward to propose as a research project. But a six-month trip to India that is based on traveling to different regions of the country is no small undertaking, especially when you are taking along a twelve-year-old boy who has lived his entire life in a small town in central Vermont and has limited experience traveling to a place with a very different culture. From the outset, I thought it would work best if we had a base location from which I could travel. But finding a suitable place turned out to be more difficult than I anticipated. Finally an Ayurvedic doctor from Vermont and a supporter of the Sustainable Herbs Program suggested that I look into an Ayurvedic center called Vaidyagrama in Tamil Nadu, south of the city of Coimbatore. I contacted the founder of the center, Ram Kumar. He assured me that we would be able to visit the villages from which plants were sourced for remedies used at the center and that this would be a good place from which to learn more about the botanical trade. He said that he would help make that possible.

We arrived at Vaidyagrama in late January 2017. It turned out it was not an ideal base because of its remoteness, both for me from research sites and for Terry and Bryce from interaction in a community. Even so, we stayed as planned until early March when we went to Kolkata for the Fulbright conference. From there we visited the AERF projects in the

Western Ghats, visited Fort Kochi in the south, and then settled in an alumni cottage at the Kodaikanal International School. Terry and Bryce stayed in Kodaikanal while I traveled to the Traditional Medicinals project in Rajasthan, the collection sites and farms south of Madurai, and Auroville. Bryce and I then returned to Vaidyagrama where I underwent a ten-day shortened panchakarma treatment, which included daily massages with herbal oils, fermented water, morning herbs, and meeting with a doctor. At the end of our time in India, we spent a month in the northern states of Uttarakhand and Himachal Pradesh looking at efforts to cultivate threatened Himalayan herbs.

The founders of Vaidyagrama wanted to create a place to practice what they called authentic Ayurveda, a center that was comfortable without compromising Ayurveda's core principles. They opened the center in 1998, the design organized according to the *vastu shastras*, literally translated as "science of architecture"—the traditional system of design used for laying out houses, towns, and cities as well as Ayurveda hospitals. The principles focus on integrating design with nature. More than almost anyplace I've been, Vaidyagrama felt like an extension of the plants and trees in and around it. The prayer hall, a round building made of sun-dried red bricks, with a red tile roof, is at the center. Covered pathways made of cement radiate out from the center. Black benches are placed along the pathways where patients can sit and look out at the forest garden planted inside the center structure. The simple rooms are situated off the pathways, each with two beds, an overhead fan, a bathroom, and a porch, designed to look out into the garden.

Vaidyagrama is on the side of a dead-end dirt road that is more like a track crossing an expanse of packed red earth than an actual road. It isn't a field or meadow, but the kind of wasteland so common in rural India. It is an hour from Coimbatore, but the city is spreading into what had been farmland. The major highway to Kerala is only ten minutes away. The land around the center is mostly barren, because people have been moving away to the cities. Ram Kumar is trying to buy this abandoned land both to expand the center and to prevent the city from encroaching.

Expectations and Faith

From the beginning, this visit to Vaidyagrama wasn't what I expected. To start with, it was hot. Tamil Nadu was in the middle of a drought. The fall monsoon had never arrived, and so temperatures in the mid-nineties had come earlier than usual. And it was dry. So dry that when we tried to play soccer with Bryce, the ball kicked up red dust that stuck to the sweat on our skin, sweat not from running but just from being outside, even at dusk. It was not the comfortable place I'd hoped to be in as we adjusted to life in India.

I was also disappointed that there was no apothecary. I'd imagined myself helping doctors with blending formulas. However, it turned out that the doctors did not make their medicines on site; they dispensed premade medicines stored in a small storeroom. The few remedies that the therapists made themselves simply involved grinding green leaves into a paste.

And I had hoped to help out in the garden and learn how to grow plants in this hot red earth, but it turned out that the garden wasn't very active, because expanding the hospital had taken precedence. The biggest disappointment, perhaps, was that Ram Kumar wasn't even at Vaidyagrama when we arrived.

Even so, the center was thoughtfully designed and implemented. Unlike much of India, with sounds of people and honking horns and music blaring, at Vaidyagrama the only sounds inside the center were birds singing at all times of day, the tinkle of the bells on the ankle bracelets of the therapist walking quietly down the cement pathways through the garden forest, the sound of overhead fans, prayers chanted at dawn and dusk. Sometimes there were muffled tones of people walking and working and talking. Everyone with whom I spoke had positive things to say about their experience and the treatments they received. It just wasn't what I expected. It was only later that I realized that letting go of my expectations, shifting the focus of my journey to what was emerging, was, perhaps, why I was here.

One of the most challenging aspects of our stay was that there wasn't much, if anything, to do. The only structured activity was prayers, held morning and evening. From the beginning I attended those, which were often the highlight of the day. Patients trickled in before dawn, coming to the sound of the bell that called us to prayer. I entered the room, rolled a yoga mat onto the ocher-colored tile floor, and took my place in a semicircle around the small altar set up on one side of the room. Ram Dass, one of the founders of Vaidyagrama, entered, wearing a long yellow tunic over his white lungi. He sat cross-legged on a low wooden prayer bench, opened his small prayer book, and began chanting with his resonant, booming voice. Patients straggled in, taking a spot on the floor or the bench around the edge of the room, joining the chants that they knew, sitting quietly otherwise. I loved the way Ram Dass sang, fully present in each syllable, even as he repeated the same chants each morning. Ram Dass's prayers were the one thing big enough to quiet my mind, which was constantly busy with worry about Bryce, worry about Terry, worry about my research. Other doctors led the prayers on Ram Dass's days off. But they seemed distracted, pausing to yawn in the middle of reading the chants, looking around the room and then losing their place. On those mornings I would go for a walk with Emily Reed, an Ayurvedic practitioner and yoga teacher who had come to the center many times to study and have treatments. We would find our prayers in the waking countryside instead.

A full week after we arrived, I finally met with Ram Kumar. We sat in a small bare office with a wooden desk and empty bookshelf. He sat behind the desk with an open laptop computer. Ram Kumar is imposing, more from his presence than his size. He is tall, bald, and quick to laugh, but also embodies what at first seemed a stern aloofness I found intimidating. Emily later described that aloofness as part the *satvic* path, a path of honesty, uprightness, and truth. Ram Kumar had always walked that path and held that energy, she told me.

I asked Ram Kumar where they sourced the plants used in the medicines at the center. He hadn't given it much thought, he said, which was not at all the answer I expected. They were working backward, he continued. Ultimately the center needed an assured supply chain of herbs or to grow the plants on-site. But they also needed physicians who understand the essence of the plants (*sara*). Today's physicians don't understand that, he said. They are stuck in the texts and in ideas that a plant has this or that property. They base their diagnosis on which plants to use for a patient's condition rather than understanding the essence of the plant and matching that with the patient.

In the twelfth century a group of teachers described the properties of six hundred herbs, Ram Kumar continued. But individual teachers characterized an herb in different ways. Ginger, for example: One teacher said it was hot. Another used the word for "very hot." And a third described it as less hot. A fourth chose the word that means "hot and cold." This is because the qualities of ginger, he continued, are more or less prominent depending on the context. How any individual experiences any given herb depends on their constitution, their condition, and the context in which they ingest the herb. Learning how these qualities will manifest in different individuals depends on understanding the essence of the plant, and how that essence will manifest. This requires careful study and the particular quality of mind called *satwa* (being on the satvic path). That's what is lacking, he said. It takes time to develop this discernment. Practitioners think they do not have enough time and so they just recommend treatments based on what is written in the texts, not what they discern themselves. He considered this to be the most threatened resource: doctors who know how to prescribe and use plants with the discernment that is the heart of Ayurveda.

"All I know is if we don't get this side right, we don't have to think about the supply chain, because there won't be any practice to use the plants. The real experts who have a conscience and who are environmentally sensitive, the *vaidyas* [Ayurvedic doctors] who think about the entire picture, are fast running out. That is what is threatened."[1] Until he can get that sorted out, he said, they are using bottled fermented medicine manufactured at a facility run by the family of one of the four founding doctors of Vaidyagrama.

Ram Kumar's comments about the role of culture reminded me of maps the Kuna Indians in Panama made when working with international conservationists to create a biosphere reserve on their territory in the late 1980s. Biosphere reserves were a model, new at the time, to address the negative impacts of national parks that excluded indigenous populations from living in and using the parklands. Biosphere reserves allowed for the presence of humans in some areas. A reserve could include a strict conservation area to protect the natural area of greatest biodiversity, a buffer zone where mixed use was allowed with some restrictions, and villages where people lived. The NGOs working with the Kuna viewed the heart of the forest as the strict conservation area and the villages as the buffer zone of mixed use. The Kuna, though, viewed their home (villages) as the area for strict preservation. The buffer zone was the forest areas that protected their home from encroachment from urban areas.[2] Culture, in other words, was at the heart. If that was protected, I took this to mean, the land would be protected as well.

In the model of Ayurvedic medicine that Ram Kumar described, the relationship between a vaidya and the plants was at the root. Protecting the plants depended on protecting the vaidya's relationship with the plants. Without the cultural value and knowledge, any practices were externally imposed; they became regulations to adhere to that depended on enforcement. Once the regulations stopped, the practices were likely to as well.

In the video series Seeding the Field, botanist and writer Robin Wall Kimmerer talks about what is known as the honorable harvest, a set of cultural practices found in many Native American cultures that frame how to harvest plants in the wild. She outlines the practices: Never take the first plant, ask permission, listen for the answer, use everything that you take, take only what you need, be grateful, share what you've taken, minimize harm.[3] Though I hadn't heard the term the *honorable harvest* before, I recognized that these were also the practices I had learned from Rosemary about wild-harvesting of medicinal plants. Stewarding that framework was the key to stewarding the plants.

Another similar concept I have encountered is that of the honorable merchant, a value, I was told, from Hamburg, Germany, where word of mouth may mean more than the written contract. This concept describes honoring your word and sticking to your agreements as the cornerstone of success—because people believe and trust in you.[4]

Both concepts—the honorable harvest, the honorable merchant—are about limits on action, limits on what we take—based on honor. These limits *arise from* the interaction between a person and a place, or between two people, and they are guided by honor, not by rules. The word *honor* holds a quality of uprightness, bringing our best self forward, a quality I associate with satwa. I also associate it with the shamans in Hedangna and their ability to see double. Acting honorably calls on humans to see more than the object at hand. It is necessary also to see the context—the other species that live in a meadow or forest, or the person to whom you give your word. That context, in a way, creates a structure for the practices of reciprocity. These examples are specific to a particular cultural framework, but they reflect qualities that most people bring to the activities and relationships they care about.

As Randy Buresh of Oregon's Wild Harvest said that sunny morning as he watched his son help harvest their certified organic Valerian root, "It is all about love, doing it from the heart, not doing it from the mind. And that's a completely different aspect when you think about it."

One morning Sebastian Pole and I walked through an araca nut forest in southern India where nutmeg, pepper, and ginger grew, the spices that first launched the trade I had come to study. During our conversation that morning, Seb said, "It's all about love—what do you love and who do you love and how you want to love them. And if you love nature and you love people, you want to take care of them."

Being a consumer is more transactional. Can knowing the larger context, developing some kind of relationship with the people and places behind the products, help make our interactions as consumers less transactional and more meaningful?

Despite what he told me, Ram Kumar *had* thought about the sourcing of plants used in the center's medicines. He was clearly aware of the challenges and complexities. He was working on solutions, and I was struck by his clarity about how to set priorities. As he said, what mattered most was the quality of the knowledge of the Ayurvedic doctors, the depth of their understanding. Thus he focused first on creating solutions that would help build their knowledge.

Most Ayurvedic practitioners in India today give patients remedies that are mass-produced in a factory. "Yet I have no connection to a bottle," Ram Kumar said. He was beginning to create opportunities for doctors to work directly with the plants. That morning he had met with a manufacturer to explore the possibility of fabricating a small burner that doctors could use to prepare the remedies in their offices. That way they would work directly with the dried herbs, which would allow them to develop and deepen their relationship with the plants. He had to provide a method that would be easy for the doctors, Ram Kumar said, or they wouldn't do it. But he was confident it was possible to figure it out.

Just as herbalists often talk about the time it takes for plants to work in the body, I was struck by how Ram Kumar brought that same quality of patience to healing the system. He often said, "We must be patient with every process. That is one of the biggest things I've learned. How to change, slowly, gradually, without getting frustrated and without giving up."

Finding Medicine, Finding Faith

Our third week at Vaidyagrama, I visited the factory that manufactures 75 percent of the medicines used at the center. The factory was run by the family of Dr. Harikrishnan, one of the four founders. Dr. Harikrishnan drove me to the small manufacturing unit, which was in his hometown, Palakkad, about an hour away, just over the border in Kerala. Harikrishnan, like most of the Indian staff I met at Vaidyagrama, didn't ask me any questions. And also like the others, he had been answering mine with as few words as possible. In the car, however, he began to speak more openly. He talked about how the practice of Ayurveda was never broken in Kerala and that the supply chain, which was disrupted everywhere else by the British and the Mughals, has remained intact. His father, an Ayurvedic doctor as well, started the factory to provide medicines for his patients. It now provides medicines for the hospital that his family also

founded, several outpatient clinics, and Vaidyagrama. When Harikrishnan first started working for the factory, twenty years ago, what he called
the "olden days," he traveled two hours by bus to Thrissur, the biggest
trading center in the region, to buy sacks of raw drugs from traders. He
returned home with the sacks on the bus.

At that time, it hadn't been hard to find the plants. Now they sometimes had to wait up to a week or so until a species was back in stock.
Fortunately, his family's operation is small enough to stop production
until plants become available. He told me he wasn't sure bigger factories
could pause production in the same way. They likely substituted with species that were more easily found. I asked what was causing the shortages.
"So many things impact the raw material supply chain," Harikrishnan
said. "Weather, rain, harvest." A few types of herbs he buys are cultivated
but most, 70 to 75 percent he guessed, were from the wild.

Dr. Harikrishnan's hometown was remarkable for its manageable
traffic, well-kept homes, tree-lined streets. I wondered why I hadn't
decided to make our travel base here, in this town where Bryce could
interact with others. The doctor dropped me at the manufacturing center,
a tall narrow building next to the house where he had grown up and his
parents still lived. He headed to the hospital to meet with patients while
I visited the factory. I sat on a bench next to a bundle of dried herbs to
wait for the manager. When he arrived, he led me into a small area where
a man was filling bottles with a traditional Ayurvedic preparation called
kashayam using a bottling machine that held around ten bottles.[5] Beyond
that, two women in blue tunics were using a press to remove the oil that
had been steeping in herbs. Chipped and faded maroon clay vessels in
which herbs were fermenting lined the wall in another room. Dried herbs
were stored in clearly labeled, covered plastic pails in a well-organized
second-floor room. On the roof, in an area covered with a canvas tent,
a machine rolled tablets from a thick doughlike mix. Outside in a small
building, a man also in a blue tunic powdered a mixture of dried herbs
in a simple grinder powered by a small gas motor. It was fascinating to
see the many ways this company was making medicine with minimal
technology. It was also impressive to see how well organized and well
used the relatively small building and rooms were.

While the manager showed me around, I asked about the plants and where they were from. The woman in charge of purchasing ordered them by email from traders, he explained. Based on Dr. Harikrishnan and his father's experience, as well as their new experience, the factory workers knew which traders were the better ones. It cost a bit more to get good quality, he added, but it was possible to find it.

A shipment arrived while I was there: an assortment of sacks of various sizes and types filled with dried roots, leaves, and stems. I gathered with four or five other employees in the front entrance, a narrow linoleum-floored hallway. A woman dressed like all the workers in a turquoise blue tunic opened and checked each bag in turn to make sure it contained what had been ordered. She weighed it on a scale. Another woman double-checked the weight against the order form to make sure the trader wasn't cheating them. Many of the sacks were reused cement bags. The manager said it didn't matter where the raw drugs originated from and that, in any case, it wasn't possible to identify that. The shop owners probably didn't know, either. "There are a lot of supply chains involved," he said, not very concerned. But, he added, they do keep track. They aren't required to by the government, but they keep receipts. If a medicine doesn't seem as good, they will trace it back and not buy from that supplier again.

This was a small-town, locally owned factory with a good reputation, not a faceless company owned by some uncaring multi-conglomerate. Yet after my visit to the factory, I couldn't help thinking of the reused bags and the many hands that had probably touched the plants on their journey from harvest to medicinal tea formula. It made me uneasy about drinking the *kashayam* I was given each morning at Vaidyagrama: I no longer swallowed the grit in the bottom of my cup, imagining it might include cement dust. I also wondered where the plants used to make that tonic had come from, what the land was like, whether there were arsenic or other heavy metals in the soil or irrigation water. I wondered where they had been dried and on what surface: left outside on a bench by the side of a busy Indian road while waiting to be picked up? I couldn't help thinking of the crowded, chaotic wholesale dealer Terry and I had visited in Bangalore on our previous trip to India. Or the woman I had watched sift through a pile of dried plants on the side of the filthy road south of Madurai, bits of garbage blowing in the wind. I wondered whether some of those plants eventually made it into the sacks shipped to Dr. Harikrishnan's factory as well.

The following week, as I talked with Dr. Ram Dass in his small doctor's office, I told him of my fears about the supply chain. He sat behind the wooden desk. Ram Dass's thick black hair was slicked back. He closed his large eyes as he spoke.

Ram Dass told me that regarding medicines, faith is the most important. As a vaidya he has to have 100 percent faith in the medicine, even if it isn't perfect. As a patient, I had to have 100 percent faith. That's what matters most. I later talked about this with Emily, the Ayurvedic practitioner who has been coming to the center since 2011. When she is at Vaidyagrama, Emily told me, she trusts the medicine 100 percent.

I met with Ram Kumar after the group session called a *satsang*. We sat cross-legged on the bench built around the edges of the interior of the community building. Several ceiling fans did their best to move the heavy, hot air. A slight breeze came through the open windows.

I asked about faith. I meant to ask about manufacturing, but I'd been thinking about what Dr. Ram Dass had said earlier that week about having faith in your doctor and the medicine. In the satsang, Ram Kumar had also said you need to have faith—to trust, for example, that the food you are served was made with love, that when it is on the table it is *prasad*, an offering, and receive it in that way.

I didn't have that faith, I said. I couldn't get past my doubts about the supply chain. I knew too much about what else might be in the medicine.

He replied that it was my ego saying, "I know this." If I begin to approach the topic from a place of *bhakti*, open heart/love, a place I will reach by focusing on my breath, he explained, I will more and more find the herbs and food that are best for me.

"I still don't get it," I said.

He told me we would keep talking.

In my study of herbal medicine at Sage Mountain, I was most deeply impressed by how empowering it is. Rather than waiting for a doctor to tell me what was wrong and what to do, I learned healing practices I could do for myself. I could make teas and tinctures to help me and my family be well. In contrast, what surprised me most about the herb industry is how disempowering it is. Over and over I was struck by the ways in which something that was so simple had become so complex. I had learned that taking an herbal product was meant to be freeing because I would no longer be dependent on the pharmaceutical industry. But I was discovering that dependence on the herbal industry was little different. So many companies increasingly depend on ingredient suppliers and contract manufacturers. Few people who work for herbal product companies actually ever see or touch the medicinal plants themselves, and many who worked in the purchasing department of herbal companies had never even seen the plants growing in the ground. Their tactile experience was handling pieces of paper or touching a keyboard or screen to place an order or retrieve a message sent via the internet. As an end user of a product of such companies, in what way was I empowered?

Ram Kumar spoke of this as well. He said they weren't making medicines themselves yet at Vaidyagrama because he wants to do it sustainably, and he hadn't figured out how yet. He commented on how complex manufacturing was, the use of fossil fuels in factories, so much plastic involved, and the unsustainable collection of wild plants. "We buy from middlemen, a wholesaler. We don't know where he collects or buys his material. There is a range of issues and a lot of work we need to do. I'm looking at preparing the kashayams now. If this works, I'll move on to the next part.

"I have no solutions," he continued, "but I know that sustainable production has to empower the physician and patient, too. It won't mean giving them ready-made stuff to dispense or to consume. There has to be a level of empowerment at every level. That is what is sustainable to me." The underlying shift needed to make the system sustainable. Empowerment at *each level*. But what did *that* mean? I wondered.

I came to Vaidyagrama with an agenda. I wanted to learn about the Ayurvedic supply network and how Ayurvedic doctors prepared remedies. I was hoping to find positive examples and interesting stories, material I could use for articles and videos for the Sustainable Herbs Program. I visited other factories and farms in India, other Ayurvedic healing centers as well. I toured the warehouses and production facilities of some of the oldest Ayurvedic companies in southern India. I saw GMP certified and non-GMP-certified manufacturing centers. I interviewed individuals at each place, including a doctor who was introduced to me as the lead in conserving Ayurvedic plants by bringing them into cultivation. I visited projects of an NGO in the north that also claimed to be working with villagers to cultivate endangered Himalayan plants. At each place I was struck by how what I observed on the ground fell short of what they claimed. Each of these projects felt like a drop in the bucket addressing the challenges of sourcing medicinal plants in ways that were socially, economically, and ecologically sustainable.

I have notebooks filled with information about each visit. Yet I wasn't clear what telling these stories would reveal about the questions I wanted to understand. Despite the challenges, I slowly was beginning to understand that Vaidyagrama called for a different way of listening and being, the kind of attention I have learned to invoke while sitting with plants or during the practice of authentic movement. You begin a session of authentic movement by closing your eyes, paying attention with what is called your inner witness, waiting for movement to arise. You continue paying attention, following the gesture to see where it leads. When the gesture winds down, you watch and wait until another arises. And so it unfolds. More than anything else, it is a practice of attention and deep listening for what is emerging. I realized I needed to bring that same quality of attention to my research, listening and following my curiosity, what was emerging, even if what emerged didn't necessarily seem related.

In a satsang one afternoon, Ram Kumar talked about the relationship between attention and light, or *prana*. Light comes from attention, he said. And it was important that we eat food filled with light. As he spoke I wondered what happens to that light if no one is paying attention to it during the food production or herbal product manufacturing process. I thought of the supply chain of botanicals. It felt dark, sludgelike, a thickness caused by a lack of attention that needed to be addressed. And yet how much of my feelings that something was wrong with the industry were simply about needing to instead change my own relationship to that industry by having more faith, as Ram Kumar and Ram Dass kept telling me? And how much of my uneasiness was an indicator of actions I needed to take in the world?

The day before we were planning to leave, I joined Rajeesh in the canteen where the doctors and staff ate their meals. The canteen was simply two long tables set under a covered area opening onto the forest garden growing between the pathways. Rajeesh was a friend of Ram Kumar's from their school days together. Ram Kumar had asked him to set up management systems for Vaidyagrama. Rajeesh had served as a navy boat captain, which made him a good choice for such organizational work.

I complimented him on the changes that he had already implemented. He thanked me. It helped that he had so much passion for it, he said. I mentioned my trip to Harikrishnan's factory and my concerns about where the herbs come from. "We aren't raised to think about things like that," he said, "or to question things. Which is good," he added, "because that means we support traditions. But it is not good because we go along with blind faith." The raw materials should be free of pesticide, he added. I mentioned studies I had been told about concerning heavy metals being found in water in the Western Ghats, far from any industry. Rajeesh acknowledged that nothing was pure. But, he added, you have to be careful about not doing anything just because it isn't perfect. It was important to find the middle way.

Most of the questions people asked during most of Ram Kumar's satsangs focused on rules. Patients asked about food and exercise and whether it was okay to read while receiving panchakarma treatment. They wanted to know whether buttermilk was good or if yogurt was okay (not at night as it kills the *agni* or digestive fire). Ram Kumar often answered with questions or practices, not prescriptions. Notice your sleep and your emotions. Pay attention to your attention, see how you spend your time and then make changes based on what you observe about, say, whether your stool floats or sinks and whether you can't fall asleep or you drift off easily. The biggest challenge is for each of us to see that the healer is within and then to take responsibility for our own health. But that takes work. And so everyone instead looks for answers and to be told what to do. It amazed me how patiently Ram Kumar answered the same questions, day after day, week after week as new patients arrived. But one afternoon, in response to yet another question about the best diet, Ram Kumar said, "Nothing is best. We don't have a best rule. Things are good in context. Look for the context."

Which seemed as good a sign as any that to understand the challenges Ram Kumar was facing and his vision to address those challenges, I needed to understand the context.

Accepting the Invitation

Barry Lopez's essay "The Invitation" proposes that every encounter we have is either an invitation to enter the world more deeply or not. What we make of that invitation depends on what we see and how we listen. Like the bear in Lopez's essay, India was an invitation into a world I often turned my back on my way to get somewhere else. But India's invitation wasn't simply into a world of beauty and grace, though that was there. It was an invitation to pay attention to a harder world. A world where the padding, the separation between human actions and their impacts on other people and the earth, is impossible to ignore. Canadian herbalist Caroline Gagnon once told me that India was on a different vibration. In Canada, her home, things were monochrome. In India it was every vibration, all at once.

As Terry and Bryce and I moved on from Vaidyagrama to Kodaikanal, called "the Princess of the Hill stations," again I experienced the disconnect between my expectations and reality. Kodaikanal was once an exclusive retreat for American and British missionaries in the hills, almost two hundred kilometers southeast of Vaidyagrama; now it is a popular destination for Indian tourists during late April and May for a family vacation away from the unbearable heat of the plains.

We stayed in a compound for the Kodaikanal International School, an elite boarding school established in 1901 for the children of missionaries in South India. A friend who was also a Fulbright scholar had been a student here and, through his connections, we were able to stay in a stone cottage beneath towering white pines spread across a wooded hillside of similar cottages where faculty and alumni stayed. The entire compound was surrounded by a tall stone wall with two gatehouses manned by gatekeepers at all times. There was a flat grassy area where we could play soccer and frisbee and a lake to walk around. The lights in our cottage were bright enough to read at night and there was a small kitchen where we could cook. We came to Kodaikanal as a place of refuge, mostly, for Bryce. And in some ways, it was a place of refuge.

But it was still India. Gripping Bryce's hand, I'd run with him across the narrow two-lane road amid the traffic jam of buses and taxis. We would keep our heads down as we passed beggars, legs amputated and dressed in rags. We gingerly stepped past overturned rubbish bins and cow pies, past the men urinating into the gutter on the side of the road. A teacher at the school told us that everyone who lives in Kodaikanal avoids restaurants during the tourist season. Since the tourists won't come back, the restaurants don't care about the quality of the food then; they just serve leftovers.

On the afternoon we arrived in Kodaikanal, I stopped to talk to a Bhutanese schoolteacher at a cottage just beyond ours as he was hanging his clothes on the clothesline. He offered to show me around. As we walked down the hill, he waved to a man with a long dark ponytail who was smoothing the bark off a spiraled piece of wood. The man beckoned us over and introduced himself as Madhu Ramnath. He was a botanist, he said. It turned out he was also an anthropologist and writer and the head of an NGO network of indigenous people focused on culture and non-timber forest projects. I was struck by the coincidence of our encounter.

When I described my research work, Madhu commented that medicinal plants in India are becoming extinct. Ayurveda is a "fraud," he said. People want their spas and facials but there aren't enough plants left to satisfy the unending desire for products and treatments. And no one cares. No one is asking about the plants. And the Ayurveda industry is a fraud as well. Big companies export these products internationally, and they don't care about the plants, either. When he asks the companies where the plants are from, they say Kashmir, Mahdu told me, but the plants don't exist in Kashmir anymore, either. And the forest department does nothing.

The teacher said, "Maybe that's what's going to happen, each thing is going to die out and the world will end."

"Well, let's hope that doesn't come to pass," Madhu said. He invited us inside his cottage for tea. The living room was small and cozy. There were books on the shelves and tables, art on the walls, a desk covered with papers and more books, a couch and chairs. It was comfortable in a way that was familiar and felt like home. His wife taught art at the Kodaikanal School, which was how they could live in such a place, he said, gesturing around the room.

Madhu said he would call so we could meet again. In the meantime I decided to track down people to meet on my own. I had come across the name of a conservation organization in Kodaikanal. I saw that Madhu served on its board of directors, and so I assumed the organization must do good work. I called the director, Ravi, to arrange a meeting. Ravi told me he was beginning to grow medicinal plants for the market, which seemed like yet another interesting coincidence. He invited me to visit.

I took the bus down the mountain the following morning, early enough to visit his land before the heat of the day. Ravi met me by the side of the road at the bus stop. He had white hair and a mustache, and was warm and friendly. I was surprised when he mentioned in passing that he no longer worked for the conservation organization, but our conversation focused on his plans to develop wild gardens for medicinal plants to sell and on building cabins for tourists, so I didn't give it much thought. His plans sounded solid and well underway.

And so when, after breakfast in his home, Ravi drove me to see his farm, I was surprised by the condition of the land, which looked no different than the scrubland we passed on our drive. He pointed out a handful of tagged medicinal plants that seemed neither healthy nor plentiful. Huge electric lines crossed above the land; I thought these would make any ecotourism venture impossible to launch. It looked like this particular vision would take a long time to manifest.

The following day Madhu invited me over. He suggested we talk while walking to the market. I mentioned that I had visited Ravi the previous day. Madhu paused, suddenly suspicious.

"Why did you do that?" he asked. "We had a lot of trouble with that guy," he added before I could reply. Ravi was quite knowledgeable, but he had gone wrong, Madhu said. His family farm was in trouble. He "mismanaged" the funds for the conservation group and was fired. Now the group was struggling to survive.

I felt chagrined by my misjudgment. To change the subject, I asked Madhu to tell me about his work. But as we walked the tree-lined path of the school compound and then through the gates into the crowded streets, past beggars squatting on the side of the dusty road, cows rummaging in garbage, the press of people, I thought about how scary it must be in India to begin slipping—to feel you are losing whatever buffer you have, a house, a private well, a car, a steady income, anything to keep you from living on the streets. There was a desperation unlike anywhere I'd ever been, heightened by the harshness of the land, especially the lack of water, and by the huge numbers of people. I was disappointed that Ravi was untrustworthy and not doing good work. But I also wondered whether this encounter was part of understanding the context that Ram Kumar spoke of—both what it took to manifest a vision and the risks of failure.

We wove through the crowds by the lake in Kodailkanal. After college in Delhi his friends were mostly going abroad into business, Madhu told me. He instead went to the jungle in central India for ten years. He studied plants and learned hunting and gathering. He tried acting and music. He got a bit lost, he admitted.

We continued walking as he talked about the loss of skills among the tribal communities where he had lived. "They can't fish anymore because they don't have the right traps. They don't have the right traps because the person who knew how to make that trap has died." It isn't just a loss of skills. They are also losing the knowledge about identifying plants and poisons, and how to find the right resources to make a bowstring.

Without bows, they are unable to hunt. "They don't have that knowledge anymore," he said. "That level of restoration is very, very complex."

His words reminded me of what Josef Brinckmann and others had said about the loss of the specific knowledge that wild collectors possess. It isn't simply a matter of making sure the plants are protected. It is ensuring that the cultural knowledge about collection and living on and with the land is sustained—not just the rules of harvesting honorably, but the detailed knowledge about how and when to harvest each species, how they regrow and what habitat they prefer. Experienced harvesters know how to divide roots and sow seeds to ensure that plants regenerate, and they know what the signs of overharvesting are. Such guidelines are passed down through relationships, either with mentors or directly with the plants. When that knowledge is lost or ignored because of market demand, restrictions must be imposed through rules and regulations and assessments, standards introduced from outside the community. Like prescriptions from doctors, these external regulations will be effective only if the collectors see the value of taking action themselves, which depends on their valuing those resources in the first place. The cascade of connections reminded me of Ram Kumar's point about the importance of empowerment on every level.

For Madhu, every thread led back to culture and ecology, politics and economics. The issues their NGO deals with are overwhelming, he said as we began our walk back to his house. Timber exploitation among tribal communities. Companies ravaging the land: palm oil plantations, hillsides being denuded by new Ayurvedic companies, mining, the list went on. There is corruption at all levels. "You can't imagine," he said. He didn't even know where to begin.

Back at his house, Madhu made tea. I asked how he managed to avoid becoming depressed. What gave him hope? He said there is always something new to learn, new plants, new practices. "I stay curious."

But then another time, he said that his depression, when it comes, is about having gone wrong eight to ten thousand years ago when humans left the forest and that kind of life behind.

In Kodaikanal I felt more powerfully than anywhere else in India how the delinking of object from place is ravaging the world. I eventually got to read Madhu's book, which had just been published, and I was struck by the quotation with which he began: "Oh what's become of the world, Zaabalawi? / They've turned it upside down and taken away its taste."[6]

What would it mean, I wonder, to live in a world with no taste? Beyond the poetic, how would it make a difference? Taste is one of the most intimate and immediate ways to interact with the world, one of the few where what is outside enters. We get clear information that bypasses our expectations or assumptions or judgments: A taste is sour, salty, bitter, or sweet. A world with no taste had none of that aliveness. Yet because taste is direct and immediate, noticing it might be a way to begin awakening the body's relationship with the world, to begin listening with the body in the way that medicinal plants helped me experience that first weekend at Sage Mountain. Where might that awakening then lead? Taste as a way of reweaving our relationship with the earth.

To my surprise, at Kodaikanal I found myself nostalgic for Vaidyagrama, despite the oppressive heat there. Dismayed by the careless, unplanned way in which Kodaikanal was growing, I longed to be in a place where prayer is literally at the center, where attention is paid daily to the point where faith becomes form and intention is manifest, where plants receive the vibration of prayer not for any specific outcome but simply because the prayers are part of the practice. A place that addresses the root cause of disease and so, in turn, the root cause of healing.

———

I left on the night bus to Pondicherry for the hour's trip to Auroville. I hadn't planned ahead to visit Auroville, but when several people mentioned that the Pitchandikulam Forest was the most inspiring project they'd seen, I decided to loosen my grip on steering my research and see what I might discover.

Auroville is an intentional community founded in 1968 by the spiritual guru Mirra Alfassa (known as "the Mother"). Born in Paris, Alfassa traveled to Pondicherry, India, in 1914 where she met Sri Aurobindo, with whom she collaborated for the rest of her life. In 1968 she established

Auroville, an experimental township whose purpose is to realize human unity. It is now home to almost three thousand people, mostly from India, France, and Germany. Many visitors pass through here. Most notable, to me, were the lush green forests, so unusual in India. The community's land was barren at the inception, and the founders began by planting trees. That effort in itself is enough to show the power of taking action.

My first morning I rode my rented bike to the Pitchandikulam Forest. It was at the end of one of the many dirt roads that wove through the forest surrounding the main temple and center of Auroville. A volunteer offered to show me around. Though different from Vaidyagrama, Auroville had the same attention to detail: the pattern of the stones in the pathway, the angle and shape of windows, the curve of the porch. A design of colored tiles had been placed in the cement floor of the bathroom. Carved or painted signs depicting animals hung along the winding paths through the forest along with large signs bearing quotations or maps of the watershed. There were small ponds of water, a nursery. Other than muffled voices of people, the only sound was birdsong. There was an aliveness that I rarely encountered, especially in the built environment in India.

I joined a tour group of foreign students. The tour was led by Joss Brooks, who established the Pitchandikulam Forest in 1973. "We all live in a watershed," Joss said, standing by a sign showing the Auroville watershed. "Know what yours is and work from there." I asked how he planned, whether he had a vision from which he worked. He said he was here every day, morning and evening. He knew what he was doing just by being there and noticing what was happening. "This is not a project," he said, echoing Ram Kumar. "It's a garden that unfolded."

The most important technology is seeds, Joss said during the tour. In older days a grandfather would give his grandchildren a watermelon. He would show them that they should spit out some seeds and save the best to plant. Now the grandson buys seeds for a huge price from a seed company. (Earlier in the day, a volunteer had showed me the forest's seed collection, each package of seeds carefully labeled and stored in drawers in a dresser.) As the tour came to a close, Joss said, "If you are passionate about something, the important thing is to stay focused and not get caught up in the politics"—a telling comment in the context of India, where politics seem to make it hard to accomplish anything at all.

Bhakti

I rejoined Terry and Bryce the following week at Vaidyagrama. It was now early May. I came to Vaidyagrama this time as a patient rather than an anthropologist. Before, I had focused on the material circumstances of the center: had asked questions about work, about sourcing plants and growing food, had listened to gossip about tensions among staff, complaints of patients. My first morning back Dr. Aruna, the thin, lovely doctor with the young daughter, came by and told me to leave my work for now. I would have to do it in the future, but that was the future. For now I needed to focus on things that gave me positive energy, like chanting mantras. Cleansing is stressful for the body, she said. Even talking to the therapists during my treatment was too much. My work was, simply, to rest.

I did my best, waking at dawn, drinking my kashayam and walking down the walkway to morning prayers. May was the off season because of the heat, up to a hundred degrees some days. Only ten or so patients were in residence at the time, compared with as many as eighty during the winter months and the height of the season. I returned to my room, had a simple breakfast, went to treatment, came back to our room and lay on the bed on the porch or on one of the benches around the edge of the porch. Terry had returned to the US to attend a conference. Bryce was helping at the summer camp for children from the village. The program turned out to be poorly organized. I'd hoped he would be occupied all day, but he wasn't, so we spent the hot afternoons lying under the fan reading aloud.

As I lay on the wooden table on my fifth day of treatment, I scanned my body. I was drawn to a point behind my solar plexus. I sense a place where a flower is growing, a small, white, forest-grown flower in a bed of moss. It is hepatica. Above the tiny hepatica towered a maple or oak or birch. I stay with the flower. I begin to sense a coating on the flower, like the coating on my tongue that the doctors note on their daily visits, an indicator of my poor digestion, though they never elaborate about what that means. But this layer was thicker, stickier, yellowish white. I've come across hepatica before in my spiritual journeys to the inside house. It feels like the part of myself that is most true, most me, most connected to the essence of who I am. But I haven't come looking for it in a long while. Certainly not since coming to India following plants through the supply chain, a journey that, though fascinating, has in many ways led me further away from the questions I thought I was asking without providing many answers.

I hear Ram Kumar's words in my head. The root cause of everything is our clouded perception, he says. Every other consequence that impacts our health follows from that clouded vision. We can address those consequences on a political, economic, social, and ecological level. But until and unless we address this root cause, any changes we make cannot be sustained. To create changes that can be sustained, we must change our consciousness.

Slightly sour-smelling warm water is being poured over my body. The room is dim. A candle by Dhanvantari, the god of Ayurveda, is the only light other than what penetrates the curtain. Two therapists, young women in their early twenties, speak to each other in hushed voices. The wood juts into my hip bone and elbow when I roll on my side as they tell me to do. I am still deep in the forest with the hepatica flower. The sticky mucuslike substance is being washed away, the petals becoming clear and clean, radiant like a flower after a storm. The little girl from my inside house is there. She is running around and exploring the forest floor, the moss and the ferns, the early-spring flowers. She tells me she will stay here, washing the petals clear.

Dr. Ram Kumar speaks eloquently about topics that range from the Sanskrit alphabet to Vedic mythology to the Ayurvedic herb industry and much more. At times his comments about bhakti (open-heartedness) and the satvic path feel divorced from the day-to-day challenges of our lives at home, say of raising a child or eating healthy food in a food desert or even the day-to-day challenges at Vaidyagrama of feeding 120 people over wood-burning stoves, in hundred-degree temperature as the cooks at Vaidyagrama must do three times daily. And yet he is one of the clearest and most articulate thinkers I have ever met, especially regarding the nature of healing.

One day when I had bombarded Ram Kumar with still more questions, he told me to ask one question and then sit with it. The answers, he told me again and again, are always inside. And yet I come from a discipline where the answers are outside. Where there is always another perspective to get, another person to talk to, always more to learn. And so rubbing up against the rigor of Ram Kumar's advice on the mind is challenging. He talks about how science constantly changes on a superficial level, so it can't change on a deeper one. That's the point, too, about doing, he said. Constant busyness because of a busy mind prevents us from dropping into being. It isn't about not doing, he clarified. It is about the place from which we do.

Another morning as I lie on the wooden treatment table, I find the hepatica flower blooming again. I know without question that that flower is just me, my self, my signature, dressed up as a flower because that is the language that speaks to me.

Knowledge and action are the children of bhakti, or open heart, or loving-kindness, Ram Kumar also told me. Bhakti is experiencing the heart as an overflowing chalice of love for the world. That is the place from which we must act in the world for our actions to take hold and make a difference. I find the little girl joyfully tending the hepatica flower inside and as I do, I feel an outpouring of love. I suddenly realize that this is what bhakti is. I kept trying to understand it with my head, but it was just this deep love for this little girl, who is, simply, myself. Just as suddenly, I realize that quality of simple openheartedness, that place of love, is the place from which to act.

Years after leaving Hedangna, I came to understand that the biggest cultural difference between me and the villagers was not linguistic. It had to do with how we inhabited our bodies. They experienced the world through their bodies. I experienced the world through my mind. I even experienced my body through my mind. But that first encounter with the little girl in that stone cottage, years ago in the workshop with Steven Buhner in Rosemary's yurt, opened me to a different way of seeing and listening. And so I began listening to the plants and trying to follow what they revealed. They didn't lead me, as I had hoped, into circles of healers and herbalists gathered in the woods. Instead they led me out of the forest and away from the meadows, into factories and warehouses and offices, deeper into the world to witness the ways that plants have been used and abused around the world. I was coming to see that my role in following these plants was less to tell the details of sourcing and production and more to tell stories about the conditions needed for connections between people and plants to be awakened and sustained. These connections happened when people showed up and paid attention: When they did, the light flowed. And this, I was coming to see, was how intention could show up in a global supply network, and how some products were filled with prana and others were not.

Coming Home

What opens the secret of anything is a kind of love.

—EMILIE CONRAD, *Life on Land*

I first attended Expo West in 2019. I'd been warned it would be overwhelming, but nothing prepared me for the scale of the stuff and the crowds of people clamoring for samples of snack bars or chocolate, for some new kind of sports drink or vitamin or coffee or kombucha, for elderberry gummies or CBD oil or herbal extracts. Each booth sported an elaborate display, some were two and three stories tall, each trying to outdo the competitors in the hope of winning the recognition of a distributor and landing a contract. Hall after hall was lined with row after row of booths, denoted by numbers etched on the floor, numbers that reached into the thousands. The entire premise of these trade shows is that growth is good: Find new markets, solidify existing ones, announce new products, make an impression. There is educational programming throughout the show, too, and though the session topics increasingly focus on sustainability, regenerative agriculture, and reducing waste, it's hard to reconcile the seemingly contradictory agendas.

In the midst of this sea of stuff, I came upon Herb Pharm's booth. Unlike other booths, here I found soil and seedlings and seeds. A display of racks filled with calendula and nettles demonstrated how they dried their herbs (though the Herb Pharm staff make a point of trying to reuse everything in their booth, they did not reuse those herbs, I was told). Large placards shared information about regenerative agriculture and why the company had been out of stock on goldenseal rather than sourcing it from unverified sources from the wild. At the front was a row of tinctures where they shared tastes of their herbs. It was like arriving at a garden in the center of downtown Manhattan.

The booth seemed to offer the seeds of a different model and so when I returned home after Expo West, I contacted Tal Johnson, CEO of Herb Pharm, to discuss the possibility of writing something for the Sustainable Herbs Program website on the philosophy behind their booth. He instead invited me to listen in on their planning for their 2020 Expo booth. That way, he said, I could write about their process for deciding how the staff translates the company's vision into the nuts and bolts of a trade show booth, the tradeoffs they make, where they compromise, and when they decide not to.

Three thousand people attended the first Expo West in 1981. Thirty-eight years later, at least eighty-six thousand attend. This doesn't count the staff working in the booths. Companies now compete to build the most creative, newest, biggest booth. The CEO of one company told me it cost them $70,000 to attend and present a booth at Expo. But they can't afford not to be there.

Tal remembered one morning a few years ago walking into the show before it opened for the day. People were handing out samples to passersby, who took only one bite before throwing the rest in the waste can and taking another sample a bit further down the sidewalk. The trash cans were overflowing. (I remembered with some chagrin that I had done the same thing myself.)

"It was really good food," he said. And it was all going to waste. "What are we doing?" he wondered. "And why isn't this getting more attention?

"On one hand," Tal continued, "You could say just don't go to Expo." But a lot of good things happen at Expo, especially around education. It's a place to learn about new and important initiatives and have face-to-face meetings with others in the industry, which is invaluable. The trade show brings people together in a way that can lead to important changes, Tal said, and so as a company they plan to stay engaged. But they are committed to reducing their environmental impact. And they want to see if their exploration can inspire the natural products industry. It is easy to stand on the outside and demand that companies act more responsibly. It is much, much harder to be on the inside and to figure out how a company can implement responsible practices. Every action has consequences. Of course it's best to make the right decision in the first place, but in a complex world that's not always possible, so it's equally important for companies to actively watch out for unintended consequences and learn from those mistakes. And so Tal invited me to listen in. "I would be really happy if we could help turn the *Titanic* and play a part in helping the industry remember its roots and the reasons why many of us got involved in this work in the first place," he said.

For three months I listened in on the details of conversations as the Herb Pharm marketing, sales, and herbalist teams weighed different options and potential impacts and watched as the designs for their booth began to take shape. The goal of their Expo West 2020 booth was to significantly reduce their climate impact in a creative way while still meeting their commercial objectives. They came up with a remarkable concept that would use every aspect of the booth to amplify their message, to challenge and engage the industry as a whole to think more creatively about taking greater action. It was unlike any booth I had seen before and I was excited to see its execution and the response it elicited.

And then the week before the 2020 Expo West was set to begin, the first case of coronavirus was reported in Southern California. Companies began to cancel. The big stores and distributors canceled first, which was disappointing for many smaller and newer brands that attend Expo West in order to be recognized—and hopefully picked up—by the big players. As company after company backed out, those smaller businesses also backed out, doubting they would see any return on their investment, which can be $50,000 or much more.

This was in the early stages of the pandemic, before events were being canceled, but the trade show was finally canceled the day before it was to begin. The economic impacts of this cancellation were tremendous, only to be dwarfed by the rapid spread of COVID-19 across the United States and around the world. By then, the innovative booth that Herb Pharm had worked on for months was already on the trade show floor and had to be shipped back to the warehouse.

Matt Palomares, the head of marketing who led the process for planning the booth, held one last meeting with the team the week after the cancellation. "I'm sure this is disappointing," he told the group. "We put so much hard work and personal passion into this. There was a lot of strong conviction for the messages we are putting out. I want you to know the idea isn't dead. The concept is not dead. It is too bad not to be able to have made a statement. But we will. I want everyone to feel really good about what we did. We should be on our way to see it all come alive, not only the booth, but everything we planned to do in the booth. Keep it alive. And be proud."

I later spoke with Stepfanie Romine, Herb Pharm's copywriter. She said that the work they did laid the groundwork for the messaging moving forward. "In the spirit of the booth, nothing will go to waste." The process, disappointing as the outcome was, helped galvanize and focus their energies. And that, she said, was invaluable.

Again and again I am told that the natural products industry is a wonderful community, that people and companies are really committed to doing the right thing. In my journeys following herbs through the supply chain, that isn't always what I have observed. But, I wondered, could the cancellation of ExpoWest and the disruptions COVID-19 was causing in the world be an opportunity for this industry to demonstrate the ways it is committed to doing the right thing? That the botanical industry is committed not just to the health of their businesses and of their customers, but to the health of the communities—human and nonhuman—on which their business depends?

These are the conversations that Herb Pharm hoped to inspire with their booth. "We all have the parts of ourselves that care deeply for the world," Matt said. "In planning our booth we asked, how can we call that part of each person to come forward? Our booth was a way of saying, 'These are our passions and concerns. What are yours?'"

Herb Pharm plans to use the booth at next year's Expo, if it is held, and so they aren't sharing the design. They still hope to find other ways to inspire a shift from focusing on a company's next great product to talking about the actions they are taking to make the world a better place. Why as a company do you exist? Whose lives and livelihoods are you supporting? What kinds of relationships and partnerships are you building? What lessons have you learned in the process that you can share with others?

———

When I was a child, my family had a Shetland pony, which we boarded at a farm about fifteen minutes from our house. While driving home after riding in early spring, my mother would sometimes pull our white Chevy van to the side of the road by a small stream. My siblings and I would tumble out of the van, jump the stream, and follow her up the steep hill, ducking beneath bare branches, too early yet for leaves, to a spot to see the spring beauties, the trout lilies, and the first wet dog trillium of spring.

This place was no place, one among many where the trillium bloomed in those Appalachian woods. Just around the bend was a ravine filled with old washing machines, broken dolls, tires gone bare. The place isn't what matters now. What matters is that week after week, my mother stopped, even with four hungry kids in the car, tired from riding and wanting to get home. Ignoring our complaints, she hiked up through the woods in the hope of seeing that trillium, leaves encircling the stem like a prayer as it pushed through the still-cold soil. What I remember now is that for my mother, the possibility of witnessing that beauty trumped all the rest.

My mother tells me now that I am reading more into those flower-hunting excursions than I should. But I'm a mother, too. I've driven home plenty of times with tired kids complaining, dinner still to make at home, dishes to clean, an evening of tasks ahead of me. I think of all the times I haven't stopped. And of all the times that my mother—and my father—did.

"Humanity is in a strong argument about the future of the earth," mystic Elizabeth Anne Hin says in one of her podcasts, *Earth*.[1] Instead of engaging with that argument, she continues, step outside under the moonlight. Stand beneath the moon in silence. Know you are part of something so mysterious and holy that if you can give your attention to that holiness, it will teach you every moment what you need to do.

To give our attention to holiness.

Hin isn't telling us to stay out under the moon. Nor is she suggesting that standing in the mystery is sufficient. She also isn't saying to do nothing. The world is a mess, and Hin is fierce about our moral responsibility to, as she says, care for all the creatures of the earth. Cleaning up the soil, the oceans, the air; making things fair; spreading the wealth; protecting freedoms and so much more is going to take time and it is going to take us all.

But she is saying that the first step to discovering our instructions about how to respond is to go outside, beneath the night sky, in a forest, with a child—in awe at the beauty and the mystery. We will not find it indoors engaging with the news of the day, in anger and in judgment. What matters, as Ram Kumar said, is the place from which we act.

My mother didn't have any grand plan or big ideas about mystery and holiness when she stopped to look at the spring ephemerals begin to bloom. It's just that she loves plants more than anything, except for birds, maybe, and her five children and eight grandchildren, and our father to whom she has been married for over sixty years. She followed what she loved. And she shared it with us. She stepped into the moonlight. But she didn't stop there. She lobbied Congress on environmental issues, was chairman of the board of the West Virginia Land Trust, marched against climate change in New York and DC and much, much more. But it started, for us, with that moment in a hollow watching the trillium begin to bloom.

Plants invited me on a journey that taught me as much about the qualities of care and attention needed to create and sustain relationships as it did about the details of processing and manufacturing. This journey has been far more complex than I ever imagined at the outset. I came to realize that the point was not to arrive at a place where I could make definitive statements about what is or isn't sustainable. It was about learning how to live in the presence of a world we did not make. Like the plants, the world is alive. And the task first is to meet that aliveness. That realization, in turn, helped me listen more deeply. Like a menstruum drawing out different constituents in a plant, this journey brought forward parts of myself that were hidden, helping me become whole in ways that I previously hadn't. The journey itself, in other words, has itself become the medicine that these plants offer. That is their promise. Whether that promise is realized depends on each of us, on whether and how we choose to participate.

ACKNOWLEDGMENTS

*T*his journey, both the research and the writing, was much more challenging than I ever expected and I am deeply grateful for the help along the way.

My deepest thanks to Rosemary Gladstar who first opened the door to the world of plants for me, inspiring me, as with everyone she teaches, to find my own ways of working with them. The early support and encouragement of Josef Brinckmann gave me the confidence and direction needed. He arranged the initial introductions that made my first trip to eastern Europe possible, and he spent countless hours explaining the nuances of the botanical industry and his vast experience sourcing botanicals from around the world for nearly four decades.

Many others have offered guidance and support by hosting me for site tours, answering my many questions, and being willing to be interviewed on camera. I can't name them all here, but I especially want to thank Jeff Bodney, Mike Brook, Randy Brown, Melanie and Jeff Carpenter, Anna Charytoniuk, David Doty, Ed Fletcher, Jennifer Gerrity, Jackie Greenfield, Danielle Hawkins, Jeff and Elise Higley, Umesh Hiremath, Nate Johnson, Sara Katz, Lizzie Matteson, Anne McIntyre, Matt Richards, Drake and Nioma Sadler, Jayant Sarnaik, Ed Smith, Deb Soule, Anastasiya Timoshyna, David Winston, and Mark Wheeler.

In one of the highlights of this journey, thanks to Sebastian Pole for his invitation to join him and Ben Heron on a trip to their projects in southern India. Conversations then and subsequently with Sebastian and Ben have helped shape this book.

I thank Claudia Welch for the introduction to Vaidyagrama, Emily Reed for good conversations on our morning walks, Geetha Mohandas, Aparna Sarma, and Drs. Ram Dass and Harikrishnan for their help during our stay. I especially thank Dr. Ram Kumar for answering my many questions with patience and insight.

Beyond these site visits, I thank those who have spoken with me on the phone about the industry. Though primarily for the Sustainable Herbs Program, their insights have been crucial to my understanding: Bill Chioffi, Steven Dentali, Ed Fletcher, Sarah Laird, Lynda LeMole, Erin Smith, and Roy Upton.

Finally, this work gained an entirely new audience and platform through the partnership with the American Botanical Council and I am grateful to Mark Blumenthal for his trust and generosity. I am also grateful for the opportunity that partnering with ABC has provided to work more closely with Steven Foster, whose workshop on sustainable herbalism in the early 2000s in many ways set me on this path.

The idea of the Sustainable Herbs Program became a reality through the incredibly generous response of the almost 1,000 Kickstarter supporters. That support, largely in $35 donations, gave me not only the resources, but also the confidence, to step into this project and make it happen. Six months of research in India were made possible by being named a 2016–17 Fulbright-Nehru Senior Research Scholar.

I am grateful for the opportunity to participate in two different writing retreats during Vermont Week at the Vermont Studio Center and a two-week Creative Writing Fellowship at Craigarden in the Adirondacks.

Conversations with Catherine Cerulli, Sienna Craig, Louise Lowe, Ann Pancake, and Woden Teachout about plants, commodities, systems of medicine and more helped clarify my thoughts on these and other themes explored in the book.

Thanks to those who have read chapters of this manuscript: Mark Blumenthal, Steven Foster, Sebastian Pole, Ben Heron, Drake Sadler, Rosemary Gladstar, Claudia Ford, Richard Mandelbaum, and Steven Dentali. And thanks to Josef for reading the entire manuscript to check for any inaccuracies and misinformation. Woden read many early versions of the manuscript and offered crucial insights as I developed the themes. My two sisters, Molly Absolon and Cornelia Brefka, offered invaluable editorial input into clarity and narrative flow. Any mistakes that are still present are my own.

I thank the circle of Authentic Movement: Amy Goodman Kiefer, Louise Lowe, Emily Medley, Cynthia Kirkwood, Pamela Kentish, Ulrike

Wasmus, Rachel Shea, and especially Jan Sandman. Here many of the ideas for this book germinated and took shape.

Thanks to Margo Baldwin at Chelsea Green for believing in this project from the outset. I couldn't have asked for a more thoughtful and conscientious editor than Fern Marshall Bradley. This book has been greatly improved by her careful editing and attention to both the details and the overall themes I explore.

I thank my parents, Ted and Calvert Armbrecht, for how they have instilled a deep sense of curiosity and adventure, and a commitment to making the world a better place. They have supported this project from the beginning.

It is one thing to let a parent work. It is another thing altogether to become part of that work, and travel to herb companies around the world. This may sound exotic but often, in fact, involves long hours on twisty roads and even more hours walking around farms in the hot sun or touring production facilities. For their patience, good company, and photographs, I thank Willow and Bryce. And I especially thank Bryce for being game enough to spend six months in India. And finally, thanks to Terry Youk, whose support for this project from the beginning has been unconditional. He became a partner in the Sustainable Herbs Program, filming and editing the many videos on the website. And he has brought a critical and supportive eye to the writing, as with the filming, pushing me to do the extra work to get it right.

NOTES

Introduction

1. Claire Morton, *Nutrition Business Journal*, email message to author, August 7, 2020.
2. Claire Morton, "The Analyst's Take: Supplement Sales Growth Expected to Spike above 12% This Year," New Hope Network, June 17, 2020, https://www .newhope.com/market-data-and-analysis/analysts-take-supplement-sales -growth-expected-spike-above-12-year.
3. Claire Morton, "The Analyst's Take: Global Supplement Sales Expected to Grow 5.6% in 2019," New Hope Network, December 9, 2019, https://www .newhope.com/market-data-and-analysis/analyst%E2%80%99s-take-global -supplement-sales-expected-grow-56-2019.
4. Tyler Smith et al., "US Sales of Herbal Supplements Increase by 8.6% in 2019," *HerbalGram* 127 (2020): 54–69.
5. NMI, 2019 Supplements/OTC/Rx Consumer Trends & Insights Report New 8th Edition USA Report, https://www.nmisolutions.com/research-reports /supplement-otc-rx-reports/usa/2019-supplements-otc-rx-consumer-trends -insights-report-new-8th-edition-usa-report. Accessed June 17, 2020.
6. Steve French, "Herbal Supplement Use and Sustainability," PowerPoint presentation, Botanical Congress, American Herbal Products Association, Las Vegas, NV, October 19, 2019.
7. *Sustainability 2019: Beyond Business as Usual* (Bellevue, WA: Hartman Group, 2019), https://www.hartman-group.com/webinars/1495124799/sustainability -2019-beyond-business-as-usual-new-report-overview.
8. Wendell Berry, "Keynote," *Watershed* (Washington, DC: Orion Society, 1996).

Chapter 1: Making Medicine

1. Steven Foster, "Echinacea," Steven Foster Group, Inc. (website), http://www.steven foster.com/education/monograph/echinacea1.html. Accessed April 12, 2019.
2. Different menstruums extract different types of constituents. For water-soluble constituents, water works fine—thus, herbal teas. If the constituents aren't water-soluble or if the herbs wouldn't make a good-tasting tea, then alcohol,

vinegar, glycerin, or milk may be used. In some systems of traditional medicine, such as traditional Chinese medicine, water is mainly used to prepare decoctions of complex formulations, while alcohol is for preparing medicated herbal wines. Both water and milk are used for making decoctions in the Indian Ayurvedic system of medicine. In other cases herbs are placed in baths for soaking in, or medicated oils are prepared for application to the skin.

3. Calum Blaikie, *Making Medicine: Pharmacy, Exchange and the Production of Sowa Rigpa in Ladakh* (PhD dissertation, University of Kent, 2014), 97.
4. Craig Holdredge, *Thinking Like a Plant: A Living Science for Life* (Great Barrington, MA: Lindisfarne Books, 2013), 114–15.
5. Holdredge, *Thinking Like a Plant*, 111.
6. Holdredge, *Thinking Like a Plant*, 101.
7. David Hoffmann, *Medical Herbalism: The Science and Practice of Herbal Medicine* (Rochester, VT: Healing Arts, 2003), 38.
8. Josef Brinckmann, "Emerging Importance of Geographical Indications and Designations of Origin—Authenticating Geo-Authentic Botanicals and Implications for Phytotherapy," *Phytotherapy Research* (2012), 1.
9. Barry Lopez, "The Invitation," *Granta*, November 18, 2015, https://granta.com /invitation.

Chapter 2: The Modern Renaissance of Herbal Medicine

1. Robert Conrow and Arlene Hecksel, *Herbal Pathfinders: Voices of the Herb Renaissance* (Santa Barbara, CA: Woodbridge, 1983).
2. Conrow and Hecksel, *Herbal Pathfinders*, 12.
3. "The New Age Movement of the 1970s was "a 'self-dispersing' movement par excellence: participants almost never affiliated exclusively with a single teacher or organization but cobbled together world views and lifestyles from an enormous menu." See Dan McKanan, *Eco-Alchemy: Anthroposophy and the History and Future of Environmentalism* (Berkeley: University of California Press, 2018), 75.
4. Hervey C. Parke, one of the directors of Parke, Davis and Company, sent expeditions to the Amazon for finding new drugs from plants, beginning in 1871. See Margaret Kreig, *Green Medicine: The Search for Plants That Heal* (New York: Bantam Books, 1964).
5. Barbara Griggs, *Green Pharmacy: The History and Evolution of Western Herbal Medicine* (Rochester, VT: Healing Arts, 1981), 235. Also see "An American Practice: Part 1–4," 2012, https://www.youtube.com/watch?v=z-rPy_0LRXE, a video series by HerbTV that provides a fascinating overview of the history of herbal medicine in America, focusing on the Eclectics and the rediscovery of their works by herbal practitioners in the 1970s and '80s.

6. Originally the word *drug* referred to dry herbs in rafters. Roy Upton said the word has been bastardized over the centuries, but originally it referred to any substance used as medicine, including plants, rather than specifically to chemicals or pills.
7. Martha Libster, *Herbal Diplomats* (Wauwatosa, WI: Golden Apple Publications, 2004), 140; Edward Price, "Root Digging in the Appalachians: The Geography of Botanical Drugs," *Geographical Review* 50, no. 1 (1960): 1–20, 12.
8. Gary R. Freeze, "Roots, Barks, Berries, and Jews: The Herb Trade in Gilded-Age North Carolina," *Essays in Economic and Business History* 13 (1995): 107–27, 109.
9. Freeze, "Roots, Barks, Berries, and Jews," 109.
10. Freeze, "Roots, Barks, Berries, and Jews," 109.
11. Freeze, "Roots, Barks, Berries, and Jews," 126.
12. Griggs, *Green Pharmacy*, 231.
13. See Karen Culpepper, "Cotton Root Bark as Herbal Resistance," *Journal of the American Herbalists Guild* 15, no. 2 (2017): 45–52; Richard Mandelbaum, "A Tree Without Roots: Lessons for the Future of Herbalism from the 19th Century," *Journal of the American Herbalists Guild* 12, no. 1 (2014): 26–30.
14. Phyllis Light, *Southern Folk Medicine: Healing Traditions from the Appalachian Fields and Forests* (Berkeley, CA: North Atlantic Books, 2018).

Chapter 3: Digging Deeper

1. Rebecca Seiferle, Centrum Writer's Conference, Port Townsend, WA, 2000.
2. Gary Nabhan, *Cumin, Camels, and Caravans: A Spice Odyssey* (Berkeley: University of California Press, 2014), 47.
3. Nabhan, *Cumin, Camels, and Caravans*, 95.
4. Nabhan, *Cumin, Camels, and Caravans*, 71.
5. Nabhan, *Cumin, Camels, and Caravans*, 71.
6. Nabhan, *Cumin, Camels, and Caravans*, 236.
7. This painting was done in 1898, four hundred years later, by well-known Portuguese artist Velosa Salgado.
8. Nabhan, *Cumin, Camels, and Caravans*, 237.
9. Nabhan, *Cumin, Camels, and Caravans*, 237.
10. Peter Frankopan, *The Silk Roads: A New History of the World* (London: Bloomsbury, 2015), 230.
11. George Masselman, *The Cradle of Colonialism* (New Haven, CT: Yale University Press, 1963), 6.
12. V. Loth, "Pioneers and Perkeniers: The Banda Islands in the 17th Century," *Cakalele* 6 (1995): 6. In 1656 the Dutch forced natives to plant 120,000 young nutmeg trees on Amboyna. Almost forty years later, in 1692, they forced them to cut many of them down. Masefield 1967: 289, as quoted in Lucile

Brockway, *Science and Colonial Expansion: The Role of the British Royal Botanic Garden* (New Haven, CT: Yale University Press, 2002), 50.

13. John Villiers, "Trade and Society in the Banda Islands in the Sixteenth Century," *Modern Asian Studies* 15, no. 4 (1981): 748.

14. Amitav Ghosh, "What Nutmeg Can Tell Us about Nafta," *New York Times*, December 30, 2016.

15. Loth, "Pioneers and Perkeniers," 14.

16. Villiers, "Trade and Society," 748.

17. Kathleen Morrison, "Pepper in the Hills: Upland–Lowland Exchange and the Intensification of the Spice Trade," in *Forager-Traders in South and Southeast Asia: Long-Term Histories*, eds. Kathleen Morrison and Laura Junker (Cambridge, U.K.: Cambridge University Press, 2002), 141.

18. See Karen Culpepper, "Cotton Root Bark as Herbal Resistance," *Journal of the American Herbalists Guild* 15, no. 2 (2017): 45–52; Richard Mandelbaum, "A Tree Without Roots: Lessons for the Future of Herbalism from the 19th Century," *Journal of the American Herbalists Guild* 12, no. 1 (2014): 26–30.

19. Herbert C. Covey, *African American Slave Medicine: Herbal and Non-Herbal Treatments* (Lanham, MD: Rowman and Littlefield, 2007). Lloyd did attribute the use of cotton bark as a uterine stimulant and emmenagogue capable of producing abortions to African Americans in the South (Claudia Ford, *Pain Pollen: The Story of Cotton*, 2018, manuscript in files of author, 3), but as in much of contemporary education about plant medicine, those uses were disconnected from the context in which that information was passed on in the African American communities that kept them alive.

20. Ford, *Pain Pollen*, 3.

21. Culpepper, "Cotton Root Bark," 49.

22. Claudia Ford, *Weed Women, All Night Vigils, and the Secret Life of Plants: Negotiated Epistemologies of Ethnogynoecological Plant Knowledge in American History* (PhD dissertation, Antioch University, 2015), 164.

23. Culpepper, "Cotton Root Bark," 50.

24. Patent medicines were medicines sold directly to the public. The ingredients were kept secret. They were promoted heavily and sold "anywhere they could find shelf space." Ethical medicines, on the other hand, like today's prescription drugs, were products bought from a pharmacist under instructions from a doctor. The contents were listed for all to see. They were not advertised to the public because the physicians believed "such marketing to be irresponsible." Ethical medicine makers sold their products thanks to the goodwill of doctors, whereas patent medicine makers sold their products by the power of their advertising. Charles Mann and Mark Plummer, *The Aspirin Wars: Money,*

Medicine, and 100 Years of Rampant Competition (New York: Alfred Knopf, 1991), 33.

25. Kevin Dunn, *Caveman Chemistry: 28 Projects, from the Creation of Fire to the Production of Plastics* (Irvine, CA: Universal Publishers, 2003), 26.1, http://cavemanchemistry.com/cavebook/chaspirin.html.

26. Selling patent medicines at the medicine shows of the late 1800s was a way for promoters to make money, much as selling popcorn makes money for movie theater owners. Though most accounts of this period focus on whether or not these doctors were quacks, historian Susan Strasser suggested that their greater impact has been in ushering in the modern world of advertising. Susan Strasser, "Sponsorship and Snake Oil: Medicine Shows and Contemporary Public Culture," in *Public Culture: Diversity, Democracy, and Community in the United States*, ed. Marguerite Shaffer (Philadelphia: University of Pennsylvania Press, 2007), 2–5.

27. Strasser, "Sponsorship and Snake Oil," 5; Virgil Vogel, *American Indian Medicine* (Norman: University of Oklahoma Press, 1970), 140.

28. Vogel, *American Indian*, 137–40.

29. James Harvey Young, *The Toadstool Millionaires: A Social History of Patent Medicines in America Before Federal Regulation* (Princeton, NJ: Princeton University Press, 1961), 98.

30. Joseph Collins and John Gwilt, "The Life Cycle of Sterling Drug, Inc.," *Bulletin History of Chemistry* 25, no. 1 (2000): 22. Because Neuralgine was a patent medicine, the company was not required to list its ingredients. No records have been kept, but Mann and Plummer guessed that acetanilide, a coal-tar analgesic, was one of these ingredients. Mann and Plummer, *Aspirin Wars*, 50.

31. Wheeling Hall of Fame: William E. Weiss, 1879–1942. Ohio Public Library, http://www.ohiocountylibrary.org/wheeling-history/4142. Accessed October 22, 2018.

32. Malcolm Goldstein, "Sterling Remedy Co. (III.1) – Neuralgyline Co.; J. W. James Co.; J. G. Dodson Medicine Co.; Drake Co.; Pape, Thompson & Pape Co.," https://onbeyondholcombe.wordpress.com/category/companies/n. Accessed October 21, 2018.

33. Mann and Plummer, *Aspirin Wars*, 50–51.

34. Mann and Plummer, *Aspirin Wars*, 44–49.

35. Mann and Plummer, *Aspirin Wars*, 49.

36. Synthetic dyes, later explosives—and also, it turns out, many pharmaceutical drugs. Mann and Plummer, *Aspirin Wars*, 18, 32.

37. Mann and Plummer, *Aspirin Wars*, 21.

38. Dunn, *Caveman Chemistry*, 26.1.

39. Mann and Plummer, *Aspirin Wars*, 25–27.

40. Mann and Plummer, *Aspirin Wars*, 58.
41. Mann and Plummer, *Aspirin Wars*, 76.
42. Mann and Plummer, *Aspirin Wars*, 109–18.
43. Rebecca Altman, "How the Benzene Tree Polluted the World," *The Atlantic*, October 4, 2017.

Chapter 4: The Herb Industry

1. T. Smith et al., "Herbal Supplement Sales in US Increase by 9.4% in 2018," *HerbalGram* 123 (2019), 62–73.
2. Anastasiya Timoshyna, Zhang Ke, Yuqi Yang, Xu Ling, and Danna Leaman, *The Invisible Trade: Wild Plants and You in the Times of COVID-19 and the Essential Journey Towards Sustainability* (Cambridge, U.K.: Traffic International, 2020), 2.
3. Timoshyna et al., *The Invisible Trade*, 3.
4. Uwe Schippmann, Danna Leaman, and A. B. Cunningham, "A Comparison of Cultivation and Wild Collection of Medicinal and Aromatic Plants Under Sustainability Aspects." In *Medicinal and Aromatic Plants: Agricultural, Commercial, Ecological, Legal, Pharmacological and Social Aspects*, eds. R. J. Bogers, L. E. Craker, and D. Lange (Dordrecht, Germany: Springer Wageningen UR Frontis Series 17, 2006), 75–95.
5. Martin Jenkins, Anastasiya Timoshyna, and Marcus Cornthwaite, *Wild at Home: Exploring the Global Harvest, Trade and Use of Wild Plant Ingredients* (Cambridge, U.K.: Traffic International, 2018), 30.
6. National Botanical Research Institute, *Devil's Claw*, 2018, http://www.nbri.org.na/sections/economic-botany/INP/sectors/Devils-claw. Accessed October 18, 2018.
7. Kerry Ploetz and Blair Orr, "Wild Herb Use in Bulgaria," *Economic Botany* 58: 2 (2004): 231–41, 232.
8. Dragana Pecanac and Hakan Tunon, *Conceptions of Sustainability in the Medicinal and Aromatic Plant Sector in Bosnia and Herzegovina* (MA thesis, International Master Programme at the Swedish Biodiversity Center, 2007), 16.
9. S. J. Dentali, "Successful Botanical Research Requires Botanical Expertise," *Clinical Pharmacology and Therapeutics* 87, no. 2 (2010): 149.
10. Josef Brinckmann, R. Marles, P. Schiff, H. Oketch-Rabah, G. Tirumalai, G. Giancaspro, and N. Sarma, "Quality Standards for Botanicals: The Legacy of USP's 200 Years of Contributions," *HerbalGram* 126 (2020): 50–65.
11. Dentali, "Successful Botanical Research," 149.
12. Dentali, "Successful Botanical Research," 149.
13. Various examples that Steven Foster and Ed Smith shared with me indicated that collectors were accidentally or deliberately passing off the wrong species

of plants as *Echinacea purpurea*, and that there's evidence in the historical
record this may have been going on for a long time.

14. Peggy Brevoort, video interview with Bethany Davis, Expo West, 2017. Files
of author.

15. Skye Lininger, video interview with Bethany Davis, Expo West, 2017. Files
of author.

16. Anne Dougherty, "Herbal Voices: American Herbalism Through the Words
of American Herbalists" (MA thesis, Health Arts and Sciences, Goddard
College, 2000), 244.

17. Steven Foster, "Echinacea in the News(papers)," *HerbalGram* 40 (1997): 11.

18. Brian Frisby, video interview with Bethany Davis, Expo West, 2017. Files
of author.

19. Peggy Brevoort, "The Booming U.S. Botanical Market: A New Overview,"
HerbalGram 44 (1998): 33.

20. Peter Landes, "Market Report," *HerbalGram* 40 (1997): 53.

21. Peter Landes, "Market Report," *HerbalGram* 43 (1998): 60.

22. Peter Landes, "Market Report," *HerbalGram* 46 (1999): 55.

23. Varro E. Tyler, "Herbal Medicine at the Crossroads: The Challenge of the 21st
Century," *HerbalGram* 54 (2002): 52–61.

24. Mark Blumenthal, Senior Editor, et al., *The Complete German Commission E
Monographs: Therapeutic Guide to Herbal Medicines* (Austin: American Botanical
Council and Boston: Integrative Medicine Communications, 1988).

25. Steven Foster, "The Complete German Commission E Monographs," *Journal of
Alternative and Complementary Medicine* 4, no. 4 (1998): 479–81.

26. "Letters to the Editor," *HerbalGram* 20 (1989): 5.

Chapter 5: Pick a Plant

1. Garbling is the final step in the preparation of a crude drug. Garbling consists of the
removal of extraneous matter, such as other parts of the plant, dirt, and added adulterants. This step is done to some extent during collection, but should be carried out
after the drug is dried and before it is baled or packaged. Although garbling may
be done by mechanical means in some cases, it is usually a semiskilled operation.
"Preparation of Drugs for the Commercial Market," in *Pharmacognosy*, 9th ed., ed.
Varro E. Tyler, Lynn Brady, and James Robbers (Philadelphia: Lippincott Williams
& Wilkins, 2011), https://archive.org/details/PharmacognosyBrady.

2. While processing companies in the certified supply chain also mix the goods,
they are required to keep records and samples of where the herbs are from.

3. Standards for the sustainable use of natural resources are authoritative or
voluntary and can range from the following: "bottom-up" locally developed

standards that are agreed upon by a particular group, collector organization, or other producers, but are not enforced; internal sourcing standards developed by traders and manufacturers; and government and private voluntary standards. FSC for wood and wood products and FairWild for wild-harvested plants fall into this latter category, as do FairTrade, FLO, FairTrade US, Fair for Life and others. Wolfgang Kathe, David Harter, and Uwe Schippmann, *Sustainability in Practice: Key Aspects, Opportunities and Challenges in Implementing a Standard for Sustainable Use of Natural Biological Resources* (Bonn, Germany: BfN-Skripten 513, Federal Agency for Nature Conservation, 2018), 8–9.

4. William Cronon, *Nature's Metropolis: Chicago and the Great West* (New York: W. W. Norton, 1991), 107.
5. Cronon, *Nature's Metropolis*, 107.
6. Cronon, *Nature's Metropolis*, 111.
7. Cronon, *Nature's Metropolis*, 107.
8. Cronon, *Nature's Metropolis*, 116.
9. Cronon, *Nature's Metropolis*, 256.
10. Verlyn Klinkenborg, "Boosted," *The New Yorker* (1991): 79.
11. Robert Pogue Harrison, "What Is a House?" *Terra Nova* 1, no. 2 (1996): 24.
12. Harrison, "What Is a House?" 24.
13. Harrison, "What Is a House?" 24.
14. Robert Pogue Harrison, *Gardens: An Essay on the Human Condition* (Chicago: Chicago University Press, 2008), 114.

Chapter 6: Harvesting the Wild

1. Traditional Medicinals, "Protecting People and Plants in Poland," https://www.traditionalmedicinals.com/articles/community/protecting-people-plants-in-poland. Accessed December 15, 2018.
2. Traditional Medicinals, "Protecting People and Plants in Poland."
3. Josef Brinckmann, California Institute of Integral Studies commencement speech, May 22, 2016, https://www.youtube.com/watch?v=xN1JRBBu2yQ. Accessed October 2, 2019.
4. Several articles address the specific impact of climate change on the herb industry through changing weather patterns that disrupt supply chains via drought, extreme rains, hurricanes, and the like; through changes in phenology and the flowering of plants; and through changes in the chemical constituents in the plants. Hannah Bauman, Tyler Smith, and Connor Yearsley, "Plants in Peril: Climate Crisis Threatens Medicinal and Aromatic Plants," *HerbalGram* 124 (2020): 44–61; Courtney Cavalier, "The Effects of Climate Change on Medicinal and Aromatic Plants," *HerbalGram* 81 (2009): 44–57; Selena

Ahmed, "Tea and the Taste of Climate Change: Understanding Impacts of
Environmental Variation on Botanical Quality," *HerbalGram* 103 (2014):
44–51; Stephen Daniells, "The Erosion of Predictability: Climate Change and
the Botanical Supply Chain," *Nutra-ingredients*, March 22, 2018, https://www
.nutraingredients-usa.com/Article/2018/03/22/The-erosion-of-predictability
-Climate-change-and-the-botanical-supply-chain.

Chapter 7: Tending the Garden

1. L. E. Sayer (1904: 5), quoted in Steven Foster, *Echinacea: Nature's Immune
Enhancer* (Rochester, VT: Inner Traditions, 1991), 116.
2. Foster, *Echinacea*, 116.
3. Foster, *Echinacea*, 118.
4. Foster, *Echinacea*, 118.
5. Josef Brinckmann, "Geographical Indications for Medicinal Plants: Globaliza-
tion, Climate Change, Quality and Market Implications for Geo-Authentic
Botanicals," *World Journal of Traditional Chinese Medicine* 1 (2015): 1–8.
6. Josef Brinckmann, "Review: Emerging Importance of Geographical Indications
and Designations of Origin—Authenticating Geo-Authentic Botanicals and
Implications for Phytotherapy," *Phytotherapy Research* (2012): 1.
7. Brinckmann, "Geographical Indications," 7.
8. The pharmacopeia set the specifications for the medicinal parts of different
plants. Companies with rigorous quality control standards use these guidelines
for preparing specification sheets when placing an order.

Chapter 8: Viriditas

1. See Christine Jones, "Creating New Soil," March 24, 2006, for an overview of
this literature. http://scseed.org/wb/media/Creating_New_Soil_Dr._Christine
_Jones_3-24-2006.pdf.
2. Josh Tickell, *Kiss the Ground* (New York: Atria, 2017), 70.
3. Tickell, *Kiss the Ground*, 54.
4. Raymond Williams, *The Country and the City* (Oxford, U.K.: Oxford University
Press, 1975), 83.
5. I contacted Organic India to arrange a visit with their farming network or
production facilities while I was in India. Unfortunately, I never received a
reply and was unable to schedule a visit.
6. Helga Willer and Julia Lernoud, *The World of Organic Agriculture: Statistics
and Emerging Trends 2019* (Research Institute of Organic Agriculture FiBL
-IFOAM-SOEL-Surveys 1999–2019, www.fibl.org), 26.

7. Willer and Lernoud, *The World of Organic Agriculture*, 25.
8. Marcin Barański et al., "Higher Antioxidant and Lower Cadmium Concentrations and Lower Incidence of Pesticide Residues in Organically Grown Crops: A Systematic Literature Review and Meta-Analyses," *British Journal of Nutrition* 112, no. 5 (2014): 794–811.
9. Norman Myers, Russell Mittermeier, Cristina Mittermeier, A. B. Fonseca Gustavo, and Jennifer Kent, "Biodiversity Hotspots for Conservation Priorities," *Nature* 403 (2000): 853–58.
10. Loren Eiseley, "The Star Thrower," in *The Star Thrower* (New York: Harcourt Brace Jovanovitch, 1978), 184.
11. Eiseley, "Star Thrower," 185.
12. Tickell, *Kiss the Ground*, 143.

Chapter 9: Supporting Supply Communities

1. J. Brinckmann and T. Smith, "Herb Profile: Senna," *HerbalGram* 120 (2018): 6–13.
2. In 2009 Traditional Medicinals partnered with Martin Bauer, Umalaxmi, Gravis, CAZRI, and WomenServe to address these social and economic issues in the Thar Desert, develop higher-quality senna, and improve best agricultural practices (https://www.traditionalmedicinals.com/plants/senna/#undefined). See also Josef Brinckmann, "Revive: Benefit Sharing in the Thar," in *Plants, People and Nature: Benefit Sharing in Practice*, ed. Denzil Phillips International (Port Louis, Mauritius: AAMPS Publishing, 2009), 38.
3. Brinckmann and Smith, "Senna," 13.
4. Other villages where they work include Dayakor village in the Phalodi Tehsil, and the villages of Khidrat, Nayagaon, and Surpura in the Bap Tehsil.
5. Brinckmann, "Revive," 38.
6. Unnikrishnan Payyappalli, a medical anthropologist and Ayurvedic doctor, guessed that 60 to 70 percent of plant material is wasted in production, and noted that this waste was the biggest issue in the Ayurveda industry in India. These companies talk about sustainability but huge amounts of waste are not being addressed, he added. And so TM is indirectly offering an approach to addressing the issue of waste as well.

Chapter 10: Conservation as Livelihood

1. Though studies have been done, in particular by FRLHT, the authors, G. S. Goraya and D. K. Ved, acknowledged that the complexity of the herbal industry especially in India was still not yet completely understood—hence

the limitations of this information. Some issues need additional research: Chains of custody of particular species aren't clear; many plants are collected and traded under different names, and so it can be hard to determine actual quantities in commerce; species are imported from other countries with no records; more information is needed on the sources of species on the IUCN Red List; and there is a need to understand the role of botanicals in international trade. The report, G. S. Goraya and D. K. Ved, *Medicinal Plants in India: An Assessment of Their Demand and Supply* (National Medicinal Plants Board, Ministry of AYUSH, Government of India, New Delhi and Indian Council of Forestry Research & Education, Dehradun, 2017), is an effort to continue gathering more information on this trade.

2. Sarah Laird and Alan Pierce, *Promoting Sustainable and Ethical Botanicals: Strategies to Improve Commercial Raw Material Sourcing* (New York: Rainforest Alliance, 2005).

3. Three important initiatives were the Guidelines on the Conservation of Medicinal Plants developed by WHO (World Health Organization), the IUCN (International Union for Conservation of Nature), and the WWF (World Wildlife Fund) (WHO et al., 1993); the Declaration of the International Conference on Medicinal Plants in Bangalore; and the Global Strategy for Plant Conservation of the Convention on Biological Diversity (CBD). Wolfgang Kathe, David Harter, and Uwe Schippmann, *Sustainability in Practice: Key Aspects, Opportunities and Challenges in Implementing a Standard for Sustainable Use of Natural Biological Resources* (Bonn, Germany: BfN-Skripten 513, Federal Agency for Nature Conservation, 2018), 13.

4. FairWild has been working to develop these quotas, as has CITES (the Convention on International Trade and Endangered Species of Wild Fauna and Flora).

5. FairWild Foundation, "Our Story," https://www.fairwild.org/our-story. Accessed June 9, 2020.

6. Rie Makita, "Applications of Fair Trade Certification for Wild Plants: Lessons from a FairWild Project in India," *International Journal of Sustainable Development and World Ecology* 25, no. 7 (2018): 619–29, 628. The operation of tribal corporation and its benefits (or lack thereof) to this community (and others) are outside the scope of this book.

7. Julie Guthman, "Unveiling the Unveiling: Commodity Chains, Commodity Fetishism, and the 'Value' of Voluntary, Ethical Food Labels," in *Frontiers of Commodity Chain Research*, ed. Jennifer Bair (Stanford, CA: Stanford University Press, 2009), 191.

8. Anthropologist Julie Guthman concluded that, despite her "abiding skepticism of labels as a vehicle of social and environmental improvement, they may be all

that there is." She continued by saying that it is important to not stop simply with promoting these standards, but to ask what sort of broader politics they invite. "Is it possible that although their apparent effects are anemic, they put processes into motion with far larger potential to effect progressive change?" (2009: 191).

9. In fact, Makita wrote that 3,813 kg were harvested in 2014–15, the first year; 4,096 kg in 2015–16; and 6,255 kg in 2016–17. Makita, "Applications," 623.
10. Makita, "Applications," 623.

Chapter 11: Medicine of Place

1. Ayurvedic formulas and medicine making are extremely complex. A few weeks later I visited SNA Oushadhasala, an Ayurvedic factory on the outskirts of Thrissur, an important herb trading center in Kerala that was established in 1920. There the head of manufacturing who showed me around also talked about how the art of Ayurvedic medicine making was being lost and that companies no longer knew how to make remedies in the traditional way as more and more opted for ready-made capsules.
2. Brian Houseal, Craig MacFarland, Guillermo Archibold, and Chiari Adrelio, "Indigenous Cultures and Protected Areas in Central America," *Cultural Survival Quarterly*, March 1985, https://www.culturalsurvival.org/publications/cultural-survival-quarterly/indigenous-cultures-and-protected-areas-central-america. Accessed March 23, 2019.
3. Robin Kimmerer, "The Honorable Harvest," Bioneers video series, Seeding the Field: 30 Years of Transformative Solutions, https://bioneers.org/the-honorable-harvest-robin-kimmerer-zstf0619. Accessed January 2020.
4. Nils Mueggenburg, personal conversation, September 2019.
5. *Kashayam* refers to a form of Ayurvedic preparation that was traditionally made from plants decocted in water. In the 1920s Vaidyaratnam P. S. Varier was the first to start processing Ayurvedic medicines in Kerala and the first to develop a way to bottle kashayams so that they wouldn't decompose. Gita Krishnankutty, *A Life of Healing: A Biography of Vaidyaratnam P. S. Varier* (New Delhi: Viking, 2001), 52.
6. Madhu Ramnath, *Woodsmoke and Leafcups: Autobiographical Footnotes to the Anthropology of the Durwa* (London: HarperCollins, 2015).

Epilogue

1. Elizabeth Hin, Monthly Contemplations: Earth, https://soundcloud.com/elizabeth-anne-hin. Accessed October 10, 2019.

INDEX

Note: Page numbers preceded by *ci* refer to the pages of the color insert section.

INDEX

Brooks, Joss, 235–36
Budapest, Hungary, TRAFFIC regional office, 103
buffer zones, 165
Buhner, Stephen, 23, 239
Bulgaria
  comfrey and lemon balm cultivation, *ci3*
  pesticides of unknown origin in, 160
  pricing competition, 117
  wild harvesting of plants, 76, 128, 129
Buresh, Randy, 148–49, 221

calamus collecting, at Runo Spólka, *ci1*
Calasso, Roberto, 151
calendula cultivation
  conventional, in Germany, *ci4*
  Oshala Farm, *ci8*
  Zack Woods Herb Farm, 131, 134, *ci4*
California School of Herbal Studies, 34, 45
capacity of producer companies, 121–22
capitalist economic systems
  conscious capitalism and certification efforts, 189, 206–7
  difficulty in achieving transparency in, 188–190
  legacy of colonialism on, 57
  questioning of, 162
  social and environmental injustices of, 50
  storytelling in, 188
Carpenter, Jeff
  milky oats harvest, 131–32
  place-based relationships with plants, 139
  Sage Mountain Herbs involvement, 133
  sustainable herb cultivation, 133–34, 136, 137
Carpenter, Mel
  place-based relationships with plants, 139
  Sage Mountain Herbs involvement, 133
  sustainable herb cultivation, 132, 133–34, 136, 137
Caveman Chemistry (Dunn), 61
Celestial Seasonings, 34
certification of plants
  as measure of attention and intention, 108, 122–23
  percentage of, 107

  See also FairWild Standard; organic certification
cGMPs (Good Manufacturing Practices), 82, 92–93
charawa, 154
Charytoniuk, Anna
  connection with plants, 116
  difficulties in sourcing herbs, 115
  herb collecting, *ci1*
  need for good partners, 120
  relationships with collectors, 111–12, 113, 114, 125, 127
  Runo Spólka roles, 103, 104, 107
chemical constituents
  dependence on place of cultivation, 139, 140
  extraction of, 17–18
  large number of, in each plant, 16
  primary and secondary, 19
  synergy of, 16–17
  variation of, with environmental stresses, 18–19, 142
Chicago grain market, industrialization of, 106
childbirth, herbs for, 58
China
  contaminants in herb supply, 72
  geo-authentic botanicals standard, 140
  international trade in medicinal plants, 7, 54, 72, 74, 75, 140
  tradition of herbal medicine in, 75, 83, 91, 139, 140
  wild harvesting of plants, 76
Christopher, John, 36, 38, 46
Clearlight, Kate, 131, 132
climate change, effects on ecosystems, 128
coal tar, role in aspirin manufacture, 63–64
coal tree imagery, 66
collectors
  attention paid by, 123–24
  elderly, 126
  FairWild Standard empowerment of, 209
  hard labor and financial risks for, 115–18
  loss of specific knowledge of, 233
  payments to, 5, 76, 117, 120, 127, 143
  precariousness of livelihood, 123–29, 195
  registered, 112, 113–14
  relationships with producer companies, 118–123

INDEX

eastern Europe
  echinacea processing, 135
  international trade in medicinal plants, 75, 98
  privatization of collection centers, after
    communism, 101
  wild harvesting in, 97, 98, 125–26, 128
  See also specific countries
echinacea
  cultivation of, 141–42, 151, 152, *ci5*
  immune system-boosting effects, 16, 17
  mechanized processing of, 135
  overharvesting of, 138
  rising popularity of, after DSHEA passage, 87
Eclectic physicians, 36–38, 43
Ecocert, 204
Egithanoff, Mary, 29
Eiseley, Loren, 167–68
Ellingwood, Finley, 43
emergent behaviors, 16
endangered species, Red List of, 74–75
energetics of medicinal plants, 134
ethical considerations
  conscious capitalism and, 189
  low payments for wild harvesting, 76
  marketing of herbal products, 77–81
  need for critical examination of the herbal
    industry, 47, 71, 197
ethically wildcrafted, as term, 197
Europe
  allowable pesticide residues for organic
    certification, 161
  longstanding tradition of botanical
    companies in, 83
  secondary processing companies in, 98
  See also eastern Europe; *specific countries*
European Pharmacopoeia, 82
Expo West trade show, 241–45
extraction of chemical constituents
  industrial scale production, 72–73
  overview, 17–18
  by producer companies, 98–99

fair trade standards
  certification efforts, 107
  pre-financing for producer companies, 120
  Traditional Medicinals support for, 102, 120

See also FairWild Standard
FairWild Foundation, 104, 197, 199
FairWild Standard
  bag requirements, 97
  bibhitaki and haritaki projects, 199, 200–201,
    210–13
  complexity of, 198
  ecological impacts of, 208–9, 211
  handwashing requirements, 118
  implementation projects, 8, 104, 191, 192
  origins of, 197
  overview, 103
  premium fund, 113–14, 198, 207, 208, 212
  questions asked by, 197–98
  record keeping requirements, 128, 205, 208,
    211–12
  traceability system, 113–14, 205–6
  training in Bhimashankar region, 204–6, *ci16*
  unsuccessful projects, 213
farming of medicinal plants. *See* cultivation of
  medicinal plants
Farnsworth, Norman, 83, 90
FDA. *See* US Food and Drug Administration
  (FDA)
financial considerations
  balancing quality and quantity, 147–48
  burdens and risks for producer companies,
    115–18
  conservation efforts intertwined with, 194, 213
  incentives for biodiversity, 195, 198, 204
  payments to collectors, 5, 76, 117, 120, 127,
    143
  prices for raw materials, 112, 113
  weeding costs, 144, 145–46, 148
finished-product companies
  relationships among buyers and suppliers,
    118–123
  role in supply chain networks, 98, 117
  samples for, *ci13*
  scale of, 123
  See also specific companies
folk healing traditions. *See* traditional medicine
  systems
Ford, Claudia, 57–59, 66, 67
forest gardens, 151
Fort Kochi (India), 51–53

— 267 —

INDEX

lead testing, 147–48
Lee, Paul, 27, 90
LeMole, Lynda, 71
lemon balm cultivation, Plovdiv, Bulgaria, *ci3*
Lewis, Walter, 90
Light, Phyllis, 40–43
Lininger, Skye, 85
Lloyd, John Uri, 36
Lloyd Brothers, 36–37
Locker, Aaron, 148
Lopez, Barry, 21, 229
Low Dog, Tieraona, 47

Madhuvaraj, N. R., 128–29, 163
Madurai, India
　author's visits to, 79–81, 216
　uncertified supply chains in, *ci2*
Makalu-Barun Conservation Project, 171
Makita, Rie, 207–10, 211
Malabar Coast, history of trading in, 51–52,
　53–54
Manali (fieldworker), 179
Mandelbaum, Richard, 38
Mann, Charles, 60, 63, 64, 65
marc (leftover material from tincture-making),
　11
marker compounds, 73, 153
marketing of herbal products
　data on, 2
　fraudulent labeling concerns, 89
　market swings after DSHEA passage, 87–89
　out of stock concerns, 123, 166
　promise of "goodness," 77–81
　storytelling and, 188
　unsupported claims in, 197
Martin Bauer Group, 159
Masselman, George, 55
Matteson, Lizzie, 151–54, 160, 168, 178
McGregor, Ronald, 138
meatpacking, industrialization of, 106–7
mechanization
　harvesting of plants, 134, 136–37, 146
　processing of herbs, 135–36
Medicinal Herb Growing & Marketing
　Conference (2016), 143–44
medicinal plants

complexity of, 6, 14, 16–17
energetics of, 134
focusing on one plant, 109–10
number of species in international trade, 74
signature of place in, 19, 139
varying personal experiences of, 88–89, 219
visions of, 22
　See also cultivation of medicinal plants; supply
　chain of medicinal plants; wild harvesting
　of plants
Meena, B., 154–56
menstruum (solvent), 11, 17–18
microbiological testing, 147–48
Mihály, Attila, 118
Mihály, Balázs, 118
milky oats harvest, 131–32
mint cultivation, in India, 162–65
modern renaissance of herbal medicine, 27–47
　countercultural impacts, 32–33
　development of community in, 44–47
　Gladstar, Rosemary contributions, 29–34,
　44–46, 66
　Hoffmann, David contributions, 45–46
　lack of attribution to original sources, 38–39
　lack of scientific rigor, 83
　Light, Phyllis contributions, 40–43
　overview, 27–28
　Smith, Ed contributions, 35–39, 66
　Winston, David contributions, 43, 45, 46, 47
Mohan (herb broker), 79–81, 158
Moore, Michael, 111, 149
Mountain Rose Herbs
　founding of, 34
　large numbers of sourced plants, 100
　relationships with collectors, 126–27

naadis (watering holes), 181, 187
Nabataeans, 53–54
Nabhan, Gary Paul, 53, 54
Nagy Mihály, 118
National Formulary, 83
National Marketing Institute (NMI), 2
Native American healing traditions
　appropriation of, by so-called Indian doctors, 61
　contributions to modern herbal renaissance,
　28, 37

INDEX

INDEX

uncertainty in growing herbs, 147
trust
  between certifiers and collectors, 114
  between customers and businesses, 190
  in supplier relationships, 102–3, 119–120,
    194, 210
tulsi cultivation, 128–29, *ci8*, *ci9*
turmeric processing, Phalada, India, *ci11*
Tyler, Varro, 90

Udavan, Goga, 182–83, 184
United Plant Savers, 34
United States (US)
  agricultural land designated as organic, 159
  cultivation and wild harvesting of medicinal
    plants, 75
  exports of medicinal plants to, 75
  loss of herbal knowledge, 83–84
  market for certified organic herbs, 159–160
  organic certification regulations, 101–3
  as price-buying market, 83–84, 85
  transparency in in herb markets, 100–103
  zero-tolerance framework for pesticide
    residues, 161
United States Pharmacopeia (USP), 82, 83
Upton, Roy, 71, 77, 78, 85, 86
Urban Moonshine, 93–94
US Department of Agriculture (USDA), 101–2
US Food and Drug Administration (FDA),
  85–86, 92, 93–94

Vaidyagrama Ayurvedic center, 215–229
  author's treatment at, 236–37
  as base location for author's research visit,
    215, 217–18
  design of, 216, 217
  factory visit, 222–25, 228
  founding of, 216
  satsangs at, 225–29
  sourcing of plants, 218–222
vaidyas (Ayurvedic doctors), 219, 220, 222
valerian, 88, *ci6*
vastu shastras, 216
Vasuduran, Dr., 192–93, 199
viriditas, 151, 152, 153, 154, 178
Viriditas Wild Gardens, 151–54, 168, 178

visualization, in sacred plant medicine, 23–24
Vitality Works, 7, 93, 147–48

Wallace Brothers, 37
Warner, John, 51
water security concerns, in India, 169, 170,
  181–83
Watershed Gathering (1996), 5
weed management
  flame machines, 148
  GPS tractors for, 146, *ci5*
  labor costs, 144, 145–46, 148
Weiss, William, 60, 61–63
Western Ghats, India
  bibhitaki and haritaki projects, 192, 198,
    199–203, *ci16*
  biodiversity of, 162, 191, 192
  deforestation in, 193
  heavy metal contamination in, 228
Westwell, Tim, 162
wheat market, industrialization of, 106
Wheeler, Mark
  estimate of US organic herb market, 159
  sustainable herb cultivation, 137, 139, 141,
    142, 157
  uncertainty in growing herbs, 147
wholesale herb markets
  India, 78–81, *ci12*
  large numbers of sourced plants, 100
wild harvesting of plants, 111–129
  bags for, 205–6, 224
  cultivation vs., 75–76
  destructive practices in, 76
  echinacea, 138
  Eclectic physicians, 36–37
  endangered livelihoods, 123–29
  as first step in herb processing, 97
  ginseng, 41–42
  impact of DSHEA on, 87
  organic certification for, 197
  overharvesting, 87, 118, 138, 195
  overview, 111–12
  relationships among buyers and suppliers,
    117–123
  scope of international trade, 74
  sustainability efforts, 195–96

THE BUSINESS OF BOTANICALS

ABOUT THE AUTHOR

TERRY YOUK

ANN ARMBRECHT is a writer and anthropologist (PhD, Harvard 1995) whose work explores the relationships between humans and the earth, most recently through her work with plants and plant medicine. She is currently the director of the Sustainable Herbs Program under the auspices of the American Botanical Council. She is the co-producer of the documentary *Numen: The Nature of Plants* and the author of the award-winning ethnographic memoir *Thin Places: A Pilgrimage Home*, based on her research in Nepal. She is a student of herbal medicine and was a 2017 Fulbright-Nehru Scholar documenting the supply chain of medicinal plants in India. She lives with her family in central Vermont.

the politics and practice of sustainable living

CHELSEA GREEN PUBLISHING

Chelsea Green Publishing sees books as tools for effecting cultural change and seeks to empower citizens to participate in reclaiming our global commons and become its impassioned stewards. If you enjoyed *The Business of Botanicals*, please consider these other great books related to health and sustainability.

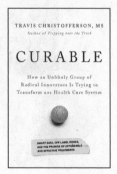

FIBERSHED
Growing a Movement of Farmers, Fashion Activists, and Makers for a New Textile Economy
REBECCA BURGESS with COURTNEY WHITE
9781603586634
Paperback

CURABLE
How an Unlikely Group of Radical Innovators Is Trying to Transform our Health Care System
TRAVIS CHRISTOFFERSON
9781603589260
Hardcover

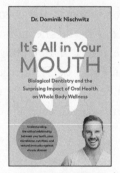

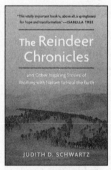

IT'S ALL IN YOUR MOUTH
Biological Dentistry and the Surprising Impact of Oral Health on Whole Body Wellness
DR. DOMINIK NISCHWITZ
9781603589543
Paperback

THE REINDEER CHRONICLES
And Other Inspiring Stories of Working with Nature to Heal the Earth
JUDITH D. SCHWARTZ
9781603588652
Paperback

the politics and practice of sustainable living

For more information,
visit **www.chelseagreen.com**.